S0-BDM-006

Systematic Evaluation

Evaluation in Education and Human Services

Editors:

George F. Madaus, Boston College, Chestnut
   Hill, Massachusetts, U.S.A.
Daniel L. Stufflebeam, Western Michigan
   University, Kalamazoo, Michigan, U.S.A.

Previously published books in the series:

Systematic Evaluation
A Self-Instructional Guide to Theory and Practice

Daniel L. Stufflebeam

Anthony J. Shinkfield

Kluwer-Nijhoff Publishing
a member of the Kluwer Academic Publishers Group
Boston/The Hague/Dordrecht/Lancaster

Distributors for North America:

Kluwer Academic Publishers
101 Philip Drive
Assinippi Park
Norwell, MA 02061

Distributors outside North America:

Kluwer Academic Publishers Group
Distribution Centre
P.O. Box 322
3300AH Dordrecht,
THE NETHERLANDS

Library of Congress Cataloging in Publication Data

Stufflebeam, Daniel L.
  Systematic evaluation.

  (Evaluation in education and human services)
  includes bibliographical references and index.
  1. Evaluation research (Social action programs)
I. Shinkfield, Anthony J. II. Title. III. Series.
H62.S7963   1984   361.6'1   84-7119
ISBN 0-89838-158-4

Copyright © 1985 by Kluwer-Nijhoff Publishing.
Second printing 1986.

No part of this book may be reproduced in any form by print,
photoprint, microfilm, or any other means without written
permission of the publisher.

Printed in the United States of America

Contents

H
62
5933s
1985

938.23

5 Jn 87
OCLC 107/0806

3 0001 00031 7117

USER'S GUIDE

A Word to the User

This book is intended for the use of a broad range of persons who are concerned with assessing, assuring, or improving the quality of programs. It is for lay groups, specialists in research, administrators, teachers, evaluators, and students. These groups can use the book to develop a broad view of the approaches that are available for evaluating programs. Beyond obtaining such a general orientation, they can use it to develop a basic level of proficiency in applying one or more of the approaches. The book may be studied in the context of group instruction or pursued independently. It can be worked through from beginning to end, or its units can be used selectively as handbook chapters. The advice throughout the book is relevant for evaluating programs, projects, and materials in education, health, and welfare.

The book contains 10 units. The first and second ones, respectively, provide an overview of evaluation and an analysis of three broad approaches to evaluation. The remaining units provide in-depth treatments of eight selected models for evaluation work.

We suggest that, at the outset, you study the first two units. This study will acquaint you with the emerging evaluation field in its historical perspective. It will also help you to appreciate the complexities and issues that in-here in the field. It will introduce you to the alternative approaches that have been used and advocated. And, in all likelihood, it will help you to consider whether your present conception of what is involved in ascertaining the value of something is overly restricted, out-of-date, in some ways il-logical, not as useful as another possible approach, or at least in conflict with some other views.

Choosing Your Own Objectives

After you have completed the first two units, we suggest that you formulate your own objectives for using and benefiting from the remainder of the text. First, you should consider what you need to gain from further study. You may need to gain in-depth knowledge of one selected approach that is already being applied in evaluating a given program so that you can thor-oughly assess it or help carry it through; or, if you or the group you are in-volved with have not yet made a commitment to any particular approach, you may need to study several alternatives in the process of choosing or adapting the one that will best suit your situation. To make such broad choices, we suggest that you carefully review the material in unit 2, since it provides a comparative analysis of alternative approaches.

After you have decided whether your initial focus will be on multiple units or an individual unit, we suggest that you then scan the initial pages of each unit you have tentatively decided to study. Particularly, you should look at the list of objectives to which each unit is directed. Subsequently, us-ing your analysis to this point and the objectives listed in the pertinent units, we suggest that you list your objectives for studying each unit on a separate sheet of paper. By keeping this sheet handy during your study of a selected unit, you will be more likely to guide your study in the direction of your own assessed needs, as well as the objectives given for each unit.

Evaluating Your Performance

You will find that each unit contains material designed to assist you to evaluate your own performance. This material is keyed to the objectives of the unit and includes self-scoring multiple-choice questions, application ex-ercises with keyed responses, and discussion questions. We encourage you to work through this material. Not only will this effort provide feedback about the extent of your mastery of the reading material, but it will also help you to increase your understanding of the contents of the unit and your ability to apply the given approach.

Beyond working through the evaluation exercises that are given, we suggest that you also engage in some self-assessment regarding the achievement of the objectives you previously set for yourself. You might list what you see as your gains regarding each objective. You might rate your attainment of each objective on a scale of none, some, considerable, and a great deal. You might list the questions that you still need to answer, and also the skills and experiences that you still need to acquire. You might list what you see as unanticipated effects on your knowledge, skills, and attitudes as a consequence of studying the material; these most likely would be positive, such as new insights, but might also be negative, such as heightened confusion. We suggest that you consider developing exercises for assessing gains that are potentially available from a study of the units. If you do that, please send us a copy, as it undoubtedly would be of use in the future when we revise this book. Finally, we suggest that you make definite plans to subject your new ideas about evaluation to field-test situations, such as planning evaluations, evaluating evaluations, or conducting workshops on evaluation.

Systematic Evaluation

1 INTRODUCTION TO EVALUATION

Evaluation is one of the most fundamental components of sound professional services. The clients of professionals deserve assistance that is directed to their needs, of high quality, up-to-date, and efficient. In order to hold professionals accountable for satisfying such standards, society must regularly subject professional services to evaluations. Some of the evaluation work that is directed at regulation and protection of the public interest obviously must be conducted by independent bodies, such as government agencies and accrediting boards. But fundamentally, the most important evaluations of professional services are those conducted (or commissioned) by the professionals themselves.

In order to keep their services up-to-date and ensure that they are effectively meeting the needs of their clients, professionals must continually obtain pertinent evaluative feedback. This process includes studying the needs of their clients, evaluating the approaches that are being proposed or used elsewhere, closely monitoring the delivery of service, assessing immediate and long-term outcomes, and searching for ways to make the services both more efficient and effective. A prime question that any outside evaluation group should pose is whether the professional maintains a self-evaluation program that produces pertinent and defensible evidence on these issues.

Unfortunately, the extent of evaluation of professional services — by the professionals and their accrediting agents — traditionally has been at best uneven and, in general, poor. Some large school districts and government agencies maintain well-funded and adequately staffed systems of evaluation, and the agency evaluators have succeeded in helping their parent organizations to be accountable to constituents and to obtain guidance for planning and administering their services. But even the most highly funded of these evaluation systems inevitably falls short of meeting the evaluation responsibilities of all the professionals in the agency. There is no escaping the fact that evaluation is a personal as well as an institutional responsibility. Offices of evaluation can meet an agency's major responsibilities for evaluation and can provide in-service training and technical support to agency staff. Ultimately, however, each professional bears responsibility for evaluating his or her own performance.

This book has been written to help professional educators and those who provide other professional services, such as health and social services, to strengthen their working knowledge of evaluation. Its basic design is that of a handbook. One can turn to any unit, independent of the others, to obtain information on a particular topic. Overall, the topics included have been chosen to give instruction about the general nature of evaluation, to provide an overview and comparative analysis of alternative approaches to evaluation, and to provide in-depth instruction in each of 8 alternative models or designs for conducting evaluations. Each unit has been written as a self-instructional guide that includes learning objectives, expository information, self-scoring test questions and exercises, and a few discussion questions.

This first unit, as an overview of evaluation, provides a broad definition of this concept and reviews the development of program evaluation, especially since 1930. It shows how the term *evaluation* has grown in both the depth and breadth of meaning attributed to it. The many definitions and roles of evaluation that have been applied depending on variations in the social and political context are described. Some key methodological developments as well as certain roles that are involved in evaluation work are identified. Finally, recent efforts to professionalize evaluation work, especially through the development of professional standards, are discussed. In general, the aim of this unit is to acquaint the reader with evaluation as a field of study and practice that is distinguishable from related fields, such as research, planning, and administration.

Objectives

This unit is directed at five learning objectives. After thoroughly studying the chapter, you should be able to meet the following objectives:

1. To define evaluation, as presented in this unit, and identify the rationale that was provided for this definition.
2. To identify several alternative methods for evaluation.
3. To identify the two major sets of standards for program evaluation and characterize the main features of the Joint Committee *Standards.*
4. To identify and describe five main periods that are used in this unit to characterize the growth of evaluation theory and practice.
5. To denote and define 12 main roles involved in evaluation work.

As with all of the units, you will find at the end of this one a set of test questions and exercises. We suggest that you complete them and assess your answers against the keyed responses. Then consider or discuss with colleagues the questions without answers. Although you can achieve all the objectives by studying only the material that is provided in the unit, we suggest that you enrich your understanding of the involved concepts by consulting the references listed at the end of each unit.

What Is Evaluation?

Many different answers have been given to the question, What is evaluation? While many of them vary only in minor ways, substantial differences exist among others. For example, some definitions essentially equate evaluation with other concepts such as research or testing, whereas others sharply distinguish evaluation from these fields. One prominent, longstanding definition states that evaluation involves comparing objectives and outcomes, whereas others call for a much broader conceptualization involving combined study of performance and values. Many of the different definitions that have been advocated are reflected in the different evaluation models presented in units 3 through 10. Moreover, unit 2 provides a comparative analysis of these models and definitions. Essentially, that analysis looks at all of the approaches against the definition given in this unit.

That definition is consistent with common dictionary meanings and, more specifically, is the one adopted by the Joint Committee on Standards for Educational Evaluation. The *Standards* definition is as follows: *Evaluation is the systematic assessment of the worth or merit of some object.*

This definition centers on the root-term value and denotes that evaluation essentially involves judgment. While evaluation optimally employs objective procedures in order to obtain dependable and unbiased information, it is not value-free. On the contrary, its essential goal is to determine the value of whatever is being assessed. According to this definition, if a study does not report how good or bad something is, it is not evaluation.

Some writers have argued against this position. They believe that this value orientation leads to threatening and subjective interpretations that give undeserved power to evaluators and impede progress. They say, so to speak, that "beauty is in the eyes of the beholder" and that one group's values should not be given precedence over another's in determining whether something is good or bad. They also argue that evaluation is too often a negative force and, in general, is poor psychology. But their arguments only convince us that evaluation is mainly indeterminant and difficult to do well; there may be many different, and possibly apparently contradictory, evaluations of a given object, depending on what value position is taken. But, inevitably, valuing is involved. And feedback, if integral to development and if directed to identifying strengths as well as weaknesses and to providing direction for improvement, can be a positive force. Indeed, evaluation is a complex enterprise.

The aspect of complexity should not be construed, we believe, to mean that evaluations should be looked upon only as naturally occurring thought processes leading to various interpretations of something's value. Instead it points to the need for great care not only in collecting information of high quality but in clarifying and providing a defensible rationale for the value perspective(s) used to interpret the findings.

In the above statement, you will note that we included the possibility of employing multiple value perspectives. We see this possibility as a fundamental concern of evaluators and of professionals in general. Often there are different publics who want or need different things from a professional service. For example, affluent families may be most concerned about the extent that public schools prepare students for entry into elite colleges and universities, whereas recent immigrants, who are poor and speak little English, may fault the schools if they do not offer bilingual education and remedial education and promote social integration. In evaluating a given school district, a competent evaluator would, according to our definition, take into account, inter alia, both of these value perspectives. In fact, we would argue that it is the shared and differential needs of the clients of a given service that should be ascertained as a basis both for determining what information to collect and what standards to invoke in determining the worth or merit of a service.

The terms *worth* and *merit* also need to be defined to enrich one's concept of evaluation. Scriven (1981) has previously pointed out their nontrivial differences and their important role in determining the value of something. At times one needs to look at the merit of something. For example, does a program for preparing history teachers succeed in producing teachers who confidently and effectively teach others about history? In general, does it do well what it is supposed to do? If so, it is meritorious, but it may not be worthy. For example, if the society has no need for history teachers because there are already more good ones than can be employed, then although the program has good merit — and may be better than many other similar ones — continuation at the same level of expansion of this program may not be a worthwhile expenditure of scarce resources. Although a meritorious program may not be worthy, we need to point out that a nonmeritorious program cannot be worthy. It would do no good to produce poor history teachers even though a great shortage of history teachers existed.

So far this discussion of what value bases should be looked at in evaluating something has identified three crucial sources of criteria:

1. Different expectations of *clients* (sometimes called stakeholders).
2. The *merit* or excellence of the service in question.
3. The extent of *need* for the service (i.e., its potential worth).

In general, we advocate considering all three sources in efforts to evaluate. But we see a need for consideration of two additional sources: *feasibility* and *equity*. While a service might be of high quality, address the different objectives of different client groups, and be directed to an area of high need, it might still fail the values of feasibility and equity.

For example, it might consume more resources than required or cause no end of political turmoil. If either is the case, then the program should, at least, be modified in these areas to make it more feasible. Obviously, a good evaluation of the service should speak to this issue and, where appropriate, provide direction for making the service easy to use, efficient in use of time and resources, and politically viable. This argument in favor of feasibility seems applicable to all societies.

The last value base to be mentioned here, *equity,* is predominately tied to democratic societies. It argues for equal opportunities for all people and emphasizes freedom for all. In the United States, an evaluation would indeed be incomplete if it did not assess whether a public service is provided for, and made available to, all members of the society. It is important to note that our concept of equity is complex. It is not enough to say that public educational services may be sought and used by all people. As Kellaghan (1982) has argued, when equality truly exists there will be seven indications of equity:

1. A society's public educational services will be *provided* for all its people.
2. People from all segments of the society will have equal *access* to the services.

3. There will be close to equal *participation* by all groups in the use of the services.
4. Levels of *attainment,* for example, years in the educational system, will not be significantly different for different groups.
5. Levels of *proficiency* in achieving all of the objectives of the service will not be noticeably different for different groups.
6. Levels of *aspiration* for life pursuits will be similar across societal groups.
7. The service system will make similar *impacts* on improving the welfare of all societal groups.

From the foregoing discussion, we can see that our proposed definition of evaluation is deceptive in its apparent simplicity. When one takes seriously the root-term value, then one inevitably must consider value perspectives as well as information, the combining of the two in efforts to reach determinations of the value of something, and, ultimately, the conversion of results to working knowledge that is used to provide or not provide (or purchase or not) certain services and to improve the ones that are offered.

Before leaving this discussion of the definition of evaluation, we want to consider three other aspects of evaluation. The first one concerns whether evaluations need be comparative, the second one concerns the main uses of evaluation, and the third concerns the extent to which evaluators need special qualifications.

A number of writers (Stake, Scriven, Cronbach) have pointed out that evaluations may focus on a single product or service or compare it to available alternatives. Moreover, they have debated the merits of these competing stances, implying that one proposition is always to be preferred. We believe that, depending on the circumstances, an evaluation legitimately may be either comparative or noncomparative.

A main consideration is the nature of the audience and what it needs to know about the object of the evaluation. If the audience is composed of consumers who need to choose a product or service, then the evaluation should be comparative — helping consumers to learn what alternatives are available and how they compare on critical criteria. If, however, the audience includes developers or consumers who are already committed to the development or use of a given program, then the evaluation might best focus intensively on the workings of the program and provide direction for improving it. Periodically, however, even if a group is firmly devoted to a certain service or product, it might get a better return from the provider of this service or find a better alternative by opening consideration to other options.

In general, we think that evaluation should be comparative before development begins or before one subscribes to a service, noncomparative during development (allowing concentration on how best to develop the service), and periodically comparative after development and/or sustained use in order to open the way for major advancements.

Broadly speaking, whether an evaluation should be comparative depends on the intended uses of the evaluation. We see three main uses: improvement, accountability, and enlightenment. The first use involves providing information for assuring the quality of a service or for improving it. Close attention must be paid to the nature and needs of the consumers and to the link between process and outcome. The evaluator here should interact closely with program staff and provide guidance for decision making. The evaluation plan needs to be flexible and responsive. When improvement is the main aim, the evaluation should resemble more a case study than a comparative experiment.

The second main role of evaluation is to produce accountability or summative reports. These are retrospective views of completed projects, established programs, or finished products. The information is aimed not at the development staff but at the sponsors and consumers. There must be an assessment of cost effectiveness, and comparisons with critical competitors are also important. Information derived from both in-depth case studies and comparative field tests is of interest to the audience in such situations.

The third use is enlightenment. Basically, evaluation and research are different enterprises. The former attempts to consider all criteria that apply in a determination of value, while the latter may be restricted to study of selected variables that are of theoretical interest. Evaluations typically involve subjective approaches and are not as tightly controlled and subject to manipulation as is the typical research investigation. However, efforts over a period of time to evaluate services may produce information of use in evolving and testing theory. And certainly, the results of evaluations often should and do lead to focused, applied research efforts. Hence, we believe it is important that evaluators, in planning their studies, take into account how their findings might be used in the context of research to promote increased understanding of the phenomena that are involved in the evaluation. With some forethought and careful planning, evaluations may serve not only to guide operating programs and sum up their contributions but to address particular research or theoretical questions as well.

To this point, that evaluation is a highly involved concept seems clear. In planning and conducting an evaluation, a number of issues have to be faced:

Whose values are to be referenced in judging results?

What particular criteria should be addressed and which should be accorded precedence?

Should the evaluation be comparative?

Should the evaluation be geared to guide development, hold professionals accountable, rank options, or promote new insights about the involved phenomena?

If these issues are to be faced so that audiences will have confidence in the findings, and want to use them, the evaluators must meet certain standards in their evaluation work. Consequently, we think the distinction between informal and professional evaluations is important. Certainly, everybody does the former whenever judging and making decisions about the things observed, thought about, interacted with, or to be purchased. But, all too often our evaluations are unsystematic and not very convincing even to ourselves. We would prefer in many cases to bring more relevance, rigor, and objectivity into our findings. These requirements, however, would often require more time, money, and expertise than we possess.

Thus, good evaluations often have to be professionally staffed. Although our definition has stated that evaluation is systematic, many of them are clearly not. What we intend to promote in this book is a kind of evaluation that is defensible. The kind of evaluation we have in mind requires systematic effort by one or more persons who have at least a certain minimum level of the requisite evaluation skills. We think that serious study of this book can help the student to attain the basic level of proficiency required to implement our concept of *systematic evaluation* and to evaluate the evaluation efforts of other persons.

Methods

One aspect that distinguishes systematic evaluation from informal evaluation is, of course, the area of methodology. When we move our consideration away from evaluations that involve quick intuitive judgments toward those that entail rigorously gathered findings and effective communications, we must necessarily deal with the complex areas of epistemology, rules of evidence, information sciences, research design, measurement, statistics, communication, and some others. Many principles, tools, and strategies within these areas have pertinence to systematic evaluation. The well-prepared evaluator will have a good command of techniques in all these areas and will be kept informed about potentially useful technological developments. Those evaluators who would exert leadership and help move their profession ahead should contribute to the critique of existing methods and the development of new ones.

Over the years, many evaluators have chosen, even championed, the exclusive use of a few techniques. Some have equated evaluation with their favorite methods, for example, experimental design, standardized testing, or site visits. Other leaders have sharply attacked narrow views of which methods are appropriate and, in some cases, have argued for substituting their favorite technique, such as the case study. We find both positions shortsighted, inadequate, and sometimes divisive.

Instead, we advocate an eclectic approach. Thus, we believe that evaluators should know about a wide range of pertinent techniques and how well they apply in different evaluative contexts. Then in each evaluative situation they can assess which techniques are potentially applicable and which ones most likely would work best to serve the particular purposes of the given evaluation.

Among the technical areas we think the professional evaluator should be proficient in are the following: interviewing, proposal writing, content analysis, observation, political analysis, cost analysis, survey research, technical writing, case study, goal-free evaluation, advocacy-adversary hearings, advocacy teams, checklists, test construction, statistical analysis, research design, system analysis, theorizing, and project administration. Convenient sources of general information about such technical areas are Scriven (1974), Anderson, Ball, and Murphy (1974), Brinkerhoff et al., (1983), and Smith (1981a and 1981b).

Standards

One characteristic of a field of professional practice is that its members are required to adhere to high standards of performance and service. Such standards typically are defined by the members of the profession and in some cases by government. Familiar examples are the standards that have been used by the fields of law, medicine, and accounting to guide and assess practice, and in some cases to reach conclusions about claims of malpractice. Until recently, program evaluators have not had to be concerned about explicit standards for evaluation, but that situation has been changing.

Recently, two sets of standards for evaluations were published. One is a set of 30 standards developed by the Joint Committee on Standards for Educational Evaluation. The other is a set of 55 standards developed by the Evaluation Research Society (ERS).

Here we concentrate on the former set for a number of reasons. Careful comparisons by independent investigators have shown that essentially everything that is included in the ERS standards is covered in more depth in the Joint Committee *Standards*. Further, the former set was developed by a joint committee whose 17 members were appointed by 12 professional organizations with total membership of about 2 million, while the ERS Standards were developed by one group with about 2,000 members. Another key difference is that the Joint Committee *Standards* speak to the client as well as the provider of evaluation services.

The *Standards for Evaluations of Educational Programs, Projects, and Materials* (Joint Committee, 1981) were developed over a five-year period. This committee involved about 200 persons concerned with the professional practice of evaluation in a systematic process of generating, testing, and clarifying widely shared principles by which to guide and govern program evaluation work in education. The results were the 30 standards, which are summarized in table 1-1. Particularly noteworthy is the ongoing process for reviewing and revising the standards. In essence, the Joint Committee determined that the 30 standards are necessary and sufficient for ensuring that evaluations will be useful, feasible, proper, and valid. The reader is advised to study the *Standards* book in depth.

In general, the Joint Committee *Standards* advise both evaluators and clients to cooperate so that their evaluations satisfy the four main conditions mentioned:

1. An evaluation should be *useful*. It should be addressed to those persons and groups who are involved in or responsible for implementing whatever is being evaluated. It should help them to identify and attend to strengths and weaknesses in the object. It should place heaviest emphasis on addressing the questions of most importance to them. It should issue clear reports in a timely manner. And, in general, it should provide not merely feedback about strengths and weaknesses but also direction for improvement.
2. It should be *feasible*. It should employ evaluation procedures that can be implemented without major disruption. It should take into account and exert reasonable controls over political forces that might otherwise subvert the evaluation. And it should be conducted efficiently.
3. It should be *ethical*. It should be founded on explicit agreements that ensure that the necessary cooperation will be provided, that the rights of all concerned parties will be protected, and that the findings will not be compromised. Moreover, it should provide a balanced report that reveals both strengths and weaknesses.

Table 1-1. Summary of Standards for Evaluations of Educational Programs, Projects, and Materials

---

A *Utility Standards*

The Utility Standards are intended to ensure that an evaluation will serve the practical information needs of given audiences. These standards are:

A1 *Audience Identification*

Audiences involved in or affected by the evaluation should be identified, so that their needs can be addressed.

A2 *Evaluator Credibility*

The persons conducting the evaluation should be both trustworthy and competent to perform the evaluation, so that their findings achieve maximum credibility and acceptance.

A3 *Information Scope and Selection*

Information collected should be of such scope and selected in such ways as to address pertinent questions about the object of the evaluation and be responsive to the needs and interests of specified audiences.

A4 *Valuational Interpretation*

The perspectives, procedures, and rationale used to interpret the findings should be carefully described, so that the bases for value judgments are clear.

A5 *Report Clarity*

The evaluation report should describe the object being evaluated and its context, and the purposes, procedures, and findings of the evaluation, so that the audiences will readily understand what was done, why it was done, what information was obtained, what conclusions were drawn, and what recommendations were made.

A6 *Report Dissemination*

Evaluation findings should be disseminated to clients and other right-to-know audiences, so that they can assess and use the findings.

A7 *Report Timeliness*

Release of reports should be timely, so that audiences can best use the reported information.

A8 *Evaluation Impact*

Evaluations should be planned and conducted in ways that encourage follow-through by members of the audiences.

Table 1-1. *Cont'nued*

B	*Feasibility Standards*

The Feasibility Standards are intended to ensure that an evaluation will be realistic, prudent, diplomatic, and frugal; they are:

B1   *Practical Procedures*

The evaluation procedures should be practical, so that disruption is kept to a minimum, and that needed information can be obtained.

B2   *Political Viability*

The evaluation should be planned and conducted with anticipation of the different positions of various interest groups, so that their cooperation may be obtained, and so that possible attempts by any of these groups to curtail evaluation operations or to bias or misapply the results can be averted or counteracted.

B3   *Cost Effectiveness*

The evaluation should produce information of sufficient value to justify the resources expended.

C   *Propriety Standards*

The Propriety Standards are intended to ensure that an evaluation will be conducted legally, ethically, and with due regard for the welfare of those involved in the evaluation, as well as those affected by its results. These standards are:

C1   *Formal Obligation*

Obligations of the formal parties to an evaluation (what is to be done, how, by whom, when) should be agreed to in writing, so that these parties are obligated to adhere to all conditions of the agreement or formally to renegotiate it.

C2   *Conflict of Interest*

Conflict of interest, frequently unavoidable, should be dealt with openly and honestly, so that it does not compromise the evaluation processes and results.

C3   *Full and Frank Disclosure*

Oral and written evaluation reports should be open, direct, and honest in their disclosure of pertinent findings, including the limitations of the evaluation.

C4   *Public's Right to Know*

The formal parties to an evaluation should respect and assure the public's right to know, within the limits of other related principles and statutes, such as those dealing with public safety and the right to privacy.

C5   *Rights of Human Subjects*

Evaluations should be designed and conducted, so that the rights and welfare of the human subjects are respected and protected.

C6   *Human Interactions*

Evaluators should respect human dignity and worth in their interactions with other persons associated with an evaluation.

C7   *Balanced Reporting*

The evaluation should be complete and fair in its presentation of strengths and weaknesses of the object under investigation, so that strengths can be built upon and problem areas addressed.

C8   *Fiscal Responsibility*

The evaluator's allocation and expenditure of resources should reflect sound accountability procedures and otherwise be prudent and ethically responsible.

D   *Accuracy Standards*

The Accuracy Standards are intended to ensure that an evaluation will reveal and convey technically adequate information about the features of the object being studied that determine its worth or merit. These standards are:

D1   *Object Identification*

The object of the evaluation (program, project, material) should be sufficiently examined, so that the form(s) of the object being considered in the evaluation can be clearly identified.

D2   *Context Analysis*

The context in which the program, project, or material exists should be examined in enough detail, so that its likely influences on the object can be identified.

D3   *Described Purposes and Procedures*

The purposes and procedures of the evaluation should be monitored and described in enough detail, so that they can be identified and assessed.

Table 1-1.   *Continued*

D4	*Defensible Information Sources*

The sources of information should be described in enough detail, so that the adequacy of the information can be assessed.

D5   *Valid Measurement*

The information-gathering instruments and procedures should be chosen or developed and then implemented in ways that will assure that the interpretation arrived at is valid for the given use.

D6   *Reliable Measurement*

The information-gathering instruments and procedures should be chosen or developed and then implemented in ways that will assure that the information obtained is sufficiently reliable for the intended use.

D7   *Systematic Data Control*

The data collected, processed, and reported in an evaluation should be reviewed and corrected, so that the results of the evaluation will not be flawed.

D8   *Analysis of Quantitative Information*

Quantitative information in an evaluation should be appropriately and systematically analyzed to ensure supportable interpretations.

D9   *Analysis of Qualitative Information*

Qualitative information in an evaluation should be appropriately and systematically analyzed to ensure supportable interpretations.

D10   *Justified Conclusions*

The conclusions reached in an evaluation should be explicitly justified, so that the audiences can assess them.

D11   *Objective Reporting*

The evaluation procedures should provide safeguards to protect the evaluation findings and reports against distortion by the personal feelings and biases of any party to the evaluation.

Source: The Joint Committee on Standards for Educational Evaluation, McGraw-Hill, 1981

4.   It should be *accurate*. It should clearly describe the object as it evolved, and in its context. It should reveal the strengths and weaknesses of the evaluation plan, procedures, and conclusions. It should be controlled for bias. And it should provide valid and reliable findings.

The Joint Committee *Standards* apply at each stage of the evaluation process: they should be taken into account, for example, in deciding whether to evaluate, in designing the evaluation and implementing it, in reporting the results, and in applying the findings. Hence, use of the *Standards* serves not only to check the quality of a completed report but to guide the evaluation along the way. A second point is that different standards are more or less important at different stages of the evaluation. Thus, users of the standards must study and internalize them so that they can apply them judiciously at each stage of an evaluation. The summary of the 30 standards presented in table 1–1 is a starting point, but we advise the reader to obtain and study the full text.

The Joint Committee worked under two basic premises: that evaluation is both an essential and inevitable human activity, and that sound evaluation should promote a more complete understanding and improvement of education. Furthermore, the committee was guided by the belief that a thoughtfully developed set of standards could play a vital part in improving the practice of educational evaluation, that is, a metaevaluative role.

Another crucial point concerning the Joint Committee *Standards* is that it is a living document. A standing joint committee, appointed by 12 organizations and based at the Western Michigan University Evaluation Center, monitors the use of the standards and is charged with the responsibility to periodically update and improve them. The committee encourages users of the *Standards* to provide feedback based on critiques and especially actual uses.

History[1]

No introduction to evaluation as a field of professional practice would be complete without giving some attention to the historical development of the field. Any profession, in order to serve the needs of its clients, must evolve in response to changing societal needs and in consideration of theoretical and technical advancements. Unless the members of a profession develop and maintain a historical perspective on their work, they are likely to perseverate in using a stagnant conception of their role and not to

---

[1]This section on the history of evaluation is based on an analysis by George Madaus and Daniel Stufflebeam, which has been summarized in George Madaus, Michael Scriven, and Daniel Stufflebeam, *Evaluation Models* (Boston: Kluwer-Nijhoff, 1983).

stimulate and contribute to innovation in their field. It has often been said that those who do not learn from their history are doomed to repeat it. We will provide only a brief historical sketch in order to sensitize the reader to the most significant developments in evaluation.

Our historical analysis is based on the seminal work of Ralph W. Tyler (see unit 3), who is often spoken of as the father of educational evaluation. Using his initial contributions as the main reference point, we have identified five major periods: (1) the Pre-Tyler Period, which includes developments before 1930; (2) the Tylerian Age, which spans 1930 to 1945; (3) the Age of Innocence, which runs from 1946 to 1957; (4) the Age of Realism, which covers the years 1958 to 1972; and (5) the Age of Professionalism, which includes developments from 1973 to the present.

The Pre-Tylerian Period

Systematic evaluation was not unknown before 1930, and neither was it a recognizable movement. The concept of evaluating individuals and programs was evident as early as 2000 B.C., when Chinese officials were conducting civil service examinations, and in the fifth century B.C., when Socrates and other Greek teachers used evaluative questioning as part of their teaching methodology. In the nineteenth century royal commissions were used in England to evaluate public services. In 1845, in the United States Horace Mann led an evaluation, based on performance testing, to assess whether the Boston schools were succeeding in educating their students. Between 1887 and 1898, Joseph Rice studied the spelling performance of 33,000 students in a large city school system and concluded that there were no significant learning gains attributable to the heavy concentration on spelling instruction then in vogue. This study is generally recognized as the first formal educational program evaluation in America. Also in the late 1800s, the movement to accredit educational institutions and programs in the United States was begun; since then the accreditation process has become one major means of evaluating educational services. Another major approach to evaluation that developed in the early 1900s was that of standardized testing. This development came as part of a major effort to make education more efficient so that great numbers of students could be served with the resources then available to schools.

The above brief account illustrates that systematic evaluation has a long history. While evaluation has only recently been identified as a field of professional practice, much of the modern evaluation work continues to draw from ideas and techniques that were applied long ago, that is, testing, commissions, accreditation, and experimental comparison of competing programs.

The Tylerian Age

In the early 1930s Ralph Tyler coined the term *educational evaluation* and published a broad and innovative view of both curriculum and evaluation. Over a period of about 15 years he developed his views until they constituted an approach that provided a clear-cut alternative to other views.

What mainly distinguished his approach was its concentration on clearly stated objectives. In fact, he defined evaluation as determining whether objectives had been achieved. As a consequence of this definition, evaluators were supposed to help curriculum developers to clarify the student behaviors that were to be produced through the implementation of a curriculum. The resulting behavioral objectives were then to provide the basis for both curriculum development and test development. Curriculum design was thus influenced away from the content to be taught and toward the student behaviors to be developed. The technology of test development was to be expanded to provide for tests referenced to objectives as well as those referenced to individual differences and national or state norms.

During the 1930s, the United States, as well as the rest of the world, was in the depths of the Great Depression. Schools, as well as other public institutions, had stagnated from a lack of resources and optimism. Just as Roosevelt tried through his New Deal program to lead the American economy out of this abyss, John Dewey and others tried to help education to become a dynamic, innovative, and self-renewing system. Called Progressive Education, this movement reflected the philosophy of pragmatism and employed the tools of behavioristic psychology.

Tyler was drawn directly into this movement when he was commissioned to direct the research component of the now famous Eight-Year Study (Smith and Tyler, 1942). This study was designed to examine the effectiveness of certain innovative curricula and teaching strategies being employed in 30 schools located throughout America. The study is noteworthy because it helped Tyler at once to expand, test, and demonstrate his conception of educational evaluation.

Through this nationally visible program, Tyler was able to publicize what he saw as clear-cut advantages of his approach over others. Since Tylerian evaluation involves internal comparisons of outcomes with objectives, it need not provide for costly and disruptive comparisons between experimental and control groups. The approach concentrates on direct measures of achievement, as opposed to indirect approaches that measure such inputs as quality of teaching, number of books in the library, extent of materials, and community involvement. And Tylerian evaluations need not be heavily concerned with reliability of differences between the scores of individual students, and they typically cover a wider range of outcome variables than those covered by norm-referenced tests. These arguments were well received throughout American education, and by the middle of the 1940s Ralph Tyler had set the stage for exerting a heavy influence on the educational scene for the next 25 years.

The Age of Innocence

Throughout the American society, the late 1940s and 1950s were a time to forget the war, leave the depression behind, build and expand capabilities, acquire resources, and engineer and enjoy a "good life." We might have called this era the period of expansion, except that there was also widespread complacence regarding serious problems in the society. As a consequence, we think this time is better referred to as the Period of Innocence or even *social irresponsibility.*

In addition to being a time of plenty, this period was a time of poverty and despair in inner cities and in rural areas, but almost no one except the victims seemed to notice. It was a period of extreme racial prejudice and segregation, but most white people seemed oblivious to the disease. It was a period of exorbitant consumption and widespread waste of natural resources without any apparent concern that one day these resources would be used up. It was a period of vast development of industry and military capabilities with little provision of safeguards against damage to the environment and future generations.

More to the point of educational evaluation, there was expansion of educational offerings, personnel, and facilities. New buildings were erected. New kinds of educational institutions, such as community colleges, emerged. Small school districts consolidated with others in order to provide the wide range of educational services that were common in the larger school systems, including mental and physical health services, guidance, food services, music instruction, expanded sports programs, business and technical education, and community education. Enrollments in teacher education programs ballooned, and generally college enrollments increased dramatically.

This general scene in society and education was reflected in educational evaluation. While there was great expansion of education, society had no particular interest in holding educators accountable, in identifying and addressing the needs of the underprivileged, or in identifying and solving problems in the educational system. While educators wrote about evaluation and collected considerable data, they seem not to have related these efforts to attempts to improve educational services. This lack of a mission carried over into the development of the technical aspects of evaluation as well. There was considerable expansion of tools and strategies for applying the various approaches to evaluation — testing, "comparative experimentation," and "congruence between outcomes and objectives." As a consequence, educators were provided with new tests and test-scoring services, algorithms for writing behavioral objectives, taxonomies of objectives, new experimental designs, and new statistical procedures for analyzing educational data. But these contributions were not derived from any analysis of what information was needed to assess and improve education, nor were they an outgrowth of school-based experience.

During this period educational evaluations were, as they had been previously, primarily the purview of local school districts. Schools could do evaluation or not depending on local interest and expertise. Federal and state agencies had not yet become deeply involved in the evaluation of programs. Funds for evaluations came from local coffers, foundations, or professional organizations. This lack of external pressures and support for evaluations at all levels of education would end with the arrival of the next period in the history of evaluation.

The Age of Realism

The Age of Innocence in evaluation came to an abrupt end with the call in the late 1950s and early 1960s for evaluations of large-scale curriculum-development projects funded by federal monies. Educators were to find during this period that they no longer could do or not do evaluations as they pleased, and that their further developments of evaluation methodologies would have to be grounded in concerns for usability and relevance. Their rude awakenings during this period would mark the end of an era of complacency and help launch profound changes, guided by the public interest and dependent on taxpayer monies for support, that would see evaluation expand as an industry and into a profession.

As a result of the Russian launch of Sputnik I in 1957, the federal government responded by enacting the National Defense Education Act of 1958. Among other things, this act provided for new educational programs in mathematics, science, and foreign language and expanded counseling and guidance services and testing programs in school districts. A number of new national curriculum-development projects, especially in the areas of science and mathematics, were established. Eventually, funds were allocated to evaluate these programs.

All four approaches to evaluation discussed so far were represented in the evaluations done during this period. First, the Tyler approach was used to help define objectives for the new curricula and to assess the degree to which the objectives were later realized. Second, new nationally standardized tests were developed to better reflect the objectives and content of the new curricula. Third, the professional judgment approach was used to rate proposals and to check periodically on the efforts of contractors. Finally, many evaluators undertook to evaluate curriculum development efforts through the use of field experiments.

In the early 1960s some leaders in educational evaluation realized that their work and their results were not particularly helpful to curriculum developers, nor responsive to the questions about the programs being raised by those who wanted to know about their effectiveness. The "best and the brightest" of the educational evaluation community were involved in these efforts to evaluate these new curricula; they were adequately financed; they carefully applied the technology that had been developed during the past decade or more. Despite all this, they began to realize that their efforts were not succeeding.

This negative assessment was best reflected in a landmark article by Cronbach (1963; see unit 5). In looking at the evaluation efforts of the recent past, he sharply criticized the guiding conceptualizations of evaluations for their lack of relevance and utility and advised evaluators to turn away from their penchant for post hoc evaluations based on comparisons of the norm-referenced test scores of experimental and control groups. Cronbach counseled evaluators to reconceptualize evaluation not in terms of a horse race between competing programs, but instead as a process of gathering and reporting information that could help guide curriculum development. Cronbach argued that analysis and reporting of test-item scores would likely prove more useful to teachers than the reporting of average total scores. When first published, Cronbach's counsel and recommendations went largely unnoticed, except by a small circle of evaluation specialists. Nonetheless, the article was seminal, containing hypotheses about the conceptualization and conduct of evaluations that were to be tested and found valid within a few short years.

In 1965, guided by the vision of Senator Hubert Humphrey, the charismatic leadership of President John Kennedy, and the great political skill of President Lyndon Johnson, the War on Poverty was launched. These programs poured billions of dollars into reforms aimed at equalizing and upgrading opportunities for all U.S. citizens across a broad array of health, social, and educational services. The expanding economy enabled the federal government to finance these programs, and there was widespread support throughout the nation for developing what President Johnson termed the Great Society.

Accompanying this massive effort to help those in need was a concern in some quarters that the investments might be wasted if appropriate accountability requirements were not imposed. In response to this concern, Senator Robert Kennedy and some of his colleagues in the Congress amended the Elementary and Secondary Education Act of 1965 to include specific evaluation requirements. As a result, Title I of that act (aimed at providing compensatory education to disadvantaged children) specifically required each school district receiving funds under this title to evaluate annually — using appropriate standardized test data — the extent to which its Title I projects had achieved their objectives. This requirement, with its specific reference to standardized test data and to an assessment of congruence between outcomes and objectives, reflects the then state-of-the-art in educational evaluation. More importantly, the requirement forced educators to move their concern for educational evaluation from the realm of theory and supposition into the realm of practice and implementation.

When school districts began to respond to the evaluation requirements of Title I, they quickly found that the existing tools and strategies employed by their evaluators were largely inappropriate to the task. Available standardized tests had been designed to rank order students of average ability; they were of little use in diagnosing needs and assessing gains of disadvantaged children whose educational development lagged far behind that of their middle-class peers. Further, these tests were found to be relatively insensitive to differences between schools and/or programs, mainly because of their psychometric properties and content coverage. Instead of being measures of outcomes directly relating to the school or a particular program, these tests were at best indirect measures of learning, measuring much the same traits as general ability tests (Kellaghan, Madaus, and Airasian, 1980).

The use of standardized tests entailed another problem. Such an approach to evaluation conflicted with the precepts of the Tylerian approach. Because Tyler recognized and encouraged differences in objectives from locale to locale, this model became difficult to adapt to nationwide standardized testing programs. To be commercially viable these standardized testing programs had to overlook to some extent objectives stressed by particular locales in favor of objectives stressed in the majority of districts. Further, there was a dearth of information about the needs and achievement levels of disadvantaged children to guide teachers in developing meaningful behavioral objectives for this population of learners.

Attempts to isolate the effects of Title I projects through the use of experimental/control group designs failed, due primarily to an inability to meet the assumptions required of such designs. And site visitation to projects by experts — while extensively employed by governmental sponsors — was not acceptable as a primary evaluation strategy because this approach was seen as lacking the "objectivity" and "rigor" stipulated in the ESEA legislation. When the finding of no results was reported, as was generally the case, there was little information on what the treatment was supposed to be and often no data on the degree to which it had in fact been implemented. Typically, the emphasis on test scores diverted attention from consideration of the treatment or of treatment implementation.

As a result of the growing disquiet with evaluation efforts and consistently negative findings, the Phi Delta Kappa set up a National Study Committee on Evaluation (Stufflebeam et al., 1971). After surveying the scene this committee concluded that educational evaluation was "seized with a great illness" and called for the development of new theories and methods of evaluation as well as for new training programs for evaluators. At the same time many new conceptualizations of evaluation began to emerge. Provus (1971), Hammond (1967), Eisner (1967), and Metfessel and Michael (1967) proposed reformation of the Tyler model. Glaser (1963), Tyler (1967), and Popham (1971) pointed to criterion-referenced testing as an alternative to norm-referenced testing. Cook (1966) called for the use of the system-analysis approach to evaluate programs. Scriven (1967), Stufflebeam (1967, 1971), and Stake (1967) introduced new models for evaluation that departed radically from prior approaches. These conceptualizations recognized the need to evaluate goals, look at inputs, examine implementation and delivery of services, as well as measure intended and unintended outcomes of the program. They also emphasized the need to make judgments about the merit or worth of the object being evaluated. The late 1960s and early 1970s were vibrant with descriptions, discussions, and debates concerning how evaluation should be conceived. The remaining units deal in depth with the alternative approaches that began to take shape during this period.

The Age of Professionalism

Beginning in about 1973 the field of evaluation began to crystallize and emerge as a distinct profession related to, but quite distinct from, its forebears of research and testing. The field of evaluation has advanced considerably as a profession, yet it is instructive to consider this development in the context of the field in the previous period.

At that time, as just discussed, evaluators faced an identity crisis. They were uncertain of their role, whether they were to be researchers, testers, administrators, teachers, or philosophers. What special qualifications if any they should possess was unclear. There were no professional organizations dedicated to evaluation as a field; nor were there specialized journals through which evaluators could exchange information about their work. Essentially, no literature about educational evaluation existed except for unpublished papers that circulated through an underground network of practitioners. There was a paucity of preservice and in-service training opportunities in evaluation. Articulated standards of good practice were confined to educational and psychological tests. The field of evaluation was amorphous and fragmented. Many evaluations were carried out by untrained personnel, others by research methodologists who tried unsuccessfully to fit their methods to educational evaluations (Guba, 1966). Evaluation studies were fraught with confusion, anxiety, and animosity. Educational evaluation as a field had little stature and no political clout.

Against this backdrop, the progress made by educational evaluators to professionalize their field during the 1970s is quite remarkable indeed. A number of journals, including *Educational Evaluation and Policy Analysis, Studies in Evaluation, CEDR Quarterly, Evaluation Review, New Directions for Program Evaluation, Evaluation and Program Planning,* and *Evaluation News,* were begun; these journals have proved to be excellent vehicles for recording and disseminating information about the various facets of educational evaluation. Unlike 15 years ago, numerous books and monographs now deal exclusively with evaluation. In fact the problem today is not trying to find literature in evaluation but to keep up with it. The May 12 group, Division H of AERA, the Evaluation Network and the Evaluation Research Society have afforded excellent opportunities for professional exchange among persons concerned with the evaluation of education and other human service programs.

Many universities have begun to offer at least one course in evaluation methodology (as distinct from research methodology). A few — such as the University of Illinois, Stanford University, Boston College, UCLA, the University of Minnesota, and Western Michigan University — have developed graduate programs in evaluation. For seven years the U.S. Office of Education sponsored a national program of in-service training in evaluation for special educators (Brinkerhoff et al., 1983), and several professional organizations have offered workshops and institutes on various evaluation topics. Centers have been established for research and development related to evaluation; these include the evaluation unit of the Northwest Regional Educational Laboratory, the Center for the Study of Evaluation at UCLA, The Stanford Evaluation Consortium, the Center for Instructional Research and Curriculum Evaluation at the University of Illinois, the Evaluation Center at

Western Michigan University, and the Center for the Study of Testing, Evaluation, and Educational Policy at Boston College. The state of Louisiana has established a policy and program for certifying evaluators (Peck, 1981), Massachusetts is currently working on a similar certification program for evaluation, and Dick Johnson (1980) issued a first draft of a directory of evaluators and evaluation agencies.

Increasingly, the field has looked to metaevaluation (Scriven, 1975; Stufflebeam, 1978) as a means of assuring and checking the quality of evaluations. As already pointed out, a joint committee (Joint Committee, 1981), appointed by 12 professional organizations, issued a comprehensive set of standards for judging evaluations of educational programs, projects, and materials, and established a mechanism (Joint Committee, 1981) by which to review and revise the *Standards* and assist the field in their use. In addition, several other sets of standards with relevance for educational evaluation have been issued (see *Evaluation News,* May 1981). And many new techniques have been introduced, as described throughout this book.

This substantial professional development in educational evaluation has produced mixed results. First, while there is undoubtedly more and certainly better communication in the field, there has also been an enormous amount of "chatter" (Cronbach, 1980). Second, although the training and certification of evaluators have improved to ensure that institutions obtain services from qualified persons, some worry that this development may result in a narrow and exclusive club (Stake, 1981). Third, the cooperation among professional organizations concerned with educational evaluation, fostered by the Joint Committee on Standards for Educational Evaluation, is a promising but fragile arrangement for promoting the conduct and use of high quality evaluation work. Fourth, while the creation of new professional organizations has increased communication and reduced fragmentation in the evaluation field, there remains a fairly sharp division between Division H of AERA, the Evaluation Network, and the Evaluation Research Society. Finally, while there has been increased communication between advocates of positivistic/quantitative approaches to evaluation and proponents of phenomenological/qualitative approaches, there is a present danger of a polarization developing between these two camps.

In spite of growing search for appropriate methods, increased communication and understanding among the leading methodologists, and the development of new techniques, the actual practice of evaluation has changed very little in the great majority of settings. The need is clear for expanded efforts to educate evaluators to the availability of new techniques, to try out and report the results of using the new techniques, and to develop additional techniques. In all of these efforts, the emphasis must be on making the methodology fit the needs of professionals and those they serve.

We have portrayed educational evaluation as a dynamic yet developing profession. While the profession is still immature, it no doubt has increasingly become an identifiable component of the broader governmental and professional establishment of education, health, and welfare. The prediction commonly heard in the 1960s that formalized program evaluation was a fad and soon would disappear proved false, and the indications are strong that this field will continue to grow in importance, sophistication and stature. The gains since the late 1960s are impressive, but there are many obvious deficiencies and needs for continued examination and growth.

Roles in Evaluation Work

Thus far we have given and discussed a basic definition of evaluation, identified some of the methods involved in evaluation work, identified standards of this profession, and provided a historical overview. Given this background, we will conclude by looking at evaluation roles.

Whether an evaluation is conducted by one person or by many, a number of roles must be implemented, and when one considers the work entailed in supporting and promoting evaluation as a profession, this view of roles becomes even broader. Importantly, then those who will be involved either as specialists or generalists in evaluation must have a broad view of the pertinent roles to enhance their participation and collaboration with the team. Perhaps nothing is so destructive of the potential contribution of evaluation as the attitude that evaluation is an independent research pursuit of an individual investigator. On the contrary, evaluation at its best involves much teamwork.

In attempting to provide a broad view of the work involved in individual evaluations and in the evaluation profession in general, we have identified 12 basic roles. While other writers might identify a different set and assign different labels, we believe our roles encompass most if not all work responsibilities that evaluators might have to implement. Further, in our experience these 12 roles have been associated with actual job assignments. Of course, there would not always be a one-to-one correspondence between role and job, but we think these 12 roles should be useful to the reader not only for thinking about the broad array of evaluation activities but also for considering possible careers in evaluation. What follows, then, are brief definitions of 12 basic evaluation roles.

Evaluation Client

Any worthwhile evaluation includes a client who is integrally involved. This is true whether the study is conducted by one person to serve his or her own purposes or by many. The client is the person or group who will use the results for some purpose such as program selection or program improvement. The client group includes whoever commissioned the evaluation in the first place as well as those who will attend to and use the results. In one way or another the time and resources required for the evaluation are provided by the client or by one or more persons in the client group. The clients are also crucial sources of the questions to be addressed and of the criteria to be employed in interpreting the results; they also bear primary responsibility for applying the findings; and often an evaluation cannot be done if the client fails to set the stage politically and to take steps to ensure that there will be full cooperation among those to be involved.

In educational, social, and health organizations, are found a variety of key clients. These include, for example, school district superintendents, hospital administrators, and agency directors; school principals, department chairpersons, and grants administrators; and teachers, psychologists, and physicians. If evaluation is to contribute maximally to the provision of meritorious and worthy services to people, this full range of clients must be involved and served. Moreover, we believe they must be actively engaged in commissioning and planning evaluations in order to derive the information they need to do their jobs well. Therefore, in order to fulfill these expectations, they must be properly trained, as must, indeed, all those persons who will be involved in implementing the other 11 roles. We wish to emphasize that perhaps the most important mission of evaluation training programs — both preservice and in-service — is to prepare clients of evaluation to carry out their evaluation responsibilities. If they do not have a sound concept of evaluation, they will likely avoid it, be passive in their associations with it, not direct it to serve their purposes, and/or find its products of little interest. But as knowledgeable clients, they can help to ensure that evaluation is a powerful and useful tool for assuring the quality of professional services.

Evaluation Designer

One of the most fascinating aspects of evaluation work is that it is a creative enterprise. Designing an evaluation to respond to a client's information requirements is far from a routine mechanical process. Among other responsibilities, one must conceptualize the questions to be addressed, size up the political scene, lay out a data-collection and analysis plan, design the reports and the reporting process, project the staffing and financial requirements, and determine how the standards of the evaluation profession will be met. No models of past evaluations nor published designs serve as all-purpose solutions to this complex set of planning decisions. On the contrary, evaluation design typically is a continuing conceptual process.

To design a good evaluation, one must be a sensitive observer of social settings, a discerning interviewer and listener, and a willing and able learner about the substance of the program to be examined. The evaluator must also be knowledgeable of a wide range of inquiry and communication techniques and able to draw together diverse pieces of specifications and information into coherent guiding rationales and practical work plans.

Next to the role of the evaluation client, we see the role of evaluation designer as the most crucial role in evaluation work. Those who become very proficient in evaluation design are often employed full time as evaluators and are in great demand as consultants to assist evaluation clients to design and commission evaluation studies.

The general evaluation conceptualizations presented in units 3 through 10 provide crucial study material for those who wish to increase their facility in conceptualizing evaluation plans. These units describe the general approaches that have been evolved by some of the evaluators who have become widely recognized as experts in designing evaluations. Beyond studying the creative contributions of others, we emphasize that development of one's evaluation design capabilities requires practice — one needs to be involved in designing a wide range of evaluations. This practice, we think, should include some individual work with a client. In addition, much can be learned by participating with teams that are charged with planning evaluations. Also, the study of a wide range of evaluation designs prepared by others provides many good examples and insights into this complex work area. We believe that evaluation training programs should include practicums and other forms of guided practice in the design of evaluations.

Evaluation Coordinator

Many evaluations involve the efforts of a number of participants, the use of considerable resources, and services to multiple clients. Hence, a need for considerable coordination of the work effort exists. This need is magnified when a given agency has a number of different evaluation projects underway. Not surprisingly, therefore, the profession includes many evaluation jobs with titles such as assistant superintendent for evaluation, coordinator of evaluation projects, director of the evaluation office, and staff director of the evaluation project.

One implication of this role is that persons specializing in evaluation should obtain training in management functions. Another is that those who are assigned to manage evaluation work must also possess or acquire basic proficiency in evaluation design. Finally, we believe that major educational, health, and social institutions should often organize their evaluation efforts into a well-managed unit of the institution.

Evaluation Caseworkers

Frequently, a crucial, and often separable, role in evaluation is that of evaluation caseworker, or fieldworker. This role involves periodic interactions with clients, review of program documents, observation of program activities, interviewing and otherwise gathering information from participants, drafting reports, and assuming primary responsibility for presenting the findings. Sometimes the caseworker is in charge of implementing the complete study design. In other cases, he or she has a narrower responsibility. But this person is vitally involved in interacting with program personnel and helping to carry out the study design.

Both technical and human relations skills are required to perform the caseworker role. Moreover, the person assigned to this role must possess or be able to develop credibility with the clients and with those who are involved in carrying out the program.

Evaluation Respondents

A role, too often taken for granted, is that of the evaluation respondent. These are the people who fill out the forms, answer the test questions, respond to interview questions, submit their work products, and allow their work to be observed. In many cases, the quality of evaluation information obtained is heavily dependent on their willingness to cooperate and to give their best effort. They are unlikely to do either of these tasks well if they are not informed about their role and convinced of the importance of the study. Consequently, those in charge of evaluations should make special efforts to ensure that the study will be of some value to the respondents as well as to other clients. They should also be careful to provide activities by which to motivate and train respondents to respond appropriately.

Technical Support Specialists

Most evaluations involve a certain amount of technical work that requires specialized expertise. For example, there may be a need to conduct and record the results of interviews; develop, administer, and score structured data collection instruments; analyze both qualitative and quantitative information; and produce audiovisual presentations of the findings.

In small-scale evaluations a single evaluation generalist must often do all such tasks without specialized assistance. The single evaluation agent is hard pressed to coordinate and do the necessary fieldwork while also fulfilling all required technical specialties. This evolution agent needs broad-gauged training in the wide range of relevant specialties. Often, this person must also be able to engage the assistance of qualified consultants.

Inevitably, however, large-scale studies must engage specialists to perform these tasks so that the evaluation caseworkers can concentrate their efforts on fieldwork with the evaluation clients and evaluation respondents. This group of experts could include test-development specialists, sampling specialists, data-processing specialists, statisticians, case-study specialists, and technical writers.

Information Specialist

One technical role that we have singled out for special attention is the information specialist. We have done so because this role involves an ongoing need for information that pertains to a series of evaluations as opposed to ad hoc technical problems that are particular to given studies. The information specialist role is especially important in agencies that maintain evaluation offices. The evaluations conducted by such offices must take into account the institutional setting and its historical context, examine current and past findings to determine trends, and avoid needless duplication of data collection efforts. What is needed, at minimum, is a good system for indexing and storing evaluation reports so that the information they contain can be easily accessed in future evaluations. In addition, many agencies would benefit by regularly collecting standardized information to help them track their inputs, processes, and outputs over time, as well as the attitudes of their constituents toward the agency's services.

Fulfillment of the information specialist role requires that the evaluator, or one or more members of the evaluation team, be proficient in information sciences. Such proficiency requires knowledge and skills in such areas as communication, information systems, data processing, financial accounting, and long-range planning. Persons who plan to specialize in evaluation should develop a general command of the information specialties, as a certain amount of work in this area is involved in even the single-person evaluation. In addition, offices of evaluation often should assign one or more persons to fulfill this important function.

Communication Specialist

At its best, evaluation is effective communication about some object's merit and worth. That is, clients' questions guide the work of the evaluators, and their message reaches and informs the client. Neither of these objectives is possible without effective communication between the evaluator and client.

All too often, however, effective communication is missing in evaluation work. Evaluators and/or clients assume that evaluators know their business and somehow will obtain and report the right message; instead evaluators often address the wrong questions. Alternatively, evaluators may do a good job of involving the clients in focusing the evaluation and collecting sound and potentially useful information, then "drop the ball" by failing to follow through and help the clients to interpret and apply the information. We wish to make emphatically clear that effective evaluation includes not only collecting and analyzing appropriate information but also ensuring through effective communication technology that the information will be presented in a useful form and subsequently used. We know that evaluators should not be held accountable for all misinterpretations and misuses of their reports, but they should be held accountable, among other things, for ensuring that their reports are relevant to the interests of audiences and understood by them.

To do so requires that evaluators be skilled in communication technology. Basically, they must be able to prepare clearly written reports that are directed to, and understandable by, the intended audience or audiences. Beyond being good writers, they need to be skilled in audience analysis and in designing different reports for different audiences. They also need facility in communicating findings through means other than printed material; for example, they need skills in public speaking, use of audiovisual techniques, and use of public media. Finally, we would mention that they need skills of political analysis and conflict management, since evaluations often are involved in controversy.

The communication specialty role has considerable implications for the training of evaluators, their use of consultants, and the staffing of evaluation offices. Clearly, evaluators should obtain training in a broad range of communication techniques. In their practice, they should, at a minimum, submit their draft reports to editors. And evaluation offices often should employ communication specialists to assist in planning evaluations and presenting the findings. Such specialists also have an important role in evaluating and helping to improve an evaluation office's performance over time in communicating its reports to its clients.

The analysis of roles to this point helps to make clear the complexity of evaluation work. A large agency, which must repeatedly do evaluations of its services over time, may have need of a full staff of evaluation specialists. Figure 1-1 is provided as an example of how an agency's evaluation office might be organized to directly provide the various evaluation functions. As seen in this organization chart, the evaluation coordinator bears responsibility for meeting the evaluation needs of the parent agency and its constituents. To assist in carrying out this role, the coordinator can direct the efforts of a variety of specialists. To the extent that their work is effectively coordinated, the office's services will be technically sound and influential. At the same time, we would emphasize that evaluations must often be done by single evaluators. To do their work well, they must become proficient in the wide range of roles already identified. Probably, the best means of encountering and learning how to address the full range of evaluation roles is by conducting single-person evaluations under the tutelage of an evaluation expert. Participation in team evaluation efforts also provides excellent learning opportunities. Evaluators must be resourceful in using the assistance of consultants, who may be available to them at low cost or no cost. Even the Lone Ranger found it necessary and beneficial to collaborate with a trusted and capable associate!

To this point in this analysis of evaluation roles, we have considered only those roles that pertain to an actual evaluation. Now we turn to four others that are involved as support roles in the professionalization of evaluation.

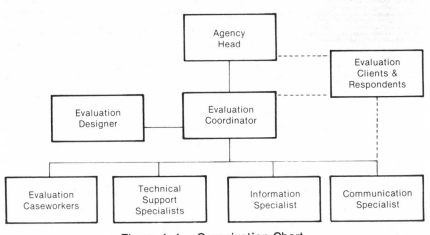

Figure 1-1.   Organization Chart

Evaluation Trainer

Throughout the preceding analysis we have referred to the training needs of those who participate in evaluation. These needs encompass orientation to specific evaluation plans as well as the development of more generalized understandings and skills, and they most definitely include understandings that are acquired through examining one's practice. Moreover, the training needs pertain to the clients and respondents in evaluations, as well as to the evaluation specialists.

Evaluation, like any other profession, must ensure that the participants in evaluation are provided with a wide range of sound evaluation training opportunities. These include specialized training programs leading to graduate degrees in evaluation; service courses that are provided to assist those who are in training for a wide range of professional roles — such as superintendent, social worker, teacher, and physician — to evaluate their professional services; continuing educational opportunities in evaluation for both evaluation specialists and generalists; and orientation sessions for the clients and respondents in specific evaluation studies. Such training should present up-to-date content that is relevant to the field problems faced by the trainees. Clearly, evaluation training is a crucial role in maintaining and advancing quality evaluation services.

Evaluation Researcher

The mission of any profession is to serve clients as well as possible, and the fulfillment of this commitment is always limited by the current state of knowledge about the field. Therefore, professions must have a research ethos. Professionals must study the profession-related needs and problems of their clients, study their services to clients, examine their practices in the light of knowledge and principles from relevant disciplines, examine their work in its historical context, theorize about the professional services, and move forward knowledge about their field through structured examination of the field's guiding assumptions and hypotheses.

Vast research programs are evident in mature professions such as medicine and law, and in business and industry. In the former case, such research is driven by the professional ethic of delivering the best possible service. In the latter case, the primary motivation is profit and survival in a competitive world. Both areas are strongly aware that improved service and competitiveness depend heavily on a dynamic program of pertinent research.

While evaluation is as old as civilization, it has existed as a formal field of practice for a very short time. Only in the last two decades have serious efforts been made to record the history of the field, theorize about evaluation practice, and conduct pertinent descriptive and hypothesis-testing studies. But there is and should be a strong trend toward establishing and maintaining a research base for the field. This trend is especially evident in the exploding literature of the evaluation field, although much of this material does not qualify as research. In any case, we wish to emphasize that research on evaluation is a vital role in ensuring that evaluators progressively improve their services and impacts.

Evaluation Developer

Another vital role is that of the evaluation developer. This role has at its base the function of helping evaluators collectively to attain and maintain the status of a profession. What is at issue in this role can be seen in a dictionary definition that characterizes a profession as "a calling requiring specialized knowledge and often long and intensive preparation including instruction in skills and methods as well as in the scientific, historical, or scholarly principles underlying such skills and methods, maintaining by force of organization or concerted opinion high standards of achievement and conduct, and committing its members to continued study and to a kind of work which has as its prime purpose the rendering of a public service."

The evaluation field is beginning to manifest the charcteristics of a profession that are contained in this definition. There are now training programs leading to masters and doctors degrees in evaluation, as well as an extensive and burgeoning literature of evaluation. The evaluation literature prescribes content and experiences to be included in evaluation training programs, as well as analyzes how the programs should draw from related disciplines, such as philosophy, psychology, sociology, and economics. Several professional organizations and two major sets of professional standards are available to evaluators. And, of course, government, the public, and service organizations are continuing to demand evaluations of professional services, as well as funds to support these services. To sustain these thrusts toward professionalization of evaluation requires national and state leadership and much support from the members of the evaluation profession. Each person who is gainfully employed as an evaluator bears a professional obligation to assist in the various efforts to develop the evaluation profession. Among the specific functions to be served are evaluation journal editor, developer of standards, provider of continuing education for evaluation generalists and specialists, and official in an evaluation society. By sharing responsibilities for these functions, evaluators can help to assure the public that services by professional evaluators will be up-to-date and of high quality.

Metaevaluator

The final role we wish to emphasize is the overarching and pervasive role of metaevaluator. Involved with evaluating evaluation, the role extends to assessing the worth and merit of all that the profession is and does — evaluation services, use of evaluations, evaluation training, evaluation research, and organizational development. Metaevaluation invokes the accepted standards of the profession and assesses and tries to assure that they are met. It also is involved when the standards themselves are examined to identify wherein they might need to be revised.

In one way or another, metaevaluation needs to be incorporated into each activity of the evaluation profession. Sometimes it is a self-assessment activity, as when evaluators, evaluation trainers, evaluation researchers, or officials of evaluation societies scrutinize their plans, work efforts, and products against the standards of the evaluation profession. In other cases it involves engaging an independent agent to assess professional evaluation services. The aim of metaevaluation is to assure quality evaluation services, to guard against or deal with malpractice or services not in the public interest, to provide direction for improvement of the profession, and to promote increased understanding of the evaluation enterprise. Clearly, all professional evaluators should maintain up-to-date knowledge of the field's standards, should incorporate them in their work, should be willing to serve as metaevaluator in relation to the work of others in the profession, and should be proactive in evaluating and trying to improve the contributions of evaluation to society.

With this brief discussion of metaevaluation we conclude our overview of evaluation roles. In a sense, we have dissected the role of the professional evaluator and have looked at its constituent parts. Rightly, we think, this has supported the impression that evaluation is often a team effort. But to conclude that evaluations need to involve team efforts would be a misinterpretation. On the contrary, evaluation is necessarily an integral part of every professional's role. Our message is that this role is as difficult as it is important. The obvious fundamental conclusion is that all professionals should develop the capability to meet their evaluation responsibilities well, whether or not they can draw assistance from a team or must perform all of the evaluation functions individually.

One basic step in the right direction is to increase one's facility to conceptualize evaluation problems and approaches to facilitate the solution of those problems. The remainder of this book has been prepared to guide this process. It presents and examines in depth a number of alternative conceptualizations of evaluation.

Knowledge Test for Unit 1

You will find that each unit concludes with three different types of questions or exercises; each, in its own way, will test your grasp of the unit. You will be presented with multiple-choice questions or statements, and explanations of the correctness or otherwise of the alternative answers. Both questions and responses should allow you to determine whether you have reached a satisfactory level in relation to the knowledge objectives of the unit. In each instance, circle the letter for what you consider to be the best response and then assess your choice against the scoring key and the interpretation of the alternative responses that follow.

After you have completed all the knowledge questions, you will be asked to review your performance and either to remediate your grasp of the unit or to continue with the other exercises. Then you will be presented with some application exercises. The unit concludes with "Questions Without Answers" and recommended supplementary readings.

Question 1. Which of the following responses encompasses what this unit maintains are the essential value bases to be considered in evaluating an object?

a. Although other criteria have a place, the essential ones are merit, need, and equity.
b. All values highly prized by evaluation personnel and their clients must be considered.
c. The evaluators may choose the value bases, based on their guiding philosophy.
d. Expectations of clients, merit, need, feasibility, and equity are the criteria for determining value bases.

Correct Response. You should have circled "d." The different expectation of *clients,* the *merit* of the object (or service) in question, the extent of the *need* for this object, the feasibility or political viability of the object, and the *equity* or equal opportunities for all to have access to the object will be guiding standards for the evaluator.

Incorrect Responses

a. Incorrect because it is incomplete.
b. Incorrect because the unit specifically identified five value bases.
c. Incorrect because the evaluators' subjectivity could give an inappropriate slant to the study, whereas if they are guided by the suggested criteria, no main value bases would be ignored.

Question 2. The stance taken in this unit is that evaluations should in general be

a. comparative of available alternatives before the program or service develops.
b. comparative both before the program starts and also periodically after development.
c. comparative before the program begins, noncomparative during development, and occasionally comparative thereafter.
d. neither comparative nor noncomparative.

Correct Response. You should have marked "c." Comparative evaluation before the program commences allows critical comparisons to be made among competing alternatives; noncomparative evaluation during development allows program personnel to concentrate on the best ways to progress; and comparative evaluation periodically after the program has been sustained will open the way for major advancements.

Incorrect Responses.

a. Incorrect as both the noncomparative and the postoperational comparative phases have been omitted.
b. Incorrect because the noncomparative phase has been omitted.
d. Incorrect because any evaluation is comparative, noncomparative, or both according to the information needs of the clients and/or the audience of the evaluation.

Question 3. Which of the following statements is most consistent with the position taken in this unit regarding the methods that may appropriately be employed in evaluation studies?

a. To avoid the slipshod work that often ensues from attempts to use multiple methods, an evaluator should specialize in using one main technique, such as experimental design or case study.
b. In general, it is appropriate to pursue an eclectic approach to the selection of methods, but the evaluator should avoid the use of unscientific approaches, such as case study and political analysis.
c. The state-of-the-art regarding methods for use in evaluation work is advanced, and evaluators should concentrate not on assessing existing methods and developing new ones but on learning and using the available methodology, especially from the fields of educational and psychological research.
d. In general, evaluators need to be proficient in using a wide range of inquiry techniques, and evaluation methodologists should develop new techniques.

Correct Response. You should have selected "d." This unit both advocates the employment of an eclectic approach to evaluation and points to the need for new evaluation tools and strategies.

Incorrect Responses

a. Incorrect because the unit advocates the use of multiple techniques.
b. Incorrect because the unit encourages the use of a wide range of techniques including case study and political analysis.
c. Incorrect because this unit advocates both employing a wide range of extant methodology and developing new methods.

Question 4. Which of the following statements *best* reflects the Tylerian age of evaluation (1930–1945)?

a. Standardized testing was introduced to make education more efficient.
b. The Tylerian approach was distinguished by a concentration on clearly stated objectives and their achievement.
c. Evaluators learned to help curriculum developers to clarify student behaviors that arose with the implementation of a curriculum.
d. Internal comparisons of outcomes with objectives proved costly.

Correct Response. You should have circled "b." This points up Tyler's philosophy and practical approach to evaluation.

Incorrect Responses

a. Incorrect because standardized testing was developed in the pre-Tylerian period (early in the 1900s).
c. While this is not incorrect, it is a narrow depiction of Tyler's alternative to earlier views of evaluation.
d. Incorrect; in fact, to the contrary, internal evaluations proved to be less costly because they didn't require the services of an evaluation specialist.

Question 5. Which statement is *most* in keeping with the period in the evolution of evaluation termed the Age of Innocence (1946–1957)?

a. While there was great expansion of education, there was no particular interest by society in holding educators accountable.
b. Evaluations were not particularly concerned with reliability of differences between the scores of individual students.
c. Federal agencies began to take a very strong interest in the evaluation of programs.
d. During this time, new test scoring services, algorithms, experimental designs, and statistical procedures were provided in response to an analysis of needs in education.

Correct Response. You should have circled "a." This statement accurately reflects the lack of evaluation for accountability or, indeed, other purposes, even though educational provisions were expanding rapidly.

Incorrect Responses

b. Incorrect; concentration on standardized testing carried a main concern for reliably ranking students.
c. Incorrect, as this development was not extensive until the 1960s.
d. Incorrect because, sadly, such was not the case; developments such as those listed paid little or no heed to the requirements, including needed improvements, of education.

Question 6. Which of the following statements is most pertinent to evaluation developments during the Age of Realism (1958–1972)?

a. From 1965, billions of dollars were poured into programs aimed at equalizing and improving opportunities in health, social, and educational services.

b. Title I of the Elementary and Secondary Act of 1965 aimed at providing compensatory education to disadvantaged children; adequate evaluation methodologies for these programs were fortunately available.
c. Emphasis on test scores directed close attention to the programs themselves.
d. Cronbach's sharp criticisms (1963) that present evaluation methods lacked relevance, and that evaluation should become a process of gathering and reporting information to guide curriculum development, was very timely.

Correct Response. You should have circled "d." Cronbach's criticisms contained in his 1963 article were a major step forward in the quest to provide appropriate methodologies to respond to the evaluation requirements of the 1960s.

Incorrect Responses

a. Incorrect, as this is a statement about a politically inspired program and not evaluation per se, even though subsequent developments forced a rapid growth in evaluation methodologies.
b. Incorrect because evaluation methodologies used to that time were quite inadequate.
c. Incorrect; the opposite is closer to the truth, as test scores diverted attention from consideration of the program or its implementation.

Question 7. Which of the following, according to this unit, best characterizes the status of evaluation in 1983?

a. Evaluators had made significant progress toward establishing evaluation as a formal field of practice.
b. Increasingly, evaluation was being recognized as a pretender to becoming a profession. This area of work had had its hayday in the 1960s; it was fast passing away from the public view and was no longer receiving much financial support.
c. In the area of methodology evaluators had reached almost complete agreement that evaluations should employ naturalistic approaches and avoid using quantitative methods.
d. In response to the major methodological developments of the past decade, thoroughgoing change and reform in evaluation practice were evident.

Correct Response. You should have selected "a." Signs of professionalizing evaluation in evidence by 1983 included established evaluation journals, numerous books and monographs on the topic, professional evaluation organizations, professional standards of practice, graduate training programs, one state program for certifying evaluators, and considerable research and development on evaluation topics.

Incorrect Responses

b. Incorrect because contrary to previous claims, that formalized evaluation was a fad and would soon fade away, the field had begun to take on the signs of a profession.
c. Incorrect because a sharp division in the field remained between those who advocated experimental/quantitative methods and those who advocated naturalistic/qualitative methods.
d. Incorrect because in spite of growing capabilities of evaluators, actual evaluation practice, according to this unit, had changed very little in most settings.

Interpreting the Knowledge Test.   Having completed the knowledge test, please check over your performance. We advise you to review relevant parts of the test for any questions you missed or doubted or for which you were otherwise confused about the appropriateness of our keyed response and explanation.

Application Exercise

This section includes one exercise designed to help you assess whether you understand and see the applicability of the main contents of this unit. We suggest that you record your response to the exercise on a separate sheet of paper and then compare your response to the sample response that follows.

Exercise 1.   Suppose the head of the welfare department in a large city engaged you to discuss the agency's plan for evaluating its programs on an ongoing basis. Suppose further that the agency head endorsed the concept of "self-evaluation," according to which each staff member in the agency is responsible for evaluating his or her own work. Also, the head noted that there would be no office of evaluation, no full- or part-time evaluation specialists, no special pay for evaluation work. Instead, he wanted to remind all of his 95 staff members that they are responsible for evaluating their work and then to provide them with an evaluation approach and training in it, so that they could get on with their evaluation efforts. The head thought this evaluation activity would be one important means of convincing the state legislature to increase support of the agency.

How would you respond, especially in light of the pertinent material in this unit?

Responses to Exercise 1 might appropriately include the following points:

a. Each professional is indeed responsible for the quality and hence the evaluation of his or her contributions.
b. While professionals do require training in evaluation, this work is far too complex to assume that individual professionals, acting independently, can do all of the evaluation needed to address the state legislature's questions about the agency.
c. Undoubtedly, appropriate methodological training would be a positive step toward professionalizing the work of the agency, but in both planning the training and deciding how to allocate resources to evaluation, the agency decision maker should consider a broad range of evaluation roles.
d. The roles involved in an agency's evaluation work are approximately as follows: evaluation client, evaluation design specialist, coordinator of evaluation services, field evaluator, technical consultant, information specialist, and communication specialist.

Questions without Answers

This section contains questions designed to assist you to think about and extend your insight into the issues contained in the unit. No answers to the questions are given. We suggest that you attempt to develop answers to the questions by pursuing such steps as reviewing the unit, consulting pertinent literary sources, including those that are listed at the back of the unit, and by discussing the questions with your fellow students and colleagues.

1. Is the definition of evaluation given in the unit equally defensible from the point of view of different philosophical schools, such as pragmatism, existentialism, and logical positivism?
2. Considering this unit's advocacy of an eclectic approach to choosing methods for use in evaluation work, are there research findings

concerning the undesirability or desirability of eclectically choosing methods from related fields — such as educational research, psychological research, accounting, and city planning — that would tend to support or refute the wisdom of the eclectic approach to choosing inquiry methods?

3. Some persons have suggested that some of the Joint Committee *Standards* for evaluations should be addressed before considering others, that is, the sequence of the presentation and consideration of the individual standards is considered by this view to be important. Do you agree or disagree? If you agree, how would you rank the *Standards* for consideration in reaching a decision about whether to perform a proposed evaluation? If you think the sequence with which the *Standards* are considered is not important, why not?

4. Consider this unit's historical account of the development of evaluation theory and practice. How would you evaluate the field's growth, regression, or stagnation regarding social responsibility, scholarship, and impact?

5. Considering the thrust of the unit and especially the analysis of roles involved in evaluation work, to what extent do you think society should invest in training and employing evaluation specialists versus evaluation generalists? Where, how, and to what extent should both types of evaluators be trained?

References

American Psychological Association. 1974. *Standards for educational and psychological tests.* Washington, D.C.: Author.

Anderson, S.; Ball, S.; and Murphy, R. and Associates. 1974. *Encylopedia of educational evaluation.* San Francisco: Jossey-Bass.

Bloom, B.S.; Englehart, M.D.; Furst, E.J.; Hill, W.H.; and Krathwohl, D.R. 1956. *Taxonomy of educational objectives. Handbook I: The cognitive domain.* New York: David McKay.

Bloom, B.S.; Madaus, G.F.; and Hastings, J.T. 1981. *Evaluation to improve learning.* New York: McGraw-Hill.

Brinkerhoff, R.; Brethower, D.; Hluchyj, T.; and Nowakowski, J. 1983. *Program evaluation: A practitioners' guide for trainers and educators.* Boston: Kluwer-Nijhoff.

Campbell, D.T., and Stanley, J.C. 1963. Experimental and quasi-experimental designs for research on teaching. In N.L. Gage (ed.), *Handbook of research on teaching.* Chicago: Rand McNally.

Coleman, J.S.; Campbell, E.Q.; Hobson, C.J.; McPartland, J.; Modd, A.M.; Weinfeld, F.D.; and York, R.L. 1966. *Equalty of educational opportunity.* Washington, D.C.: Office of Education, U.S. Department of Health, Education, and Welfare.

Cook, D.L. 1966. *Program evaluation and review technique: Applications in Education.* Washington, D.C.: Government Printing Office.

_____ . 1971. *Educational project management.* Columbus, Ohio: Charles E. Merrill.

Cronbach, L.J. 1963. Course improvement through evaluation. *Teachers College Record, 64,* 672–683.

_____ . 1980. *Toward reform of program evaluation.* San Francisco: Jossey-Bass.

Eisner, E.W. "Educational objectives: Help or hindrance?" *The School Review,* 75 (1967):250–260.

_____ . 1975. *The perceptive eye: Toward the reformation of educational evaluation.* Stanford, California: Stanford Evaluation Consortium, December.

Glaser, R. "Instructional technology and the measurement of learning outcomes: Some questions." *American Psychologist, 18* (1963):519–521.

Glass, G. 1976. Primary secondary and meta analysis of research. *Educational Researcher, 5* (10), 3–8.

Guba, E.G. "A Study of Title III activities: Report on evaluation." (National Institute for the Study of Educational Change, Indiana University, October, 1966) (mimeo).

Guba, E.G., and Lincoln, Y.S. 1981. *Effective evaluation.* San Francisco, Washington, London: Jossey-Bass.

Hammond, R.L. 1967. "Evaluation at the local level." Address to the Miller Committee for the National Study of ESEA Title III.

Johnson, R. 1980. *Directory of evaluators and evaluation agencies.* New York: Exxon Corporation.

Joint Committee on Standards for Educational Evaluation. 1981. *Standards for evaluations of educational programs, projects, and materials.* New York: McGraw-Hill.

Kaplan, A. 1964. *The conduct of inquiry.* San Francisco: Chandler.

Kellaghan, T. 1982. "Los sistemas escolares como objecto de evaluación." In Daniel Stufflebeam; Thomas Kellaghan; and Benjamin Alvarez (eds.), *La Evaluación Educativa.* Bogota: Pontificia Universidad Javeriana.

Kellaghan, T.; Madaus, G.; and Airasian, P. 1982. *The effects of standardized testing.* Hingham, Mass.: Kluwer-Nijhoff Publishing.

Krathwohl, D.R.; Bloom, B.S.; and Masia, B.B. 1964. *Taxonomy of educational objectives: The classification of educational goals. Handbook II: Affective domain.* New York: David McKay.

Metfessel, N.S., and Michael, W.B. "A paradigm involving multiple criterion measures for the evaluation of the effectiveness of school programs." *Educational and Psychological Measurement, 27* (1967):931–943.

Peck, H. "Report on the certification of evaluators in Louisiana." Paper presented at the meeting of the Southern Educational Research Association, Lexington, Kentucky, Fall 1981.

Popham, W.J. 1971. *Criterion-referenced measurement.* Englewood Cliffs, N.J.: Educational Technology Publications.

Provus, M. 1969. *Discrepancy evaluation model.* Pittsburgh, Pennsylvania: Pittsburgh Public Schools.

Reinhard, D. 1972. *Methodology developments for input evaluation using advocate and design teams.* Unpublished Doctoral Dissertation, Ohio State University.

Rice, J.M. 1897. The futility of the spelling grind. *The Forum, 23,* 163–172.

_____. 1914. *Scientific management in education.* New York: Hinds Noble and Eldredge.

Roth, J. 1977. Needs and the needs assessment process. *Evaluation News, 5,* 15–17.

Scriven, M.S. 1967. The methodology of evaluation. In *Perspectives of curriculum evaluation (AERA Monograph Series on Curriculum Evaluation,* No. 1). Chicago: Rand McNally.

_____. 1974. Prose and cons about goal-free evaluation. *Evaluation Comment, 3,* 1–4.

_____. 1975. *Evaluation bias and its control. Occasional Paper Series* No. 4, Western Michigan University, Evaluation Center.

Smith, E.R., and Tyler, R.W. 1942. *Appraising and recording student progress.* New York: Harper.

Smith, N.L. 1981a. *Metaphors for evaluation: Sources of new methods.* Beverly Hills: Sage.

_____. 1981b. *New techniques for evaluation.* Beverly Hills: Sage.

Stake, R.E. 1967. The countenance of educational evaluation. *Teachers College Record, 68,* 523–540.

_____. 1975. *Program evaluation, particularly responsive evaluation. Occasional Paper Series* No. 5, Western Michigan University, Evaluation Center.

_____. 1978. The case-study method in social inquiry. *Educational Researcher, 7,* 5–8.

_____. "Setting standards for educational evaluators." *Evaluation News* no. 2, *2* (1981):148–152.

Stufflebeam, D.L. "The use and abuse of evaluation in Title III." *Theory Into Practice, 6* (1967):126–133.

_____. 1978. Metaevaluation: An overview. *Evaluation and the Health Professions, 1* (2), 146–163.

Stufflebeam, D.L., et al. 1971. *Educational evaluation and decision making.* Itasca, Ill.: Peacock.

Suarez, T. 1980. *Needs assessments for technical assistance: A conceptual overview and comparison of three strategies.* Unpublished doctoral dissertation, Western Michigan University.

Tyler, R.W. 1967. Changing concepts of educational evaluation. In R.E. Stake (ed.), *Perspectives of curriculum evaluation* (Vol. 1). New York: Rand McNally.

Webster, W.J. 1975. *The organization and functions of research and evaluation units in a large urban school district.* The Dallas Independent School District, Dallas.

2 AN ANALYSIS OF ALTERNATIVE APPROACHES TO EVALUATION

Three major approaches to evaluating programs are set forth in this unit. The first — pseudoevaluation — includes attempts to mislead through evaluation. The second — quasievaluation — encompasses studies that are preoccupied with answering given questions of interest instead of assessing the value of something. The third — true evaluation — considers what we see as comprehensive efforts to examine the worth and merit of an object. Particular study types that are associated with each approach are examined in detail and contrasted with each other. In general, this unit provides an overview of 12 types of evaluation studies.

Typically, clients want a politically advantageous study (pseudoevaluation), evaluators prefer to conduct a questions-oriented study (quasievaluation), and consumers want a values-oriented study (true evaluation). Evaluators should be keenly sensitive to their own agendas for an evaluation as well as those held by developers and consumers.

Among the most important developments in the field of evaluation are the diverse ways in which evaluation has been conceptualized. This unit provides an overview and analysis of three general approaches that have been advocated or employed under the label of systematic evaluation. These ap-

45

proaches are unique and comprise most efforts to evaluate services. Whereas two of the approaches are typically used in legitimate efforts to assess worth and merit, one of them is often used illegitimately to create a false impression of an object's value. Not surprisingly, the various types of studies delineated in the remainder of this book are those that we see as fitting into the two legitimate categories of evaluation. We have included commentary on the other approach because it is widely employed and, we feel, should be exposed as inappropriate practice. Under the guise of systematic evaluation, this approach often misleads audiences. In general, the material in this unit is derived from a previous study by Stufflebeam and Webster (1980).

Objectives

This unit has been designed to help you achieve the following objectives:

1. When given the unit's definition of evaluation and a set of descriptions of evaluation studies, you should be able to classify them as pseudo-evaluation, quasievaluation, or true evaluation and identify the study type with which each one is most closely associated.
2. When given labels associated with two or more of the study types reviewed in this chapter, you should be able to contrast them in terms of advance organizers, purposes served, sources of questions, types of questions addressed, methods typically used, and key developers and proponents.
3. When given the names of selected study types, you should be able to list the general strengths and weaknesses of each one, with regard to the conduct of evaluation as it is defined in this book.

After you have studied the body of this unit, you will encounter a set of self-scoring test questions and exercises with keyed responses that partially reflect the above objectives. We suggest that you work through these evaluation exercises in order to assess your mastery of the material in the unit. At the end of the unit you will also find "Questions Without Answers" and suggested readings, which are intended to guide your further study of the concepts treated in the unit.

Alternative Conceptualizations of Evaluation

The study types reviewed here and throughout this book were selected to represent broadly the diverse views and practices to evaluate education, especially, but also health and welfare programs. The various study types were classified according to their degree of conformity to a particular definition of evaluation. Consistent with our explanation in unit 1, we define evaluation here as a *systematic study that is designed, conducted, and reported in order to assist a client group to judge and/or improve the worth and/or merit of some object.* We think this definition should be widely acceptable because it agrees with definitions of evaluation that appear in most dictionaries. However, the following analysis shows that many studies done in the name of systematic evaluation either do not conform to this definition or directly oppose it.

Using the proposed definition, each of the study types presented in this book was examined to see whether it fitted into one (or perhaps more) of three broad but distinct groups. The first group includes politically oriented evaluations, which either are surreptitiously conducted or used to promote a positive or a negative view of an object, irrespective of its objectively assessed worth or merit. The second group includes evaluations that are oriented to answer specified questions whose answers may or may not assess an object's worth or merit. The third group includes studies that are designed primarily to assess and/or improve the worth or merit of an object. For convenience in referencing the three groups of approaches, they have been labeled, respectively, as pseudoevaluation, quasievaluation, and true evaluation.

Each of the approaches and the associated study types were further analyzed in terms of seven descriptors: (1) advance organizers, that is, the main cues that evaluators use to set up a study; (2) the main purpose served; (3) the sources of questions that are addressed; (4) the questions that are characteristic of each approach and study type; (5) the methods that are typically used; (6) the persons who pioneered in conceptualizing each approach and study type; and (7) other persons who have extended the development and use of each approach and study type. In addition, each approach and study type was judged, in general terms, against the 30 standards that have been issued by the Joint Committee on Standards for Educational Evaluation.

Pseudoevaluations

Many have said that liars figure and figures lie. Likewise, hucksters and manipulators often use evaluation inappropriately to achieve their aims. They may either collect information rigorously but withhold the findings or release them selectively, or they may falsify the findings and deceive everyone, including themselves. Two types of pseudoevaluation are characterized below.

Covert Investigations

The first type is labeled "covert evaluation," although it might just as well be called politically controlled evaluation. Its advance organizers are implicit or explicit threats faced by the client for an evaluation. The client's purpose in commissioning a covert evaluation is to secure assistance in acquiring, maintaining, or increasing a client's sphere of influence, power, or money. The questions addressed are those of interest to the client and certain groups that share the client's interest. Two main questions guide this type of evaluation: What information would be advantageous in a potential conflict? And, What data might be advantageous in a confrontation? Typical methods of conducting covert evaluations include document analysis, participant observation, simulation studies, private investigations, and maintenance of secret files. Generally, the client wants information obtained to be as technically sound as possible but also wants to be guaranteed the ability to control the dissemination of the information. Because the information might be released selectively to create a distorted picture of an object's value or not released in order to cover up a situation, this approach must be labeled "pseudoevaluation."

We have not nominated persons to receive credit for pioneering or developing covert investigations. But unfortunately, many actual studies deserve this label.

To counter the possible claim that the covert evaluation is imaginary, we invite you to consider the following example. A superintendent of one of the nation's largest school districts once confided that he possessed an extensive notebook of information about each of the schools in his district. The information encompassed student achievement, teacher qualifications, racial mix of teachers and students, average per-pupil expenditure, socioeconomic characteristics of the student body, average length of tenure in the system for teachers in the school, and so forth. These data revealed a highly segregated school district. When asked why all the entries in the notebook were in pencil, the superintendent replied that it was absolutely essential that he be kept informed about the current situation in each school. However, he said, it was also imperative that the community at large, the board, and special interest groups in the community, in particular, not have access to the information — for any of these groups might use the information to harm the district and to threaten his tenure there. Hence, one special assistant kept the record up-to-date; only one copy existed, and the superintendent kept it locked in his desk. The point is that the superintendent's ongoing covert investigation and selective release of information was clearly not a case of true evaluation, for it did not include full and open disclosure. In our view, this was an instance of pseudoevaluation.

Public-Relations-Inspired Studies

A similar case of pseudoevaluation is the study that is planned, conducted, and used to serve public-relations purposes. In this type of study, the advance organizer is the propagandist's information needs. The purpose of the study is to help the client create a positive image for an institution, program, process, and the like. The questions that guide such a study are derived from the public-relations specialists' and administrators' conceptions of which questions would be most popular with their constituents. In general, the public-relations study seeks information that would be most helpful in securing public support. Methods typically used in public-relations studies are surveys, experiments, and the use of "expert" consultants. A pervasive characteristic of the public-relations evaluator's use of dubious methods is a biased attempt to nurture a good picture of the object of the evaluation.

A contact with an urban school district illustrates this second type of pseudoevaluation. A superintendent, in requesting a community survey for his district, stated quite openly that he wanted a document that would yield a positive report on the performance of the school district. He said that such a positive report was urgently needed so that community confidence in the school district would be restored. The superintendent's request for the survey (and positive report) was summarily dismissed, but why he thought one was needed soon became clear. Several weeks after making the request, he was suddenly discharged.

Before addressing the next group of study types, we wish to offer a few additional comments concerning pseudoevaluations. Perhaps you are confused as to why we have discussed these two study types. We certainly are not recommending their use. We have considered these types of studies because they are unfortunately a prominent part of the evaluation scene.

Sometimes evaluators and their clients are coconspirators in performing the first two types of studies. On other occasions, evaluators, believing they are doing an unbiased assessment, discover that their client has other intentions. When the time is right, the client steps in to subvert the study in favor of producing the desired biased picture. It is imperative that evaluators be more alert than they often are to these kinds of potential conflicts; otherwise, they will be unwitting accomplices in efforts to mislead through evaluation.

Quasievaluations

Quasievaluation studies are so labeled because sometimes they happen to provide evidence that can be used to assess the worth or merit of an object, while in other cases their focus is too narrow or is only tangential to questions of merit or worth. The key point is that these studies start with a particular question and then move to the appropriate methodology for answering the given question. Consideration of whether the obtained information is sufficient to support a judgment of the value of something is definitely a secondary concern. Quasievaluation studies have legitimate uses apart from their relationship to evaluation; hence, the main caution is that these types of studies not be equated to evaluation.

Two units in this book discuss quasievaluation study types: unit 3 on the Tylerian tradition and unit 4 on Suchman's scientific approach. We will analyze these versions of quasievaluation in this unit; the first falls into the category of quasievaluation that we have termed objectives-based studies, while Suchman's is keyed heavily to experimentation. Other examples of quasievaluation approaches, identified by Stufflebeam and Webster (1980), are accountability studies, testing programs, and management information systems.

Objectives-based Studies

As seen in unit 1, the objectives-based study has been perhaps the dominant force in the movement to systematize evaluation work. In this type of study some statement of objectives provides the advance organizer. The objectives may be prescribed by the client, developed by the persons whose work is being assessed, formulated by the evaluator, or developed cooperatively by those involved in the evaluation. The usual purpose here is to determine whether the objectives have been achieved and, accordingly, to conclude whether the effort being assessed has been successful. Program developers, sponsors, managers, and service providers are typical audiences for such studies.

The methods used in objectives-based studies essentially involve the collection and analysis of performance data relative to specified objectives. Ralph Tyler is generally acknowledged to be the pioneer in the objectives-based study. Many people have furthered the work of Tyler by developing variations of his objectives-based evaluation model. A few of them are Bloom et al. (1956), Hammond (1972), Metfessel and Michael (1967), Popham (1967), and Provus (1971). In unit 3, we offer an extension of the Tylerian model developed by Metfessel and Michael (1967).

Undoubtedly, the objectives-based type of study has been the most prevalent type used in the name of evaluation. It has good commonsense appeal, professionals have had a great amount of experience with it, and it makes use of technologies of behavioral objectives and standardized testing. Common criticisms are that such studies yield mainly terminal information that is delivered too late to be of use in improving services and that this information is often far too narrow in scope to constitute a sound basis for judging the value of a service.

Experimentally Oriented Studies

The experimental research type of study is quite prominent in evaluation. We have labeled it as quasievaluation because it starts with questions and methodology that may or may not be related to assessing value. The experimental research type of study calls to mind Kaplan's (1964) famous warning against the so-called "law of the instrument," wherein a given method is equated to a field of inquiry. Consequently, the field of study is restricted to the questions that are answerable by the given method. Fisher (1951) specifically warned against equating his experimental methods with science.

The advance organizers in experimental studies are problem statements, hypotheses, and study questions. The usual purpose of an experiment is to determine or demonstrate causal links between certain independent and dependent variables, such as a given instructional method and documented professional performance or test scores. Particularly noteworthy is that the sources of questions, investigated in experiments, are researchers, the developers of education programs, and journal editors, and not usually the constituents, practitioners, or financial sponsors.

The frequent question in the experiment is, What are the effects of a given intervention on specified outcome variables? Typical methods used are experimental and quasiexperimental designs. Pioneers in using experimentation to evaluate programs are Linquist (1953), Campbell and Stanley (1963), Suchman (1967), and Cronbach and Snow (1969). Other persons who have developed the methodology of experimentation substantially for use in evaluation are Glass and Maguire (1968) and Wiley and Bock (1967). In unit 4, we have specifically reviewed the contributions of Suchman in applying experimentation to the evaluation of social programs.

The main advantage of experimental studies in evaluation work is that they provide strong methods for establishing relatively unequivocal causal relationships between program and outcomes. The problems, however, are that the approach is often not workable in field settings and provides a much narrower range of information than is needed to evaluate education, health, and welfare programs. In addition, experimental studies tend to provide terminal information that is not useful for guiding the developmental process.

Before leaving our discussion of the objectives-based and experimental design approaches, we wish to emphasize that these are only two of the approaches that qualify as quasievaluation. We have concentrated on these two approaches because subsequent units on the works of Tyler and Suchman are operationalizations of these approaches. As mentioned previously in this unit, the other study types that qualify as quasievaluations are testing programs, management information systems, and accountability studies.

True Evaluations

The majority of units in this book are devoted to study types that we have classified as true evaluation. As opposed to pseudoevaluations, they emphasize the need to guard against biased studies, and in contrast to quasievaluation they advocate comprehensive investigations of worth and merit questions.

Decision-oriented Studies

We begin our examination of true evaluation or values-oriented studies by looking at the decision-oriented approach. It emphasizes that evalution should be used proactively to help improve a program as well as retroactively to judge its value. Decisions to be made — whether by a manager, a policy board, a program staff, or an electorate — provide the advance organizers for decision-oriented studies. Basically, the purpose of the studies is to provide a knowledge and value base for making and defending decisions.

The source of questions addressed by the decision-oriented studies is involved decision makers, which include administrators, citizens, students, teachers, physicians, policy boards, voters, and all others who decide about funding, conducting, and using services. The main questions addressed are, What needs to be accomplished? How should a given enterprise be planned? How should the plan be carried out? When and how should the enterprise be revised? Answers to these questions are based on underlying value positions, for example, educational enterprises should excel in fostering human growth and development while being frugal in the use of resources and while serving both individual goals and the common good. Many methods are appropriate for conducting decision-oriented studies. These include surveys, needs assessments, case studies, advocate teams, structured observations, and quasiexperimental and experimental designs.

Cronbach (1963) first introduced evaluators to the idea that evaluation should be reoriented from its objectives-based history to a concern for helping educators make better decisions about how to educate. Later, Stufflebeam (1966, 1967) introduced a conceptualization of evaluation that was based on the idea that evaluation should help educators make and defend decisions that are in the best interests of meeting students' needs. Many other persons have since contributed to the development of a decision-oriented concept of evaluation. Included among them are Alkin (1969), Reinhard (1972), Taylor (1974), Guba (1978), and Webster (1975). Units 5 and 6 provide extensive information about the strategies that have been developed by Cronbach and Stufflebeam.

A main advantage of the decision-oriented strategy is that it encourages professionals in groups, as well as government organizations, to use evaluation continuously and systematically in their efforts to plan and implement services that meet constituents' needs. It also presents a rationale for helping professionals account for decisions made in the course of developing and offering a service.

A main limitation is that the collaboration required between an evaluator and decision maker introduces opportunities for biasing the evaluation results. External metaevaluation (evaluation of the evaluation) has been employed to offset such opportunities for bias.

Client-centered Studies

Whereas the decision-oriented study is addressed more often to management levels than to staff levels in an organization — because more authority for decision making often exists at the higher levels — the client-centered approach is centered more on "where the action is." Studies that adhere to this approach concentrate mainly on helping the people who are involved on a day-to-day basis in implementing a service to assess and improve their contributions. The advance organizers are concerns and issues in the program of service. The purpose of the study is to help the people in the local service context to understand the functioning of their service activities and the degree to which the services are respected by experts and valued by the clients.

Community and practitioner groups in the local environment plus external experts are the sources of questions that are addressed by the client-centered study. In general, the groups usually want to know about the history and status of a service program and the ways in which a variety of stakeholder groups have judged it. Typical methods used in the client-centered study are the case study, adversary reports, sociodrama, and what Stake (1975) has called "responsive evaluation."

Stake (1967) is the pioneer of the client-centered type of study, and his approach has been developed by MacDonald (1975) in England, Rippey (1973), and, most recently, Guba (1978). In unit 7, we have provided an extensive review and analysis of Stake's proposals for conceptualizing and conducting evaluation work.

The main strength of the client-centered approach is that it is an action-research approach in which people implementing programs are helped to conduct their own evaluation. Its main weakness is its lack of external credibility and its susceptibility to bias on the part of people in the local setting, since they, in effect, have great control over the evaluation.

Policy Studies

We see the policy study as a third major type of true evaluation. We have so classified this approach because it sets out to identify and assess, for society or some segment of society, the merits of competing policies. The advance organizer for the policy study is a given policy issue, for example, What is the best or at least an effective means to meet federal guidelines for equal educational opportunity? The purpose of the policy study is usually to identify and assess the potential costs and benefits of competing policies for a given institution or for society.

Legislators, policy boards, and special interest groups often posit the questions that are addressed by policy studies. A main question they pose is, Which of two or more competing policies will maximize the achievement of valued outcomes at a reasonable cost? Methods used in policy studies include the Delphi Technique (described by Anderson, Ball, Murphy, and Associates, 1973), experimental and quasiexperimental design, scenarios, forecasting, and judicial proceedings.

Joseph Rice (discussed in Anderson, et al., 1973) can be mentioned as the pioneer in this area, as he conducted massive studies around 1900 to help education decide on the merits of continued concentration on spelling. Other persons who have contributed substantially to the methodology for conducting policy studies are Coleman, Campbell, Hobson, McPartland, Moor, Weinfeld, and York (1966), Jenks, Smith, Adand, Bane, Cohen, Gintis, Heynes, and Mikelson (1972), Clark (1965), Owens (Note 1), Wolf (1973), and Weiss (1972). Unit 10 describes the study type that has been advocated by Owens and Wolf and that we view as a policy study approach.

The main advantage of policy studies is that they are essential in guiding institutions and society. The main problems are that policy studies, over and again, are corrupted or subverted by the political environment in which they must be conducted and reported.

Consumer-oriented Studies

In the consumer-oriented study, the evaluator is the "enlightened surrogate consumer." Advance organizers are societal values and needs. The purpose of a consumer study is to judge the relative values of alternative goods and services and, thereby, to help taxpayers and practitioners to make wise choices in their purchase of goods and services.

Questions for the consumer-oriented study are derived from society, from constituents of service institutions, and especially from the evaluator's frame of reference. The general question addressed is, Which of several alternative consumable objects is the best buy, given their costs, the needs of the consumer group, and the values of society at large? Methods include checklists, needs assessments, goal-free evaluation, experimental and quasiexperimental designs, modus operandi analysis, and cost analysis (Scriven, 1974). Also a popular method is for an external independent consumer advocate to conduct and report findings on studies of publicly supported programs.

Scriven (1967) pioneered the consumer-oriented approach in education, and there are strong parallels between his work and the concurrent work of Ralph Nader in the general field of consumerism. Glass has been an avid supporter and developer of Scriven's work.

One of the main advantages of this approach is that it is a hard-hitting, independent assessment intended to protect consumers from shoddy products and services. The approach has high credibility with consumer groups. The main disadvantage of this approach is that it can be so independent from practitioners that it may not assist them to do a better job of serving consumers. Moreover, the consumer-oriented study requires a highly credible and competent expert plus sufficient resources to allow the expert to conduct a thorough study. Often this approach is too costly to be carried out well and produces faulty, unrealistic data.

Conclusion

This completes our review of what we consider to be the three major approaches to evaluation. Contained within a discussion of these approaches have been the various study types depicted in this book. We reiterate that none of these approaches conforms to pseudoevaluation. In summary, the ideas and procedures for evaluations put forward by Tyler (unit 3) and his adherents, Metfessel and Michael (unit 3), Hammond and Suchman (unit

4), are examples of quasievaluation. Those advocated by Cronbach (unit 5), Stufflebeam (unit 6), Stake (unit 7), Owens and Wolf (unit 8), and Scriven (unit 10) conform to our depiction of true evaluation. Many of the evaluation procedures advocated by Weiss — particularly those related to politics and interpersonal relationships — are very much in line with our concept of a true evaluation. In general terms, we consider that writers who advocate the holistic approach to evaluation such as MacDonald and Stake (unit 9) are also presenting examples of true evaluation, provided that the lack of external credibility is recognized and acknowledged.

As stated at the beginning of this unit, a critical analysis of these study types has important implications for both the practitioner and the student of evaluation. Both need to strengthen their abilities to assess and apply evaluation plans, models, and so on, that have been advanced in the literature of evaluation. Not only does such study identify alternative plans that one might choose or adapt, but it also should increase sensitivity about the strengths, weaknesses, and trade-offs among given schemes. And it should heighten one's alertness and resistance to plans that involve subterfuge (the pseudoevaluations).

Evaluators should particularly note that they may encounter considerable difficulties if their perceptions of the study being undertaken differ from those of their clients and audiences. Typically, clients want a politically advantageous study (pseudoevaluation) performed, whereas evaluators prefer to conduct questions-oriented studies (quasievaluation), since they allow evaluators to exploit the methodology in which they were trained. Moreover, the consumers of the assessed services usually want values-oriented studies (true evaluation) that will help them to determine the relative values of competing goods and services or to judge the merit and worth of an existing program or object. If evaluators are ignorant of the likely conflict in purpose, the evaluation is probably doomed to failure from the start. The moral is that at the onset of the study, evaluators must be keenly sensitive to their own agendas for an evaluation study as well as those that are held by client and audience. Further, evaluators should advise involved parties of possible conflicts in the purposes for doing the study and should negotiate a common understanding at the start. Presented alternatives could be legitimately either a quasievaluation study directed at assessing particular questions or a true evaluation study directed at searching for all evidence that could help the client and audience assess the worth of the object.

It is not believed, however, that politically inspired and controlled studies serve appropriate purposes in the evaluation of health, welfare, and education. Granted, they may be necessary in administration and public relations, but they should not be confused with, or substituted for, evaluation. Finally, it is imperative to remember that no one type of study is consistently the best in evaluating something. Another point to be gleaned from the review of the various study types presented in this book is that they have both strengths and weaknesses. In general, the weaknesses of the politically oriented studies are that they are prone to manipulation by unscrupulous persons, and may help such people mislead an audience into developing a particular opinion of a program's worth that is unfounded and perhaps untrue. The main problem with questions-oriented studies is that they often address questions that are narrower in scope than the questions needing to be addressed in a true assessment of value. However, it is also noteworthy that these types of studies are frequently superior to true evaluation studies in the efficiency of methodology and technical adequacy of information employed. Finally, the values-oriented studies undertake an overly ambitious task. For it is virtually impossible to assess the true value of any object. Such an achievement would require omniscience, infallibility, and a singularly unquestioned value base. Nevertheless, the continuing attempt to consider questions of value certainly is essential for the advancement of society.

Knowledge Test for Unit 2

Below are 4 multiple-choice questions and 12 matching statements that have been designed to assist you to test and strengthen your mastery of the lessons in unit 2. For each question, please circle the letter of what you consider to be the best response and then assess your choice against the explanations of the correct and incorrect responses that immediately follow each question. A scoring key for the questions follows the multiple-choice questions.

When all the knowledge questions have been completed, you will be instructed to review (and if indicated, to remediate) your overall performance. Then you will be advised to attempt a number of application exercises. The unit is concluded with several "Questions Without Answers" and a list of recommended readings.

Question 1.   Which of the following characterizations of evaluation is most consistent with the way evaluation is defined in this unit?

a.   Evaluations should concentrate on determining the worth or merit of an object irrespective of the interests or wishes of any particular group.
b.   The primary, nearly exclusive responsibility of professional evaluators is to answer the questions that are advanced by their clients.
c.   Evaluators must avoid addressing questions in given evaluations that have been the focus of similar evaluations, because such practice would not add to extant knowledge.

d. Evaluators should both make an extensive assessment of the worth and merit of an object and address the information needs of their audiences.

Correct Response. You should have chosen "d." The definition of evaluation given in unit 2 preserves authority for the evaluator to assess everything that needs to be considered in judging the worth and merit of an object, but also directs the evaluator to ensure that the evaluation highlights the information that would be of most service to the client group.

Incorrect Responses

a. Incorrect because this unit emphasizes that true evaluation involves serving clients and making comprehensive assessments.
b. Incorrect for the same reason as was given for response "a."
c. Incorrect because the definition of evaluation given in this unit excludes no type of information as long as it bears on questions about the worth and merit of the object of interest and would be of potential use to the client group.

Question 2. Which of the following is *not* characteristic of pseudoevaluations?

a. They may involve the withholding or the selective releasing of findings.
b. They often involve independent and publicly reported assessments of the merit and worth of the evaluation.
c. They often involve trumping up findings to gain support for a product or service.
d. They may involve the collection of highly valid and reliable information.

Correct Response. You should have chosen "b." Since pseudoevaluations, by definition, are inappropriate uses of evaluation by certain persons to achieve their aims, opening such evaluation work to independent and public scrutiny would almost never occur, except in the rare case in which the perpetrator of the pseudoevaluation was not only unethical but also largely unintelligent.

Incorrect Responses

a. Incorrect because withholding or selectively releasing findings is essentially what is involved in the type of pseudoevaluation study that was labeled covert investigations.

c. Incorrect because the type of pseudoevaluation labeled the public-relations study involves precisely the manipulative use of evaluation to achieve one's aims.
d. Incorrect because in the covert investigation the previous offense against the ethical use of evaluation concerns not the quality of data collected but the failure to report the full set of findings without biasing their message.

Question 3.   Which of the following is *not* characteristic of a quasievaluation study?

a. It addresses a broad range of questions about the worth and merit of the object of interest.
b. It is designed to answer some particular questions that are given before the search for information begins.
c. The information obtained may or may not be sufficient to support a value claim about the object of interest.
d. There are legitimate uses for the results from such studies.

Correct Response.   You should have chosen "a." According to this unit, the information yielded from quasievaluation studies often is too restricted to support value claims about the object of interest.

Incorrect Responses

b. Incorrect (the statement is characteristic of quasievaluation) because quasievaluations usually start with a given question, then employ methods that will answer the question; only at the end of the study might the evaluator consider whether the obtained information is sufficient to support judgments about the worth and merit of the object.
c. Incorrect because while the information gathered to answer particular questions is often too narrow to support broad value judgments, sometimes the questions have sufficient scope to guide the collection of the wide range of information necessary to support judgments of worth and merit.
d. Incorrect because quasievaluations have legitimate uses in helping clients to answer questions that are of importance to them, whether or not the obtained information would be sufficient to support broad value claims.

Question 4.   Which of the following is *not* characteristic of true evaluations?

a. Their designs include safeguards against collecting or reporting biased findings.
b. They consistently generate a broad range of information.
c. Whereas quasievaluations often trade off the collection of a wide scope of information in favor of gathering highly accurate data on a few questions of interest, true evaluations often sacrifice a certain amount of rigor in order to obtain the range of information relevant to judgments of worth and merit.
d. The dominant method used in true evaluation is true experimental design.

Correct Response.   You should have selected "d." Experimental design is one method sometimes used in true evaluation, but it is usually used in conjunction with other techniques, such as document review, survey, case study, site visits, and hearings. Experimental design certainly is not the dominant technique used in true evaluations. Indeed, no technique dominates this approach, as the choice of techniques is typically pragmatic and eclectic.

Incorrect Responses

a. Incorrect (this statement is characteristic of true evaluation) because there is a pervasive concern in true evaluation for assuring that the evaluation work be sound, fair, and useful.
b. Incorrect because, by definition, true evaluations are attempts to obtain and report a sufficiently broad range of information in order to support claims about the worth and merit of an object of interest.
c. Incorrect because there are always trade-offs in evaluation work, and because those doing narrowly focused quasievaluations find it easier to succeed in making their findings more highly accurate than those evaluators who, in the pursuit of true evaluations, must allocate their time and resources to the often intractable tasks of collecting the full range of information required to support broad value judgments.

Questions 5 to 16.   For each description in numbers 5–16 select the most applicable study type listed below. In the space provided at the left of each description write the letter of the selected study type. You may use an answer more than once.

A. covert investigation
B. public-relations–inspired study

C. objective-based study
D. experimentally oriented study
E. decision-oriented study
F. client-centered study
G. policy study
H. consumer-oriented study

_____ 5. The major guiding questions are associated with needs to be served, the relative merits of alternative ways that the needs might be addressed, adequacy of program implementation, and extent and quality of results.

_____ 6. This type of study assesses products and services from the point of view of those who are intended to benefit from the use of the products and services.

_____ 7. This type of study is designed to assist clients to obtain accurate information that they can control and selectively release in order to further their aims.

_____ 8. This study type has dominated the efforts to systematize evaluation.

_____ 9. The main problems with this study type are that it often isn't workable in field settings and yields a very narrow range of information.

_____ 10. This study type is centered on where the action is and is directed toward concerns and issues pertaining to the product or service to be evaluated that are seen from the perspective of the various stakeholders.

_____ 11. This study type might be termed an "image-building" approach.

_____ 12. This study type is illustrated by a study that has been designed to identify and assess two or more legislative proposals for health care for the poor.

_____ 13. This study type was basically developed by Tyler.

_____ 14. This study type has been advocated by Scriven and Nader.

_____ 15. Robert Stake has been the main advocate of this study type.

_____ 16. Cronbach and Stufflebeam have advocated this type of study.

Correct Responses. You should have responded as follows, for the reasons given:

_E_ 5. Concern for needs, alternative plans, implementation of plans, and outcomes are the main categories of information that are associated with Stufflebeam's *decision-oriented conceptualization* of evaluation.

__H__   6. Assessments from the consumer's perspective, with the evaluator serving as enlightened surrogate consumer, are precisely what are involved in *consumer-oriented evaluation*.

__A__   7. Covert investigations do deal in accurate information as well as selective release of the information.

__C__   8. The *objectives-based study* as advocated by Tyler has been the dominant strategy for evaluating programs since the 1940s.

__D__   9. *Experimentally oriented studies* use designs that involve laboratory-like controls, which often cannot be imposed in field settings because they would interfere with the delivery of service, and they are usually focused on only a few carefully defined independent and dependent variables and thus yield only a very narrow range of information.

__F__   10. Stake's *client-centered* approach to evaluation is focused on a careful study of ongoing program operations and is devoted to addressing and providing continuous feedback to those who are involved in and concerned about the particular program.

__B__   11. The *public-relations*-inspired type of study is devoted to collecting evidence and reporting information so as to garner support for an object; it seeks not to present a true picture, but to project a positive image.

__G__   12. *Policy-oriented studies* essentially project and assess the relative costs and benefits of two or more policy proposals, such as optional strategies for providing health care to the poor.

__C__   13. Ralph Tyler is the person most often mentioned in the literature of evaluation as being responsible for keying evaluation work to carefully stated objectives.

__H__   14. *Consumer-oriented studies* are consistent with the evaluation philosophy advanced by Scriven and with the many evaluations of products and services that Ralph Nader and his associates have conducted.

__F__   15. The *client-centered* label is consistent with the thrust of Robert Stake's evaluation philosophy, which is more often called "responsive evaluation."

__E__   16. Both Cronbach and Stufflebeam have proposed an approach to evaluation that provides guidance for *decision making*.

Scoring of the Knowledge Test.   Having completed the knowledge test, we suggest that you total the number of correct responses. We would evaluate your initial performance as follows: 15–16 excellent, 13–14 very good, 10–12 good, 7–9 fair, 0–6 poor.

After you have obtained an overall estimate of your initial performance, we suggest that you direct your attention to those questions that you missed. We suggest that you reread each of these questions and its keyed response and then review the text material to strengthen your understanding of the involved concepts.

Application Exercises

This section contains application exercises that have been designed to help you understand whether you have understood our presentation and analysis of alternative conceptualizations of evaluation. Following each question is a sample response or a list of pertinent points that might have been included in your response. Reviewing these answers will help you assess your responses.

Exercise 1. Below is a partially completed table of information that contrasts study types in terms of six descriptors. Demonstrate your grasp of the essential similarities and differences among these study types by filling in the missing information.

Study Types	Objectives-Based Studies	Decision-Oriented Studies	Consumer-Oriented Studies	Client-Centered Studies
Advance Organizers	Objectives			
Purpose		To provide a knowledge and value base for making and defending decisions		
Source of Questions			Society at large, consumers, and the evaluator	
Main Questions				What is the history of a program and how is it judged by those who are involved with it and by those who have expertise in the program area?

Study Types	Objectives-Based Studies	Decision-Oriented Studies	Consumer-Oriented Studies	Client-Centered Studies
Typical Methods	Comparison of performance data to objectives			
Pioneers		Cronbach and Stufflebeam		

Correct Response to Exercise 1. Your completed matrix of information should approximate the one that appears below.

Study Types	Objectives-Based Studies	Decision-Oriented Studies	Consumer-Oriented Studies	Client-Centered Studies
Advance Organizers	Objectives	Decision Situations	Societal Values and Needs	Localized Concerns and Issues
Purpose	To relate outcomes to objectives	To provide a knowledge and value base for making and defending decisions	To judge the relative merits of alternative goods and services	To foster understanding of activities and how they are valued in a given setting and from a variety of perspectives
Source of Questions	Program developers and managers	Decision makers, their constituents, and evaluators	Society at large, consumers, and the evaluator	Community and practitioner groups in local environments and experts
Main Questions	Which students achieved which objectives	How should a given enterprise be planned, executed, and recycled in order to foster human growth and development at a reasonable cost?	Which of several alternative consumable objects is the best buy, given their costs, the needs of consumers, and the values of society at large?	What is the history of a program and how is it judged by those who are involved with it and by those who have expertise in the program area?
Typical Methods	Comparison of performance data to objectives	Surveys, needs assessments, case studies, advocate teams, observations, and experimental design	Checklists, needs assessment, goal-free evaluation, experimental design, and cost analysis	Case study, adversary reports, socio-drama, responsive evaluation

Study Types	Objectives- Based Studies	Decision- Oriented Studies	Consumer- Oriented Studies	Client- Centered Studies
Pioneers	Tyler	Cronbach and Stufflebeam	Scriven	Stake

Exercise 2. List what you see as the main strengths and weaknesses of the experimental approach to evaluation.

Sample response to Exercise 2. According to the position taken in the unit, your response should be approximately as follows:

a. Strengths
  1. Assesses causal relations.
  2. Provides for reliable and objective information.
  3. Yields data that are amenable to analysis.
  4. Promotes precise and objective reporting.
  5. Guards against political manipulation.
b. Weaknesses
  1. Not attuned to audiences' information needs.
  2. Not geared to yielding timely feedback.
  3. Yields a narrow view of an object's value.
  4. Often fails to document and assess a program's implementation.
  5. Often guided by impractical procedural plans.

Exercise 3. List what you see as the main strengths and weaknesses of the client-centered strategy for evaluating programs.

Sample response to Exercise 3. According to the position taken in this unit, your response should be approximately as follows:

a. Strengths
  1. Yields continual feedback.
  2. Serves multiple audiences.
  3. Is flexible and responsive.
  4 . Promotes self-evaluation.
  5. Stresses effective communication of findings.
  6. Takes context into account.
  7. Assesses process.
  8. Assesses intended and actual outcomes.
  9. Assesses side effects.
  10. Yields a broad scope of information.

11. Assesses strengths and weaknesses.
12. Reports judgments from many sources.
13. Stresses validity.
14. Stresses full description.
15. Stresses clear communication.
16. Is applicable by small institutions.
b. Weaknesses
1. Depends on audiences' cooperation.
2. May neglect summative evaluation.
3. Is not supported by fully developed and validated methods.
4. Often produces information of questionable reliability.
5. Objectivity of the evaluation is often in doubt.
6. Allows employment of biased or untrained evaluators.
7. Often yields equivocal or contradictory findings.
8. Sometimes vulnerable to political manipulation.

Questions Without Answers

This concluding section includes four questions that are intended to help you to think critically about the contents of this unit. Answers are not provided. Instead, we suggest that you read and think about each one and, if possible, discuss it with your fellow students or colleagues. In addition, you may find these questions useful as a guide to your further study of the readings that are listed at the back of the unit.

1. Can an internal, self-evaluation ever approximate the requirements of a true evaluation? If so, what has to be done to meet these requirements?
2. Is this unit's distinction between quasievaluations and true evaluations artificial, especially if one considers that evaluation typically involves not a single study but a program of studies?
3. Are there any fundamental philosophical issues that separate consumer-oriented studies from client-centered studies? If so, what are they?
4. Is it crucial that evaluators distinguish between pseudoevaluation, quasievaluation, and true evaluation? If so, why? If not, why not?

References

Alkin, M.C. 1969. Evaluation theory development. *Evaluation Comment*, 2, 2-7.
Anderson, S.; Ball, S.; Murphy, R.; and Associates. 1973. *Encyclopedia of educational evaluation*. San Francisco: Jossey-Bass, p. 142.

Bloom, B. S.; Englehart, M. D.; Furst, E. J; Hill, W. H.; and Krathwohl, D. R. 1956. *Taxonomy of educational objectives. Handbook I: Cognitive domain.* New York: David McKay.

Campbell, D. T., and Stanley, J. C. 1963. Experimental and quasi-experimental designs for research on teaching. In N. L. Gage (ed.), *Handbook of research on training.* Chicago: Rand McNally.

Clark, K. *Dark ghetto.* New York: Harper and Row, 1963.

Coleman, J. S.; Campbell, E. Q.; Hobson, C. J.; McPartland, J.; Mook, A. M.; Weinfeld, F. D.; and York, R. L. 1966. *Equality of educational opportunity.* Washington, D. C.: U. S. Department of Health, Education, and Welfare, Office of Education.

Cook, D. L. 1966. Program evaluation and review techniques, applications in education. *U. S. Office of Education Cooperative Monograph, 17* (OE–12024).

Cronbach, L. J. 1963. Course improvement through evaluation. *Teachers College Record, 64,* 672–683.

Cronbach, L.J. and Snow, R.E. Individual Differences in Learning Ability as a Function of Instructional Variables. Stanford, Calif.: Stanford University Press, 1969.

Ebel, R.L. 1965. *Measuring educational achievement.* Englewood Cliffs, N. J.: Prentice-Hall.

Fisher, R. L. 1951. *The design of experiments* (6th ed.). New York: Hafner.

Glass, G. V., and Maquire, T. O. 1968. Analysis of time-scires quasi-experiments. (U. S. Office of Education Report No. 6–8329.) Boulder, Col.: Laboratory of Educational Research, University of Colorado.

Guba, E. G. 1978. Toward a methodology of naturalistic inquiry in educational evaluation. *CSE Monograph Series in Evaluation*, Los Angeles, Calif. Center for the Study of Evaluation.

Hammond, R. L. 1972. Evaluation at the local level (mimeograph). Tucson, Ariz.: EPIC Evaluation Center.

Jencks, C.; Smith, M.; Adand, H.; B., M J.; Cohen, D.; Gintis, H.; Heynes, B.; and Michelson, S. *Inequality:* A reassessment of the effect of family and schooling in America, New York: Basic Books, 1972.

Kaplan, A. 1964. *The conduct of inquiry.* San Francisco: Chandler.

Lessinger, L. M. 1970. *Every kid a winner: Accountability in education.* New York: Simon & Schuster.

Linquist, E. F. 1953. *Design and analysis of experiments in psychology and education.* Boston: Houghton Mifflin.

McDonald, B. 1975. Evaluation and the control of education. In D. Tawney (ed.), *Evaluation: The state of the art.* London: Schools Council.

Metfessel, N. S., and Michael, W. B. 1967. A paradigm involving multiple criterion measures for the evaluation of the effectiveness of school programs. *Educational and Psychological Measurement, 27,* 931–943.

Owens, T. 1971. Application of adversary proceedings to educational evaluation and decision making. Paper presented at the annual meeting of the American Educational Research Association, New York.

Popham, W.J. 1969. Objectives and instruction. In R. Stake (ed.), *Instructional objectives. AERA Monograph Series on Curriculum Evaluation* (vol. 3). Chicago: Rand McNally.

Provus, M.N. 1971. *Discrepancy evaluation.* Berkeley: McCutcheon.

Reinhard, D.L. Methodology Development for Input Evaluation Using Input Evaluation Using Advocate and Design Teams. Ph.D. dissertation, Ohio State University, 1972.

Rippey, R.M. (ed.). *Studies in Transactional Evaluation.* Berkeley: McCutcheon, 1973.

Scriven, M.S. 1967. The methodology of evaluation. In R.E. Stake (ed.), *Curriculum evaluation. AERA Monograph Series on Curriculum Evaluation* (vol. 1). Chicago: Rand McNally.

Stake, R.E. 1967. The countenance of educational evaluation. *Teachers College Record, 68,* 523–540.

Stake, R.E. *Program Evaluation, particularly Responsive Evaluation.* Occasional Paper Series No. 5, Western Michigan University, Evaluation Center 1975.

Stufflebeam, D.L. 1966. A depth study of the evaluation requirement. *Theory into Practice, 5* (June), 121–134.

————. 1967. The use and abuse of evaluation in Title III. *Theory into Practice, 6* (June), 126–133.

Stufflebeam, D.L. and Webster, W.J. "An Analysis of Alternative Approaches to Evaluation." Educational Evaluation and Policy Analysis, no. 3.2 (May–June 1980), 5–19. Copyright © 1980, American Educational Research Association, Washington, D.C.

Suchman, E.A. 1967. *Evaluative research.* New York; Russell Sage Foundation.

Taylor, J.P. 1974. An administrator's perspective of evaluation. Kalamazoo: Western Michigan University. (Occasional Paper #2).

Thorndike, R.L. 1971. *Educational measurement* (2nd ed.). Washington, D.C.: American Council on Education, 1971.

Webster, W.J. "The Organization and Functions of Research and Evaluation in Large Urban School Districts." Paper presented at the annual meeting of the American Educational Research Association, Washington, D.C., March 1975.

Weiss, C. *Evaluation Research: Methods of Assessing Program Effectiveness,* Englewood Cliffs, N.J.: Prentice-Hall, 1972.

Wiley, D.E. and Bock, R.D. "Quasi-experimentation in Educational Settings: Comment. *The School Review,* Winter, 1967, *35* 3–66.

Wolf, R.L. "How teachers feel toward evaluation." In E.R. House (ed.), *School evaluation: The Politics and Process.* Berkeley: McCutcheon, 1973.

3 OBJECTIVES-ORIENTED EVALUATION: THE TYLERIAN TRADITION

Ralph W. Tyler developed the first systematic approach to educational evaluation. This evolved from his work in the 1930s and early 1940s on the Eight-Year Study at Ohio State University (Smith and Tyler, 1942). Since that time, Professor Tyler has continued to develop aspects of evaluation, particularly at the national level following the growth of federally funded programs in education. The extent of the esteem in which he is held can be gauged, in part, by the large number of highly reputable evaluators who have based their methodology on the Tylerian approach.

Before Tyler published his model for evaluation in 1942, studies focused on the student and the measurement of student attainment. Evaluation was therefore virtually identical to measurement. Tyler endeavored to swing the emphasis to a wide range of educational objects, such as curricula and facilities. He also emphasized the necessity to establish, classify, and define objectives in behavioral terms as initial stages of an evaluation study. Evaluation then became the process of determining the congruence betweeen these objectives and performances.

The Tylerian concept has often been applied with a narrowness of approach that Tyler never intended. Most significantly, whereas Tyler offered a practical means to provide feedback during the course of an evaluation study, attention became fixed on data (usually connected with student achievement), which became available only when the program had run its full cycle. Despite the disadvantages of evaluation being construed as a terminal process and of a narrow focus being placed on objectives, Tyler's work stands as a milestone in the growth of evaluation as a science.

Ralph W. Tyler is generally considered the father figure of educational evaluation. There are possibly two main reasons for this. First, he proposed, described, and applied a developed approach to evaluation — something that had not been done earlier. And second, his methodological approach has been both pervasive and influential. Outstanding contributors to the field of educational evaluation, such as Michael and Metfessel, Provus, and Hammond, have provided further dimensions to Tyler's work while retaining his basic philosophy and technology.

In general terms, Tyler considered that evaluation should determine the congruence between performance and objectives. Tyler reached this conclusion following his work in the 1930s and early 1940s on the Eight-Year Study at Ohio State University. Some years later (1950, p. 69) he summarized his deliberations in these words:

> The process of evaluation is essentially the process of determining to what extent the educational objectives are actually being realized by the program of curriculum and instruction. However, since educational objectives are essentially changes in human beings, that is, the objectives aimed at are to produce certain desirable changes in the behavior patterns of the student, then evaluation is the process for determining the degree to which these changes in behavior are actually taking place.

In this unit major aspects of the Tylerian approach to evaluation are presented. In addition, the work of Michael and Metfessel, adherents of the model conceived by Tyler, are briefly outlined. After you have completed the body of this unit, you will be directed to complete a knowledge test of the Tyler assignment, checking your answers against those provided, and an application exercise, comparing your responses with those provided. Finally, the unit ends with discussion topics (and their possible uses) under "Questions Without Answers" and suggested readings.

Objectives

The following are the objectives of this unit:

1. To develop an understanding of the intention of Tyler's approach to evaluation by considering his procedure for evaluation design, advantages of the Tylerian approach, and uses of the Tyler model.

2. To point out some limitations of the Tylerian approach; in particular, evaluation as a terminal process; technical constraints — screening process to obtain objectives, and placing objectives into behavioral terms; behaviors as the ultimate criterion; and the narrow focus of evaluation.
3. To review an extension of the Tylerian approach by Metfessel and Michael, by considering their eight-step procedure for evaluation, and Appendix (of multiple criterion measures).

The Intention of the Tylerian Approach

In his general statement on evaluation published in 1942, Ralph Tyler laid the foundation for an "objectives-oriented" style of evaluation. He concluded that decisions about programs had necessarily to be based on the congruence between the objectives of the program and its actual outcomes. If objectives are achieved, decisions will be taken in a particular direction. If they are not achieved, or only partially so, then different decisions will be made. Tyler's main concern was that the teacher, administrator, or curriculum developer should arrive at rational judgments about program areas given to their direction.

Procedure for Evaluation Design

The advantage of the congruence definition of evaluation is that it evolved from an organized rationale of program development. Tyler considered that evaluation should be an essential stage in this development. Moreover, he considered that there must be a series of logical steps by which the actual evaluation process takes place. According to Tyler, the procedure for program evaluation is the following:

1. To establish goals or objectives.
2. To place objectives in broad classifications.
3. To define objectives in behavioral terms.
4. To establish situations and conditions in which attainment of objectives can be demonstrated.
5. To explain the purposes of the strategy to relevant personnel in the selected situations.
6. To choose or develop appropriate measurement techniques.
7. To collect performance data (in the case of educational programs these would be of student performance).
8. To compare data with behavioral objectives.

It should be noted that Tyler's definition of evaluation is very much in line with these procedural steps. If the aim of a program of curriculum and instruction is to produce change in the behavior patterns of those who benefit by it, then a method of measuring the extent of change is necessary. Before this can happen, "goals and objectives" must be clearly determined and defined. Placed in behavioral terms, objectives can then be field tested after appropriate conditions for their testing are established.

Tyler did not differentiate between goals and objectives in his strategy. One can infer from his writings, however, that program goals are ideals to be striven for, while objectives state subgoals that can be expressed as measurable entities.

Advantages of the Tylerian Approach

Before Tyler developed his approach, educational evaluation had focused almost exclusively on the student. What students achieved was the basis of the evaluation of the program. Achievement, or merit, was sometimes based entirely on measurements such as those provided by test scores and occasionally was based on a synthesis of various measures and subjective impressions. In this measurement-oriented method of discovering the merit of the program, the student was the dominant focus of attention. Moreover, evaluation was limited to those variables for which measures could be invented.

The Tylerian approach, in theory, moved the spotlight to other aspects of the program apart from the student. In particular, knowledge about program intentions, its goals and its behavioral objectives, and procedures for its successful implementation had to be considered closely. The fact that objectives had to be defined gave firm reference points for evaluation and decision making. Definitions of objectives also implied criteria for measuring their success. Any valid evidence about behavioral objectives could be construed as a valid method of evaluation. In general terms, he accepted any procedure for gathering evidence about the behavior of subjects of an evaluation. He was nevertheless especially interested in non-paper-and-pencil approaches, such as observation, interviews, and the assessment of student handwork and exercises.

Tyler provided a practical means for *feedback* (a term he introduced into evaluation language). Thus, Tyler viewed evaluation as a recurring process. Evaluation, he considered, should provide program personnel with useful information that may enable objectives to be reformulated or redefined. If modification to objectives occurs, a corresponding revision must be made in the plans for the evaluation.

Tyler's strategy also gave scope for the evaluator with initiative to explore data relevant to the process by which the program was evolving. However, as will be pointed out below, this potentially valuable aspect of program evaluation was never stressed by Tyler nor put into effect by his immediate contemporaries. It was left to others, including Scriven (*formative evalua-tion*) and Stufflebeam (*process evaluation*), to emphasize the full importance of evaluation having the utility to judge the processes of a program as well as its end results.

Tyler stressed that an evaluation study need not necessarily be considered in isolation from similar studies. He saw real value in information derived from earlier studies being used to help define objectives, select appropriate conditions where achievements of objectives can be displayed, and help in the interpretation of measured outcomes. He therefore considered that a good evaluator should develop skills in apt use of appropriate precedents in evaluation studies or measurement techniques.

As has been mentioned earlier, Tyler laid the foundation for the first systematic approach to evaluation. This was later to emerge as the "management by objectives" approach to developing and monitoring organizations or aspects of organizations. One of the strongest aspects of the systems approach has been its rational appeal. In education, particularly, the notions of the systematic steps of objectives formulation, feedback, ongoing evaluation, and recycling (based on goal or objective modification) were appealing. Moreover, the process has been found to be usable by the classroom teacher who wishes to make program decisions. External agents have rarely been needed, although the Eight-Year Study was a marked exception.

Uses of the Tylerian Model

Tyler envisaged that his approach to evaluation would be used primarily by teachers and curriculum developers. Following the advent of federally funded programs in the 1960s, he also considered that his method would be appropriate for professional evaluators.

Apart from curriculum modification and classification of objectives, as outlined above, the Tylerian approach has been useful in the classroom situation. Much, however, has depended upon the acuity of the teacher to use the method positively — no matter what the extent of discrepancy revealed between objectives and performance outcomes, decisions to improve education must remain the paramount use of evaluation.

Tyler's approach could be useful for the guidance of student learning. It could support the diagnosis and subsequent remediation of weaknesses in the learning process either by individuals or groups. It could also enable a teacher to modify learning objectives in keeping both with the learning capacities and the needs of students, thus making the curriculum generally more realistic. The grading of students, it should be noted, was never mentioned by Tyler as a use for his approach to evaluation.

Tyler also saw evaluation as useful in the provision of information about aspects of a school to its patrons. In one sense, he was foreshadowing the use of evaluation for accountability purposes. However, he was more concerned with positive change resulting from the evaluation than with supplying parents and other members of the community with ammunition for use against school-based personnel. "Information derived from a rational process of evaluation should be put to good effect — that is, educational improvement."

Some Limitations of the Tylerian Approach

Tyler saw the purpose of evaluation as providing a check "as to whether these plans for learning experiences actually function to guide the teacher in producing the outcomes desired." This has the flavor of a developmental or formative intent. In reality, the Tylerian approach has been used in a much more summative way. Herein lies the most prevalent criticism of the model.

Evaluation as a Terminal Process

It is ironical that a procedure that so strongly suggested feedback and its utilization in educational improvement should have been used almost exclusively to judge *final* success only. With its full range of possibilities never emphasized by Tyler, the objectives-oriented approach tended in practice to make evaluation a terminal event, allowing final product judgments only. Any process data gathered were not necessarily wasted, as they could be used after goals had been realigned. However, the opportunity was lost to use such data for refinement of the program in its ongoing state.

Thus, the Tylerian concept of evaluation in congruence terms, relating outcomes to objectives, gave predominance of attention to a terminal process that yielded information only after the full cycle of the program had occurred. There is little doubt that the way in which Tyler conceptualized his method of evaluation and the way in which it was practiced differed markedly — and too often to the disadvantage of the full potentiality of the Tyler approach.

Technical Constraints

To obtain an operational set of objectives for outcome congruence purposes, the evaluator was required to select, and refine, appropriate objectives. Clearly, all possible objectives for a program could not be investigated in an evaluation. Tyler suggested, therefore, that an initial screening process takes place "through a philosophy and a psychology." He never specified exactly what form this process would take; the disadvantage to his vague approach is obvious. Attempts by later writers to interpret this refining process have tended only to confuse the issue. Perhaps it is sufficient to conclude that this initial screening should expose the most important aspects of a program from points of view like content and learning and development theory and that such aspects should be expressible in behavioral terms.

The evaluator's main contribution was to reduce the generally screened goals into measurable, behavioral objectives. For the Tyler strategy to work, objectives had to be stated in operational terms. The skill necessary for this basic component (by which the whole evaluation process would either stand or fall) proved to be too demanding for some teachers. As a result, the criterion for stating objectives became the ease with which the statement could be utilized directly as test items. As a result, important objectives, particularly those dealing with the less concrete aspects of the program such as attitudes, were often ignored.

Behaviors as the Ultimate Criterion

From his definition of evaluation, Tyler gave special emphasis to objectives being statements about behaviors, and invariably about student behaviors. Although, as has been stated above, the Tylerian model gave theoretical promise of placing focus on educational procedures as well as on students, evaluators felt compelled to evaluate everything in terms of effects on students. This occurred even when the actual object of the evalaution was a new building design as an innovative administrative procedure. Everything tended to be viewed from the point of view of the students and their change in behavior (which, if positive, was called "achievement"). Thus, taking the above example, the question to be answered was whether the new building structure, or administrative procedure, added to student achievement. The narrow, technical approach to evaluation in congruence terms focused too much attention on behaviors as the ultimate criterion.

The Bias and Narrow Focus of Evaluation Components

Some critics have considered that the Tylerian approach is fallible in areas such as selection of the most important objectives, openness to value bias in this selection, and the basic standards by which discrepancies between objectives and performance outcomes are measured.

There can be little doubt, moreover, that the procedure focused narrowly onto the classroom primarily, and onto the teacher as the expected agent for the study. If the choice of objectives was too restrictive, there was little chance that a more realistic, and open, study would emerge. The evaluation was, in effect, locked into the pattern of initial objectives. One likely, unfortunate outcome was that the program would develop mainly with emphasis upon the chosen objectives, thus stultifying program creativity for the sake of evaluation demands.

Too often, the choice of objectives was restricted to the more readily quantifiable behavioral objectives, those easily specifiable. Nonoperationally defined worthwhile activities, such as appreciating, judging, and thinking reflectively — those more difficult to quantify — were seldom included as specified objectives for curriculum evaluation. It was difficult to place students in situations where these latter activities could be displayed in a measurable way. With precise quantification and behavioral specification difficult, or even felt to be impossible, with these less tangible elements of the program evaluation tended to become lopsided and therefore incomplete.

Metfessel and Michael — An Extension of the Tylerian Approach

Like Tyler, Metfessel and Michael (1967) believed that measurement of outcomes should improve educational decisions. As an appendix to an interesting paper (1967), Metfessel and Michael listed multiple criterion measures that could be used to evaluate programs. By specifying the range of possible criteria for measurement of outcomes, Metfessel and Michael went considerably further than Tyler. Nevertheless, their evaluation paradigm is basically similar to the Tylerian approach.

The Eight-Step Procedure for Evaluation

Metfessel and Michael developed an eight-step paradigm for evaluation for the purpose of helping school-based personnel (teachers, administrators,

and consultants) in evaluating the attainment of objectives in school programs. The fourth segment of this paradigm used the multiple criterion
measures referred to above. The eight major steps in the evaluation process
are as follows:

1. To involve members of the total school community as participants, or
    facilitators, of the evaluation.
2. To construct a cohesive list of broad goals and specific objectives ar-
    ranged in a hierarchical order from general to specific desired outcomes
    by (a) setting goals that broadly encompass theoretical intentions for
    the program; (b) stating specific objectives in operational terms to
    allow objective measurement whenever possible; and (c) developing
    judgmental criteria that permit the definition of significant and relevant
    outcomes, the establishment of realistic priorities in terms of societal
    needs, of pupil readiness for learning, of pupil-teacher feedback, and
    of the availability of staff and material resources.
3. To translate the specific behavioral objectives into a communicable
    form, applicable to facilitate learning in the school environment.
4. To select or construct a variety of instruments that will furnish mea-
    sures from which inferences can be drawn about the effectiveness of
    programs to meet planned objectives.
5. To carry out periodic observations through the use of the varied instru-
    ments to gauge the extent of behavioral change that is valid with respect
    to the selected objectives.
6. To analyze the data provided by the measures of change through use of
    appropriate statistical methods.
7. To interpret data that are relative to the specified objectives in terms of
    particular judgmental standards and values considered appropriate to
    desirable levels of performance; in this way, to draw conclusions that
    provide information about the direction of growth, the progress of stu-
    dents, and the effectiveness of the total program.
8. To make recommendations that provide a basis for further implemen-
    tation, modifications, and revisions of broad goals and specific objec-
    tives with the purpose of program improvement; to provide feedback,
    based on recommendations, to all individuals involved in the program;
    and to make provision for the cycle of the evaluation process to recom-
    mence once outcomes are given to right-to-know audiences.

The paradigm also gave details of those individuals who would be
primarily responsible for evaluation at each of the successive stages of the
process. These responsibilities, in the form of facilitating roles, were indi-

cated by the letter "L" for lay personnel, "P" for professional staff personnel, and "S" for students. When more than one of these groups had responsibility for a stage of the evaluation process, those who were to act as secondary or indirect agents were designated as such. For example, whereas all three groups would have primary responsibility for the first stage, only professionals would be involved in stage six, and professionals would have the main responsibility for stage eight, with lay and student personnel having secondary, facilitating roles.

Metfessel and Michael also stressed that *judgmental* decisions should be involved throughout all phases of the evaluation process, "as participants of each stage may be expected to make adjustments in their activities in terms of the amount and kinds of feedback received."

In addition, Metfessel and Michael pointed out that evaluators need to be aware that measures may indicate false gains or false losses that are correlated with the following:

1. Experiences within and without the school environment that fall outside the intention of the specific behavioral objectives.
2. Uncontrolled differences resulting from the effects of teachers and other school-based personnel (often motivational in nature).
3. Inaccuracies in the various aspects of data collection and analysis.
4. Errors in research design and statistical methodology.

With such pitfalls ever present, the wisdom and judgment of the evaluator must be "particularly helpful and necessary" if honest and meaningful conclusions are to be derived from evaluation data.

The Appendix of Multiple Criterion Measures

The appendix to the 1967 paper contained multiple criterion measures for the evaluation of school programs. These criterion measures were an excellent contribution on instrumentation, as they listed the various sources and types of criterion measures necessary to give a rounded and complete grasp of the various aspects of a school program. Importantly, although Metfessel and Michael did not move beyond the Tylerian approach in principle, they did broaden the focus for the judgment of a program.

The appendix provided five main dimensions (criterion measures) for evaluating school programs. In each instance, these were measures that if applied to a program, would indicate either the status or change of an aspect of a program by comparison with specific objectives set for the program. These five dimensions of indicators, with sufficient examples to demonstrate criterion measures applicable to each, were presented as follows:

1. Indicators of status or change in cognitive and affective behaviors of students in terms of standardized measures and scales: for example, standardized achievement tests, standardized self-inventories, standardized rating scales, and standardized tests of psychomotor skills.
2. Indicators of status or change in cognitive and affective behaviors of students by informal or semiformal teacher-made instruments or devices: for example: interviews, questionnaires, self-concept perceptions, and teacher-made achievement tests or rating scales.
3. Indicators of status or change in student behavior other than those measured by tests, inventories, and observation scales in relation to the task of evaluating objectives of school programs: for example, absences, anecdotal records (critical behavioral incidents), assignments (number and types completed), books (number and types checked out of library), disciplinary actions taken (type and frequency), peer group participation, referrals by teacher to counselor, and skills (demonstration of new or increased competencies).
4. Indicators of status or change in cognitive and affective behaviors of teachers and other school personnel in relation to the evaluation of school programs: for example, attendance (frequency of, at professional meetings, or at inservice training programs), memberships, including elective positions held in professional and community organizations; and records and reporting procedures practiced by administrators, counselors, and teachers.
5. Indicators of community behaviors in relation to the evaluation of school programs: for example, attendance at special school events; conferences (frequency of parent-teacher or parent-administrator meetings sought by parents); parental response to letters and report cards; and telephone calls from parents, the community, and personnel in the communications media.

The appendix suggested that a wide variety of lay and professional-individuals and groups would be involved in the evaluation — as definers of criterion measures and audiences for final reporting. Metfessel and Michael have stressed a need for a cohesive model of broad goals and objectives, together with a wide range of indicators of the degree of their successful attainment.

Knowledge Test for Unit 3

Objective questions, and correct and incorrect responses to them, are given in this section. The purpose of the section is to determine whether you have a sufficient grasp of the knowledge objectives of the Tylerian approach to evaluation. The test may be self-administered; circle the letter you consider to be the best response. A comparison should then be made with the responses that follow each question. When all questions have been completed, you will be instructed to assess your performance.

Question 1.   According to Tyler, evaluation is

a.   the process of determining the extent to which valued goals have been achieved.
b.   the process of delineating, obtaining, and providing useful information for judging decision alternatives.
c.   the process of describing the background, monitoring the process, measuring the outcomes, and interpreting the full set of information.
d.   the assessment of merit.

Correct Response.   You should have circled "a." This statement captures the essential definition of the Tylerian approach to evaluation — namely, the discrepancy between performance as against goals (or objectives).

Incorrect Responses

b.   Incorrect because the information which is gathered in the Tylerian approach must be related to behaviorally stated objectives.
c.   Incorrect because the Tylerian approach neither describes the background nor interprets any information apart from that related to behavioral objectives.
d.   Incorrect because the Tylerian approach is based on a tighter, and less flexible, definition of evaluation (as the correct response indicates).

Question 2.   Which of the following statements *best* describes Tyler's position about the kinds of evidence admissible for educational evaluation?

a.   Only test scores known to be valid and reliable are admissible.
b.   Test scores are the most useful kinds of evidence, but they must be appropriately balanced with interview and observational data.

c. Any valid evidence about behaviors provides an appropriate method of evaluation.
d. None of the above.

Correct Response. You should have responded with "c." Tyler stressed the wisdom of gaining evidence about behavioral objectives as widely as possible. This included the use of both objective tests and observations.

Incorrect Responses

a. This response limits the scope of admissible evidence to objective testing.
b. This response gives an incorrect emphasis, as circumstances will dictate the kinds of admissible evidence that can be gathered; if it is available and valid, evidence about objectives should be used.
d. Question "c" is a correct response.

Question 3. The Tylerian approach to evaluation endeavored to display advantages over previous approaches because it

a. focused almost exclusively on the student.
b. made judgments of achievement based entirely on measurements such as those provided by test scores.
c. remained uncluttered by standards for measuring successful outcomes.
d. considered knowledge about the program's intentions, its broad goals and behavioral objectives, and about procedures for its successful implementation.

Correct Response. You should have circled "d." This statement contains the main advantages over earlier procedures for educational evaluation in which the measurement of student achievement was the predominant focus (that is, evaluation is identical to measurement). With objectives defined, firm referral points for evaluation and decision making were available.

Incorrect Responses

a. Although in practice the Tylerian approach tended to become student-centered, in theory any aspect of education could be the subject of scrutiny in a study.
b. Incorrect — see the correct response.
c. Incorrect because the definition of objectives also implied criteria for measuring their successful outcomes.

Question 4.   Which of the following *best* characterizes Tyler's opinion about feedback?

a.   Tyler viewed evaluation as a recurring process.
b.   Provided that congruence between objectives and performance could be established, the intervening process was of little importance.
c.   Feedback almost inevitably leads to confusion about the behavioral objectives that are the basis of the evaluation.
d.   Despite reformulation of objectives following feedback of information, the plans for the evaluation should remain unchanged if the study is to keep its credibility.

Correct Response.   You should have responded "a." Tyler considered that evaluation should provide program personnel with ongoing, useful information that could lead to the reformulation or redefinition of objectives.

Incorrect Responses

b.   Incorrect because Tyler provided a practical means for feedback even if this was not frequently used by those who used his approach.
c.   Incorrect because this statement runs contrary to Tyler's stated opinion that goal (or objective) clarification may result from feedback.
d.   Incorrect because Tyler considered that, with modification of objectives, corresponding revision in the plans for the evaluation must ensue.

Question 5.   Which of the following is *not* a use for which the Tylerian model could be applied?

a.   To evaluate large federally funded programs.
b.   To clarify and modify the purposes of a curriculum.
c.   To guide student learning, including the diagnosis and subsequent remediation of perceived weaknesses.
d.   To present a balanced account of the pros and cons of introducing a new program into a classroom.

Correct Response.   You should have circled "d." Tyler, and those who adhered to his approach, did not have a strategy for evaluating the merit of broad goals and selected objectives.

Incorrect Responses

a. Incorrect because Tyler considered his approach to be useful for professional personnel to evaluate federally funded programs.
b. Incorrect because goal and objective revision was a possible use of the Tylerian approach.
c. Incorrect because guidance and support of student learning was one of the main uses to which Tyler wished to see his model applied.

Question 6. Which of the following *best* describes the list of steps that Metfessel and Michael have suggested for the proper performance of an evaluation study?

a. Involve a wide range of community representatives; formulate goals, specify objectives; obtain data-collection instruments; collect, analyze, and interpret data; and formulate recommendations.
b. Define the problem, define alternative action responses to the problem; define and operationalize multiple criteria; collect criterion information about each alternative; and judge the relative merits of the alternatives.
c. Model the program to be evaluated; specify objectives; determine the information requirements; specify multiple criterion measures; and collect, analyze, and report data.
d. Describe the program's antecedents; identify and assess the program's objectives; modify the objectives; select multiple criterion instruments; gather process and output data; and utilize the data to modify the program.

Correct Response. You should have selected "a." This statement represents a brief but accurate synthesis of the Metfessel and Michael progressive stages for evaluation.

Incorrect Responses

b. Incorrect because the emphasis is on evaluation as a problem-solving strategy — rather than the evaluation of a definite program or object.
c. Incorrect because the first three steps show a markedly different approach from that of Metfessel and Michael.
c. Incorrect because this list of steps differs at almost every stage from the approach outlined by Metfessel and Michael.

Interpreting the Knowledge Test.   Having completed the knowledge test of the Tylerian approach, review those questions you missed and those that puzzle you despite your choice of the correct response. We suggest that you review the pertinent sections of the unit to strengthen your grasp of its message.

Application Exercises

This section includes one essay exercise aimed at determining your understanding of Tyler's model and an exercise directed at the Metfessel and Michael section of the unit. Following each exercise is a list of points that should have been included in your response. Reviewing these should help you assess your work. A more complete assessment of your answers will result from your rereading of the relevant part (or parts) of this unit.

Exercise 1.   Select an educational program or object, whether real or hypothetical, to be evaluated. Imagine that you intend to carry.out the study yourself using the Tylerian approach and philosophy toward evaluation. Write an essay outlining the procedures you intend to use. Your answer should contain two main elements: (a) comments of a general nature, about Tyler's philosophy toward the uses of evaluation; (b) conformance with the Tylerian model.

Response to Exercise 1 should include the following:

a.   Concerning the uses of evaluation:
   1.   The general desire to improve the curriculum or object as a result of the evaluation should be emphasized.
   2.   In the case of curriculum evaluation, the improvement of student learning (including remediation of weakness) is an important outcome related to modification of learning objectives.
   3.   Revision of goals and objectives may result from feedback; Tyler viewed evaluation as a recurring process.
   4.   The study could provide useful information for patrons of the educational institution in which the program or project takes place.
b.   Concerning the Tylerian model, the steps should be given in the order specified by Tyler (with particular emphases according to the area being investigated):
   1.   The establishment of broad goals and specific objectives.

2. The broad classification of objectives.
3. The definition of objectives in behavioral terms.
4. The establishment of appropriate conditions in which attainment of objectives can be shown.
5. The planning of explanations of the purposes of the study to key personnel in the selected situations (above).
6. The selection of appropriate measurement techniques.
7. The collection and analysis of performance data.
8. The comparison of analyzed data with the defined behavioral objectives.

Exercise 2. Suppose that before commencing the evaluation of the program or objective you selected for Exercise 1, you decided to explore multiple criterion measures that would be used to aid evaluation. In note form, select two or three such criteria (appropriate to your subject of evaluation) under each of the following broad classification areas suggested by Metfessel and Michael.

a. Indicators of status or change in cognitive and affective behaviors of students in terms of standardized measures and scales.
b. Indicators of status or change in cognitive and affective behaviors of students by informal or semiformal teacher-made instruments or devices.
c. Indicators of status or change in student behavior other than those measured by tests, inventories, and observation scales in relation to the task of evaluating objectives of school programs.
d. Indicators of status or change in cognitive and affective behaviors of teachers and other school personnel in relation to the evaluation of school programs.
e. Indicators of community behaviors in relation to the evaluation of school programs.

Responses to Exercise 2 may include items such as the following according to the areas of classification listed above:

a. Standardized achievement and ability tests; standardized self-inventories yielding measures of attitudes; standardized rating scales for judging quality of products.
b. Incomplete sentence technique; questionnaires; measures of self-concept perceptions (semantic differential, for example); self-evaluation measures.

c. Anecdotal records; attendance; case histories; extra-curricular activities; grade-point average; referrals by teacher to counselor; demonstration of skills.

d. Attendance at professional meetings; elected positions in various organizations; rating scales of attitudes, work efficiency and perceptions of various members of the total school community.

e. Frequency of attendance at school-related events; conferences with school personnel requested by parents or initiated by school personnel; frequency of requests for information and parental response to letters or report cards.

Questions Without Answers

Four questions are given in this section but answers have not been provided. The questions could be used as subjects for group discussion or as individual assignments. Each question can be attempted at two levels: first, by reference to the material contained in this unit, and second, by wider reference to the list of books and articles that concludes this unit.

1. What were Tyler's most useful contributions to the state-of-the-art of evaluation?

2. Tyler stated that an evaluation is *the process of determining to what extent the educational objectives are actually being realized by the program of curriculum and instruction.* What deficiencies do you perceive in such an approach? What are some suggestions for improvement?

3. As a guide to measurement techniques, how useful is the Metfessel and Michael appendix (1967)? Discuss procedures that might be adopted to use some criterion measures in each of the five categories as aids to the evaluation of the attainment of objectives in programs.

4. Tyler proposed that a classroom teacher can use his or her approach to curriculum evaluation. Do you think this is so? (In your discussion, you may wish to suggest points at which the teacher could need help from others.)

References

Krathwohl, D. R. 1965. Stating objectives appropriately for program, for curriculum, and for instructional materials development. *Journal of Teacher Education, 12,* 83–92.

Metfessel, N. S., and Michael, W. B. 1967. A paradigm involving multiple criterion measures for the evaluation of the effectiveness of school programs. *Educational and Psychological Measurement, 27,* 931–943.

Michael W. B., and Metfessel, N. S. 1967. A paradigm for developing valid measurable objectives in the evaluation of educational programs in colleges and universities. *Educational and Psychological Measurement, 27,* 373–383.

Smith, E. R., and Tyler, R. W. 1942. *Appraising and recording student progress.* New York: Harper & Row.

Stufflebeam, D. L., Foley, W. J., Gephart, W. J., Guba, E. G., Hammond, R. L. Merriman, H. O., and Provus, M. M. 1971. *Educational evaluation and decision making in education.* Itasca, Ill.: Peacock.

Tyler, L. L., and Klein, M. F. 1967. Recommendations for curriculum and instructional materials. Los Angeles: University of California, Los Angeles. (mimeo)

Tyler, R. W. 1942. General statement on evaluation. *Journal of Educational Research, 35,* 492–501.

_____. 1950. *Basic principles of curriculum and instruction.* Chicago: University of Chicago Press.

_____. 1953. Some persistent questions on the defining of objectives. In C. M. Lindvall (ed.), *Defining educational objectives.* Pittsburgh: University of Pittsburgh Press.

_____. 1966. The objectives and plans for a national assessment of educational progress. *Journal of Educational Measurement, 3,* 1–10.

Tyler, R., Gagne, R., and Scriven, M. 1967. *Perspectives of curriculum evaluation.* Chicago: Rand McNally.

Worthen, B. R., and Sanders, J. R. 1973. *Educational evaluation: Theory and practice.* Worthington, Ohio: Charles A. Jones.

4 EDWARD A. SUCHMAN AND THE SCIENTIFIC APPROACH TO EVALUATION

A research scientist and a firm believer in the necessity to base conclusions primarily on scientific evidence, Edward Suchman considered that evaluation must be approached with the logic of scientific method. His work and writings during the 1960s, however, emphasized the need to assess programs in relation to their practical setting. For this reason he suggested specific criteria for assessing program success. His studies in the field of social sciences, particularly public health, made him recognize that evaluation research is attended by practical constraints. Moreover, he stated that evaluation researchers, in their attempts to expose desirable and undesirable consequences, must consider relevant values, especially those in conflict.

Suchman's contribution to the field, Evaluative Research: Principles and Practice in Public Service and Social Action Programs (1967), *makes it clear that he considered that an evaluator should use whatever research techniques are available and appropriate to circumstances and needs of a particular evaluative study.*

While Suchman believed the ideal study would adhere to the classic experimental model, he also stressed that, in reality, evaluation research projects usually utilize some variation or adaptation of this model. To a large extent, the formulation of the objectives and design of an evaluation re-

search study will depend upon who conducts the study and the anticipated use of the outcomes.

Edward Suchman believed that evaluation, like all research, must rest upon the logic of the scientific method. He expected that an evaluator would use whatever research techniques are available and feasible according to the circumstances of a particular evaluation. Suchman, who held the position of Professor of Sociology at the University of Pittsburgh (before his untimely death in 1971), worked extensively in the field of social sciences, particularly public health. His publications focused on the area of social research, and his main contribution to evaluation is his interesting and informative book *Evaluative Research: Principles and Practice in Public Service and Social Action Programs* (1967).

Suchman was not alone in his belief that while evaluators are basically researchers, they must strike a balance between rigorous method and the situation in which they must function. Earlier writers who had advocated a similar approach to evaluation methodology included Klineberg (1955), James (1958), Herzog (1959), and Fleck (1961).

Suchman distinguished between evaluation and evaluation research. The former he referred to generally as the "process of making judgments of worth," while he considered evaluation research to be "those procedures for collecting and analyzing data which increase the possibility for proving rather than asserting the worth of some social activity." When he discussed the *process* of evaluation, he proposed a scientific approach. He saw evaluation as a continuous social process, inherently involving a combination of basic assumptions underlying the activity being evaluated and of the personal values of the study participants as well as of the evaluator. Evaluation, he maintained, must necessarily become a scientific process to account for this intrinsic subjectivity since it cannot be eliminated.

Objectives

The objectives of this unit are to characterize what Suchman considered to be the three main aspects of evaluation:

1. *Conceptual aspects*, which include purposes and principles of evaluation, values and the evaluation process, assumptions for evaluation studies, types of evaluation, and categories of evaluation.
2. *The methodological aspect*, which includes evaluation versus nonevaluation research, methodological approaches to evaluation, variations in

evaluation research design, principles of evaluation research design, and the measurement of effects (with emphasis on reliability and validity).

3. *The administrative aspect*, which includes evaluation and administrative science, the administration of evaluation studies (some problem areas), and compromises to meet administrative constraints.

These objectives may be achieved by reading the material offered in this unit. However, a more complete grasp of Suchman's theories and philosophies of evaluation will be gained by reading his original works listed at the end of this unit.

The problems included here should test understanding of the Suchman approach to evaluation. It is advisable not to attempt these problems until (at the least) the material is thoroughly understood.

Conceptual Aspects of Evaluation

As has been stated, Suchman viewed evaluation as a scientific process. Consistent with this stance, he did not consider that the field of evaluation has any methodology different from the scientific method. He therefore conceptualized evaluation research as "first and foremost *research*, and as such it must adhere as closely as possible to currently accepted standards of research methodology." The same procedures that were used to discover knowledge could be utilized to evaluate the degree of success in the application of this knowledge. Suchman held strongly to the concept that by adopting the scientific method, an evaluator will produce findings that are more objective and of ascertainable reliability and validity.

Suchman stated that basic research has a different purpose from evaluation research. Basic research is the discovery of knowledge; administrative action is not a necessary consequence. But evaluation research is applied research, and its purpose is to determine the extent to which a specified program is achieving the desired result. The results will always be used by the administrator for decisions about the future of the program. Bearing in mind the dominant role of administrative criteria in determining the worthwhileness of the study undertaken, the evaluator needs to be constantly aware of the potential *utility* of findings.

This emphasis upon the necessity for usefulness of findings could give rise, in Suchman's opinion, to a very real problem for the evaluator. Because of a strong vested interest, the program administrator will endeavor to control the evaluation, at least to the extent of defining the objectives of the program to be evaluated. To a far greater extent than the basic researcher, the evaluator loses control over the research situation. Thus, it is not the concepts of research per se that make evaluation studies difficult, "but rather the practical problems of adhering to these principles in the face of administrative considerations."

When he explored whether evaluation research is ready to play a more significant role, Suchman concluded that this was not so. Systematic analysis of the *theoretical, methodological,* and *administrative* principles underlying the evaluator's objectives and procedures was needed before positive and meaningful steps forward could be taken confidently. Some aspects of Suchman's views of these three (connected) aspects of evaluation research will now be outlined.

Purposes and Principles of Evaluation

Suchman supported the purposes of evaluation listed by Bigman (1961):

1. To discover whether and how well objectives are being fulfilled.
2. To determine the reasons for specific successes and failures.
3. To uncover the principles underlying a successful program.
4. To direct the course of experiments with techniques for increasing effectiveness.
5. To lay the basis for further research on the reasons for the relative success of alternative techniques.
6. To redefine the means to be used for attaining objectives, and even to redefine subgoals, in the light of research findings.

These purposes, in Suchman's opinion, suggested an intrinsic relationship between program planning and development on the one hand, and evaluation on the other. The means of attaining Bigman's purposes, namely, evaluation research, must provide the basic information for designing and, if necessary, redesigning programs. Just as traditional research should lead toward increased understanding of basic processes, so evaluation research should "aim at an increased understanding of applied or administrative processes." Suchman also maintained that programs in action are greatly influenced by administrative processes.

A principle espoused strongy by Suchman is that different situations warrant different evaluation approaches — including different technical methods and criteria for measuring the success in attaining desired objectives. Based on the assumptions that an evaluation study may take several forms and also that the primary function of most studies is to help the design, development, and operation of programs, Suchman drew the distinction (already given) between evaluation and evaluation research. The former designates the process of judging the merit of some activity, regardless of the method employed. Evaluation research, however, designates the specific use of the scientific method for the purpose of making an evaluation. In other words, evaluation can be considered a goal, while evaluation research can be considered a particular means of attaining that goal.

While Suchman considered that the use of scientific methodology needed particular emphasis, he did not rule out the use of nonscientific methods. He acknowledged that in program design and implementation, many evaluation questions can be answered without research. Nevertheless, he maintained that if the basic requirements of evaluation research could be met — that is, underlying assumptions of objectives examined, measurable criteria developed specifically related to objectives, and a controlled situation instituted — then conclusions based on convincing research, and not just subjective judgment, would be the outcome.

Values and the Evaluation Process

A precondition to any evaluation study, Suchman maintained, is the presence of some activity whose objectives are assumed to have value. He defined value as "any aspect of a situation, event, or object that is invested with a preferential interest as being good, bad, desirable, undesirable, or the like." Values may therefore be construed as modes of organizing human activity based on principles that determine both the goals and the implementation of programs, together with the means of attaining these goals.

Suchman considered that the evaluation process stems from, and returns to the formation of values, as shown in figure 4-1.

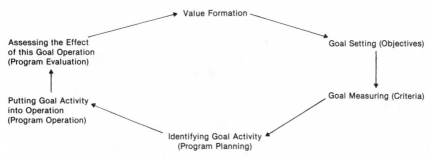

Figure 4-1.   Evaluation Process

Evaluation starts with a particular value (either explicit or implicit), then proceeds to goal-setting activity, that is, a selection among possible alternative goals. Goal-setting forces are necessarily in competition with each other for resources and effort. Next, criteria are selected to measure goal attainment; the nature of the evaluation will determine the type of measure used. The next steps are the identification of some kind of goal-attaining activity (the treatment) and the operationalizing of this activity. At some point in the process this goal-directed operation is appraised. This stage includes the evaluation of the degree to which the operating program has achieved the predetermined objective. Finally, based on this evaluation, a judgment is made whether the goal-directed activity was worthwhile.

The act of judgment returns the activity to value formation. Suchman's concept of the cyclic movement of the evaluation process emphasizes the very close interrelationship between evaluation and the value-laden nature of program planning and operation. As a result, there is the ever-present possibility of conflict in values between the program administrator and the evaluator. This problem will be discussed later in the unit. In general terms, it may be said that values play a large role in determining the objectives of social service programs (such as those of an educational nature) and that the evaluation process that exposes desirable and undesirable consequences of such programs must take social values, especially conflicting values, into account.

Assumptions for Evaluation Studies

Suchman's main assumption for evaluation studies is that every program has some value for some purpose. It follows that the most identifying feature of evaluation research "is the presence of some goal or objective whose measure of attainment constitutes the main focus of the research problem."

When a clear statement of the program objective to be evaluated has been explicated, the evaluation may be viewed as a study of change. The program to be evaluated constitutes the causal or independent variable, and the desired change is similar to the effect or dependent variable. Characterizing an evaluation study this way, Suchman postulated that the project may be formulated in terms of a series of hypotheses that state that "activities A, B, and C will produce results X, Y, and Z."

Objectives and assumptions of an evaluation study are closely tied when the following difficult questions need to be answered before a study commences: What *kind* of changes are desired? What *means* will be used to effect this change? What *signs* will enable the change to be recognized? Before these questions can be addressed adequately, the evaluator must be able to diagnose the presence or absence of a social problem and its underlying value system, and to define goals indicative of progress in ameliorating that condition.

Suchman outlined six questions that must be answered when formulating the objectives of a program for evaluation purposes and, indeed, the design of the study itself:

1. *What* is the nature of the content of the objective (e.g., change in knowledge, attitudes, and/or behavior)?
2. *Who* is the target of the program (e.g., large-scale or discrete groups)?
3. *When* is the desired change to take place (e.g., short-term or long-range goals or cyclical, repetitive programs)?
4. Are the objectives *unitary* or *multiple* (e.g., programs similar for all users or different for different groups)?
5. What is the desired *magnitude* of the effect (e.g., widespread or concentrated results)?
6. *How* is the objective to be attained (e.g., voluntary cooperation or mandatory sanctions)?

Many of the answers to these questions will require an examination of the underlying assumptions of the stated objectives. Suchman saw it as the duty of an evaluator to challenge these assumptions if necessary, for only then can the scientific label truly be applied to the evaluation process.

He classified assumptions into two types: value assumptions and validity assumptions. Value assumptions pertain to the system of beliefs that determines what is "good" within a society or part of that society. For example, a new educational program may be viewed favorably or unfavorably by various groups within a school district. The question the evaluator must answer before investigating the program is, What is success, and from whose point of view?

Validity assumptions are specifically related to program objectives. Such assumptions, for example, underlie the belief of educators that early elementary programs must be consonant with the home influences of each child. Suchman stressed that answers to all validity questions can never be discovered before a program is initiated. The administrator should call upon his or her experience and skill to develop practical programs whose assumptions are clearly laid down. The task of the evaluator is then to prove or disprove the significance of these assumptions.

Types of Evaluation

Following Herzog (1959), Suchman spoke of three types of evaluation studies. *Ultimate evaluation* refers to the determination of the overall success of a program vis-à-vis its stated objectives. *Preevaluative research* deals with intermediate problems (for example, development of reliable and valid explications of the problem, the definition of goals, and the perfection of techniques) that must be solved before ultimate evaluation may be attempted. *Short-term evaluation* seeks specific information about concrete procedures in terms of immediate utility.

Whatever type of evaluation is used, there is a tendency, Suchman pointed out for the objective(s) of the study to be idealized. Without diminishing the obvious significance of the idealized ultimate objectives, Suchman pointed out that it is the practical immediate objectives that most often represent the translation from purpose to program. He advocated that program evaluation should consist essentially of the measurement of success in reaching these practical objectives.

Suchman referred to a prevalent error that evaluators make when they move from a global evaluation of a program to segmental evaluations of their component parts. Too often the practice exists of evaluating program components in terms of ultimate criteria of success rather than according to relevant intermediate criteria. The concept should therefore exist of a cumulative chain of objectives progressing from the most immediate practical objective to the ultimate (perhaps idealized) goal. Moreover, knowledge is never complete, and there must be gaps between the cause-effect links of this chain, which can be filled only by making assumptions concerning the validity of the linking steps. Thus, the validity assumptions (discussed earlier) become the "indispensable cement which binds the hierarchy of objectives together."

Categories of Evaluation

In addition to varying levels of objectives, Suchman considered that evaluation research could be conducted in terms of different categories of effect. These categories represent various criteria of success (or failure) by which a program is judged. He proposed five categories:

1. *Effort.* Evaluations in this category have as their criterion of success the quantity and quality of program activity that takes place. This is an assessment of input regardless of output. It indicates, at least, that something is being done to meet a problem.

2. *Performance.* Criteria in this area measure results of effort rather than the effort itself.
3. *Adequacy of performance.* This criterion of success refers to the degree to which effective performance is adequate by comparison with the total amount of need (according to defined objectives).
4. *Efficiency.* Evaluation in this category addressed the question, Is the capacity of an individual, organization, facility, operation, or activity to produce results in proportion to the effort expended?
5. *Process.* The purpose of this category is to investigate basic explanations for reasons leading to the findings. Suchman outlined four dimensions of an analysis of process: (a) the attributes of the program, (b) the population exposed to the program, (c) the context within which the program occurred, and (d) the different kinds of effects produced by the program (e.g., multiple or unitary effects and duration of effects).

In summary, in discussing types and categories of evaluation, Suchman outlined a basic process to be followed in conducting an evaluation study. This process entails stating objectives in terms of ultimate, intermediate, or immediate goals, of examining the underlying assumptions, and of instituting criteria of effort, performance, adequacy, efficiency, and process.

The Methodological Aspects of Evaluation

Evaluation versus Nonevaluation Research

Suchman clearly delineated inherent differences between the objectives and research conditions of evaluation as opposed to nonevaluation (i.e., basic, or pure) research. He saw the difference not as one of right versus wrong, but rather "a complex mixture of differing values, purposes, and resources."

Evaluation research is a special kind of applied research whose goal, unlike nonevaluation research, is not to discover knowledge but to test the application of knowledge. With its main emphasis on utility, evaluation research should provide information for program planning, implementation, and development. Evaluation research also assumes the particular characteristic of applied research that allows predictions to be an outcome of investigation. Recommendations made in evaluation reports are examples of predictions.

By comparison with nonevaluation research, the evaluation study contains an array of variables over which the evaluator has little, if any, control. Suchman stressed that in evaluation research, the observable and measurable variables are *the* phenomena of interest; the implemented program has as its goal the changing of the values of these measures. Whereas the underlying concept is of prime importance in basic research, such is not the case in applied research, of which evaluation research is a form.

Suchman contended that program evaluation may have very little generalizability, as the evaluation is applicable solely to the program being evaluated with its contextual ramifications. A reason therefore exists why so many evaluation studies appear repetitive — the uncertainty is always present that a program that is effective in one situation may very well not be in another. Moreover, when the problem-solving objective of evaluation research is considered to "place a premium upon administrative decision making for some *immediate* and specific need," further difficulties for external validity present themselves.

Methodological Approaches to Evaluation

The inherent difference between evaluation and nonevaluation studies, Suchman maintained, is reflected in the form taken by the statement of the problem. Whereas pure research (nonevaluation research) questions whether A is related to B and tests this relationship experimentally (under controlled conditions), applied research (evaluation research) questions whether A works effectively to change B and attempts to answer this question empirically by manipulating A and measuring the effect on B. In nonevaluation research, crucial importance is given to an analysis of the process whereby A relates to B, but in evaluation research "it becomes relatively unimportant to understand why A produced B." Readers should note that in making this statement, Suchman conflicts with a view to be expressed shortly (and repeated later), that evaluation emphasis must be given to the *process* that occurs between program initiation and findings.

The differences, moreover, between evaluation and nonevaluation research are not absolute, but may be considered to exist on a continuum. Suchman thought that an evaluator should therefore adhere as closely as is practical to the rules of scientific inquiry, but the evaluator must define and justify where and when these rules have had to be adapted to reality.

It may very well be argued, however, that if A is falsely assumed to cause B, an expensive program based on A may be instituted, only to find that the desired effect does not occur because of a change in the "true" cause, which may have been minimally related to A. Suchman advocated that to test for such a spurious cause, the evaluation design must include an analysis of the *process* that intervenes between program initiation and outcomes. This approach demands an evaluation research design that becomes "an inherent part of the service program itslf." An ongoing evaluation is a recognition that many changing conditions govern the operation of a program, including forces beyond the control of the program administrator but also feedback from the evaluation itself, which may influence both program objectives and processes. Bearing this in mind, an evaluator must make allowance for such contingencies and developments by making provision, in the design, for the collection of additional data if it proves necessary.

Variations in Evaluation Research Design

Suchman stated that evaluation research has no special methodology of its own; being research, it holds to the tenets of scientific method as closely as possible. It therefore uses a variety of recognized research designs and available scientific techniques for data collection and analysis. The important question to be asked (as Suchman saw it) was not whether evaluation research is scientific, but to what extent evaluation research can make the best use of available research designs and techniques.

Emphasizing the connection between a program's causes and effects on the one hand, and design on the other, Suchman proposed a model that shows that the intended causal sequence of the evaluation study becomes only one of many possible sets of actions and events leading to outcomes. Diagrammed in figure 4–2, the model is an open-system, naturalistic, multi-causal concept (as opposed to the closed-system of nonevaluation research).

This model has great implications for the design of evaluation research studies. For example, it indicates that social programs are inevitably evaluated within the context of other programs or events that affect the desired object. Thus, the study's design must make provision to consider the preconditions and intervening events that will influence the initiated program

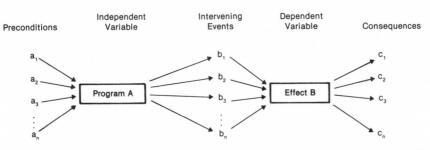

Figure 4–2.   Multi-causal Concept of Evaluation

activity. Effects, both desirable and undesirable, are likely consequences of the lack of experimental control inherent in a natural setting. Again, the design must make provision for these effects to be investigated.

Principles of Evaluation Research Design

Suchman presented a list of principles to be observed in laying out the design of an evaluation study, the main ones are as follows:

1. A good design is one that is the most suitable for the purpose of the study; whether or not it is scientific is not an issue.
2. There is no such thing as a single correct design; hypotheses can be studied by different methods using different designs.
3. All research design represents a compromise dictated by many practical considerations.
4. An evaluation research design is not a highly specific plan to be followed without deviation, but rather a series of guidelines to ensure that main directions are followed.

In Chapter 6 of his 1967 book, Suchman gave details of possible variations in evaluation research design. Interested readers may wish to investigate these designs. It will be found that while Suchman believed that the ideal study would adhere to the classic experimental model, he also stressed that, in reality, evaluation research projects usually utilize some variation or adaptation of this model. To a large extent, the formulation of the objectives and design of an evaluation research study will depend upon who conducts the study and the anticipated use of the outcomes. He emphasized that while designing a study, an evaluator must be aware that validity considerations are crucial.

The Measurement of Effects

According to Suchman the measurement of the effects of a program requires specification relating to four major categories of variables:

1. Component parts or processes of the program.
2. Intended population and actual groups reached.
3. Situational conditions within which the program occurred.
4. Differential effects of the program.

Suchman pointed out that determination of both the reliability and validity of the criteria of effectiveness of these variables causes particular problems. For the most part, the evaluator does not measure directly the phenomena being studied, but rather indices of these phenomena. Two obvious problems present themselves. First, how does the evaluator decide on indicators for the criteria of achievement of program objectives? And second, how does the evaluator select from all possible indicators, those to be used for a particular purpose?

In presenting ways to solve these problems, Suchman discussed aspects of the methodological concepts of reliability and validity at considerable length. In particular, he emphasized that evaluators should be aware of, and endeavor to control, the main sources of unsystematic variation in evaluation research:

1. Subject reliability: attitudes and behavior affected by moods, fatigue, and so on.
2. Observer reliability: personal factors influence interpretation of subject's responses.
3. Situational reliability: conditions of measurement produce changes in results, which do not reflect "true" change in presentation being studied.
4. Instrument reliability: all of the above (combined) or specific aspects of the instrument itself (e.g., poorly worded questions) affect reliability.
5. Processing reliability: coding errors, and so on, occurring randomly lower reliability.

Validity presents a much broader problem than reliability, as it refers not only to specific measures but also to the significance of the whole evaluation process. The validity of an evaluation study refers to validity of its specific measures; it also refers to the theory underlying the hypotheses relating the evaluation activities to its objective. The following are the sources of bias leading to validity concerns in evaluation studies:

1. Propositional validity: the use of incorrect or inappropriate assumptions or theories.
2. Instrument validity: the use of irrelevant operational indices.
3. Sampling validity: lack of population representativeness in the sample.
4. Observer (evaluator) validity: introduction of a consistent bias based on personal bias or preconceived notions.
5. Subject validity: habits and predispositions of subjects introduce invalid biases.

6. Administration validity: conditions of the study (e.g., methods of data collection) constitute a source of invalidity.
7. Analysis validity: deliberate or unintended bias causes invalidity.

The differential effects of a program encompass what Suchman terms *unanticipated* or *unintended effects*. Social phenomena are so complex and interrelated that to change one of its aspects becomes impossible without producing a series of connected changes, which Suchman terms *secondary effects*. These secondary effects of a program can be particularly troublesome when the program is intended to be widely disseminated. Federally funded programs in education fall into this category. The evaluator and program administrator must therefore be wary of easy acceptance of secondary positive effects as justification for a program's *intended* objectives being achieved; decisions concerning generalizability should be made on this basis. However, it is also important to understand that research is a learning process and that the secondary effects (desirable or undesirable), and the analyzing of these effects, is an integral part of this process.

Evaluation and Program Administration

As was mentioned earlier, Suchman considered that the purpose of evaluation is usually one of utility. Its main objective is to increase the effectiveness of program administration. Connected to this objective is the concept that the conduct of an evaluation study itself is a form of program activity; consequently, planning and execution of evaluation studies require administrative resources. Suchman recognized a close nexus between evaluation research, on the one hand, and administrative theory and practice, on the other.

Evaluation and Administrative Science

Evaluation research can challenge traditional practice and perform the useful function of making these activities more efficient. Evaluation studies of past programs serve the important function of exposing unproductive effort. In regard to present programs, evaluation research can appraise the current progress and indicate promising new strategies. And concerning future programs, evaluation research can make a major contribution by defining objectives.

Suchman pointed out that evaluation has traditionally been considered as the final process of the administrative function of program planning, the earlier processes being research, planning, demonstration, and operation. However, he stressed that evaluation, as a study of effectiveness, may occur at *each* stage of the total process. For example, an administrator may wish to evaluate, or have evaluated, the findings of a research study or the feasibility of the program during its development stage. Of the various processes, Suchman held the opinion that planning and operation required the most careful evaluation, with higher priority being given to established operating programs.

The evaluation of the operational stage — "to provide a measure of the extent to which the program attains the desired results" — serves, among others, these valuable functions:

1. Points out specific strong and weak points of program operation and suggests changes and modifications of procedures and objectives.
2. Examines the efficiency and adequacy of programs compared with other methods in the light of total needs.
3. Suggests new approaches for future programs.
4. Establishes priorities among programs in terms of scarce resources such as funds, personnel, and time.
5. Provides public accountability.
6. Builds morale and critical attitudes of staff by involving them in the evaluation of their efforts.

It should be noted that each evaluation function has a very real connection with administrative functions.

Suchman warned that evaluation research, fraught as it is with administrative considerations, may be undertaken with purposes other than program improvement in mind. For instance, an administrator may attempt to justify a weak program with biased reporting ("eyewash"), to cover up program failure by avoiding objective approaches ("whitewash"), or to destroy a program regardless of its worth in order to be rid of it ("submarine"). Because administrative structures tend to perpetuate themselves, it should also be considered that the results of an evaluation will most likely be resisted if the study has the potential to weaken the power of the organization. Suchman saw no easy solution to this ever-present problem.

Administration of Evaluation Studies: Some Problem Areas

An evaluation is "a form of social activity encompassing a number of highly significant interpersonal relationships between and among research workers, program personnel, and subjects." The evaluator cannot escape these interrelationships. In addition to the normative aspects of research, an evaluator deals with issues very close to vested interests. Less the objective scholar, therefore, than judge of success or failure, the evaluator's recommendations may affect the continuation or change of a program. The accuracy of the evaluator's judgment may very well depend on the quality of the interface activities between the evaluator and personnel important to the study.

If role relationships do deteriorate between an evaluator and an administrator, various ameliorative strategies are possible; some suggestions were given by Suchman:

1. Develop an optimal initial orientation level of expectation by both parties.
2. Clarify the roles of both parties to the undertaking.
3. Increase the interpersonal skills of all participants by an initial training program (organized by both parties).

Suchman warned that particularly when external evaluations occur, evaluators need to be aware that program personnel feel that they are on trial and therefore threatened. Coordination between the evaluator and administrators can go a long way toward averting conflict. "The evaluator and the program personnel are advised to sit down together before the evaluation takes place to discuss the objectives and plan of procedure."

The question, Who should do the evaluation?, Suchman maintained, is not easily answered. Both internal and external evaluations have advantages and disadvantages. Though experiencing less ego involvement and less pressure to make compromises in research design or interpretation, the outside evaluator is less likely to understand the objectives and procedures of the program or the practicality of recommendations. An inside evaluator will be more informed about the program, but loss of objectivity is an ever-present danger. While circumstances will dictate which strategy is preferable, Suchman advised that, whenever possible, a combination of both has many advantages.

Another ever-present problem concerns the different value positions of the evaluator and the administrator concerning definition of objectives. In general, the evaluator will seek to measure achievement, whereas the program administrator will be more likely to emphasize effort and technique. The evaluator is likely to be more concerned with ultimate objectives, whereas the program administrator will be more involved with immediate objectives. Suchman emphasized that evaluation is intended to aid, and not to hamper, a project. Thus, the evaluator may produce a report of little real value if obsessed with precise summative measurements. On the other hand, preoccupation with day-to-day techniques, and loss of sight of the project's total meaning, is equally poor practice. An explication by evaluator and administrator of the study's goals is crucial to the solution of the problems arising from differing value stances as in the examples given above.

Compromises to Meet Administrative Constraints

It has been pointed out that Suchman considered that evaluation studies should be the best possible compromise between the demands of science and the realistic conditions of research. Often, however, compromise decisions have to be made at least partly in terms of administrative constraints or pressures. If it is assumed that evaluation research is carried out to give the basis for administrative decisions, then the study's design must accommodate administrative policies and other constraints. The evaluator needs to keep in mind that an evaluation takes place under natural conditions and its research techniques must necessarily adapt to the realities of data collection and analysis. The ingenuity and alertness of the evaluator are needed, nevertheless, to maintain scientific controls to the extent possible.

Finally, in his discussion of evaluator and administrator concerns, Suchman stated that both parties should consult about the practicality and implementation possibilities of findings, while the results of an evaluation must be translated into judgments concerning program success or failures. To have real value, the results should indicate clear guideposts for future directions. One serious error an evaluator can make is to draw up a list of recommendations without consulting the program administrator and personnel. Such a consultation would avoid a presentation of findings that fails to take into account the many contingencies necessary for practical action, including interpersonal and administrative functions.

Knowledge Test for Unit 4

This knowledge test contains two parts. The true-false questions will assess whether you have grasped the basic premise of Suchman's approach to evaluation. Having decided whether a statement is true or false, you will then be directed to answer a further question based upon your answer. Compare your answer with the correct response that follows each question.

The second part of the knowledge test consists of two multiple-choice questions. Once again, each question is followed by the correct response and the reasons for this as well as explanations about the incorrectness of the other responses.

After you have completed all questions in both parts, we suggest that you review and remediate your performance, using the guidelines that appear after the questions.

Question 1. Suchman's main objective in writing was to make obvious a need for the critical reevaluation of the role and methodology of evaluation research in the areas of public service and social action.

True _____   False _____

If true, what were Suchman's conclusions concerning the relationship between evaluation research and the basic tenets of research methodology? If false, what is Suchman's main objective in writing about evaluation research?

Correct Response. The statement is true. Suchman constantly stressed that evaluation research should adhere to the principles of research methodology. Evaluation research must therefore be a scientific process in which every effort must be taken to "control" both the subjectivity of the evaluator and participants and the influence of extraneous variables. Ultimately, the significance of evaluation results will be determined by the "same scientific standards used to judge nonevaluation research."

Question 2. The main purpose of evaluation research, according to Suchman, is to provide useful information for administrators seeking to make more effective program decisions.

True _____   False _____

If true, list five important concerns an evaluator must have to ensure that information derived from an evaluation study is accurate and useful for decision-making purposes. If false, state the main purpose of evaluation research according to Suchman.

Correct Response. The statement is false. Suchman considered that the primary objective of evaluation research is to determine the extent to which a program or procedural strategy is achieving a desired result. Emphasis is certainly placed on the potential utility of the evaluator's findings, but the primary purpose of an evaluation study is to discover program effectiveness when compared with program objectives in the light of the relationship of objectives to their underlying assumptions.

Question 3. Suchman considered that a very close relationship should exist between evaluation and program planning and development. Pure research leads toward the increased understanding of basic processes, whereas evaluation research aims at increased understanding of applied processes and strategies thus enabling rational changes to be made.

True ____   False ____

If true, state the basic requirements necessary (in Suchman's opinion) to carry out evaluation research that can accurately propose suggestions for program development. If false, state whether Suchman saw *any* type of relationship existing between evaluation and program development and/or improvement.

Correct Response. The statement is true. Suchman envisaged evaluation research providing the basic information necessary for designing and redesigning action programs. Then evaluation, in a sense, should involve more than judging success or failure of a program; it also should encompass understanding and redefinition. To achieve these ends, Suchman maintained that evaluation research should become increasingly scientific, that both program objectives and their underlying assumptions should be thoroughly understood before an evaluation study commences, that criteria specifically related to those objectives must be developed, and that a controlled situation should be instituted to determine the extent to which these objectives (and any negative side effects) are achieved. At this point, according to Suchman, the stage has been set for meaningful program development.

Question 4. Suchman believed that a "value is any aspect of a situation or object that is given an orientation such as being 'good,' 'bad,' 'desirable,' or 'undesirable.' "

True ____   False ____

If true, what is the significance, in Suchman's opinion, of values with respect to evaluation studies? If false, what was Suchman's definition of a "value," and what importance does an understanding of the term have in the carrying out of an evaluation?

Correct Response. The statement is true. Suchman saw values as modes of organizing human activity — meaningfully charged principles that determine the goals of social action programs and the most acceptable means of attaining these goals. For any evaluator, an understanding of these principles is of paramount importance, for only with such understanding can the exact meaning of program goals, their underlying assumptions, and program operation be grasped. An evaluator must necessarily, therefore, be very much aware of any conflicting values that exist before a study commences or that arise during its progress. Unless taken fully into account, conflicting values can introduce problems so serious that the effectiveness of the evaluation results either diminish or cease to exist.

Question 5.   Suchman was not concerned that the success of an evaluation of a social action program rested on the diagnosis of the presence or absence of a social problem and the definition of goals indicative of a desirable path to ameliorate that condition.

True _____   False _____

If true, what (if any) importance did Suchman attach to problem diagnosis and goal definition? If false, what are some of the general considerations involved in the formulation of goals and objectives for evaluation research?

Correct Response. The statement is false. Suchman thought that without problem diagnosis and, subsequently, goal definition, evaluation research would be aimless. To formulate goals and objectives for evaluation research, Suchman advocated six main considerations: (a) *What* is the nature of the content of the goal (or objectives)? (b) *Who* is the target of the program? (c) *When* is the desired change to take place? (d) Are the objectives *unitary or multiple*? (e) Are *widespread or concentrated* results sought? (f) *How* are goals and objectives to be attained?

Question 6.   Because evaluation research has a particular concreteness by comparison with the more abstract basic research, significant questions can be raised about the meaning of data collected in either type of study. Evaluation research stresses the underlying concept as the primary variable of interest; study data must have the ability to represent this concept reliably and validly. Basic research, however, stresses that the observable and measurable indices are *the* phenomena of interest.

True _____   False _____

If true, discuss which of the two types of research — evaluation or basic — lends itself more readily to generalizability. If false, given an accurate account of the "meaning" of the data collected in either type of study.

Correct Response. The statements that follow the opening sentence are false. Evaluation research is primarily concerned with observing and measuring outcomes; the program being evaluated is usually aimed directly at changing the values of these specific measures and only indirectly at the underlying concept. By contrast, basic research is concerned primarily with translating a concept into observable units (i.e., operational indices of the underlying concept) whose worth depends on their ability to represent the concept reliably and validly.

Question 7. Because Suchman so strongly supported basic research procedures as the ideal for evaluation research, he supported only the classic experimental design approach for evaluation studies.

True _____   False _____

If true, outline the basic procedures one would follow to adhere to the classic experimental model. If false, state whether Suchman considered that adaptations of the ideal experimental design were feasible.

Correct Response. The statement is false. Suchman considered that the classic experimental model is an ideal research design from which adaptations may be derived according to particular sets of circumstances. Thus, there is not one but a set of research designs, for there is no one best way to design all evaluation studies. As examples of adaptations of the classic experimental model, Suchman referred to Campbell's quasiexperimental designs.

Question 8. In evaluation, reliability is affected not only by chance errors of the measuring instrument, but also by actual fluctuations of the object being measured.

True _____   False _____

If true, mention at least three kinds of change factors that contribute to unreliability of measures of change. If false, alter the statement so that it reads correctly.

Correct Response. The statement is true. Some major sources of unreliability of measures of change result from the following factors: (a) Subject reliability: the subject's moods may affect his attitude toward the program. (b) Observer reliability: the observer's moods may affect the way in which he makes his measurements. (c) Situational reliability: certain environmental conditions may account for observed changes. (d) Instrument reliability: poorly worded questions, for instance, may produce inaccurate responses. (e) Processing reliability: coding and other mechanical errors reduce reliability.

Question 9. Suchman believed that "outside" evaluators should be used exclusively because personnel closely connected with the organization and maintenance of a program have too much ego involvement in the outcomes of an evaluation to be entrusted with its commission.

True _____   False _____

If true, mention three ways in which "inside" evaluators, purposely or otherwise, could distort evaluation information. If false, outline Suchman's true stance on this issue.

Correct Response. The statement is false. Suchman maintained that the question concerning who should do the evaluation cannot be answered in any clear-cut fashion. There are advantages and disadvantages to both internal and external evaluations. Outside evaluators may be less ego involved in outcomes, but they are less likely to understand the objectives or procedures of the program and less aware of the practical implications of recommendations stemming from the evaluation study. On the other hand, while insiders may be very aware of program goals, organization, and potentiality, they may find it extremely difficult to maintain objectivity. Circumstances of a particular situation must therefore dictate inside versus outside evaluation. Whenever possible, Suchman considered, a combination of both can have many advantages. He envisaged a rational, professional division of labor.

Question 10. It was Suchman's opinion that program decisions often have to be made in terms of administrative pressures. Consequently, if an evaluator wishes to conduct a study that gives the basis for inferences about decision making, a concern with administrative policy and pressures cannot be ignored. Indeed, it should be built into the research design.

True _____   False _____

If true, state the main reason why Suchman was willing to accept administrative "interferences" during an evaluation research study. If false, give the precise relationship Suchman thought should exist between evaluation on the one hand and administrative decision making on the other.

Correct Response. The statement is true. Suchman's stance was that evaluation research is applied research; it has to take place in the field under natural conditions and must therefore adapt itself as best it can to the practical conditions that exist. One such condition very often is administrative pressure. If this is not understood and allowance is not made for it in the research design, the evaluation study will be less useful for decision-making purposes.

Multiple Choice

Question 11.   In regard to criteria for assessing programs, Suchman proposed that:

a.   the main concern is to isolate, analyze, and judge a treatment as it operates in practice.
b.   the surest route to the formulation of sound evaluation conclusions is systematically to generate and test hypotheses about relationships between intervening variables and immediate outcomes.
c.   the success or failure of a program should be evaluated in terms of cost effectiveness, recidivism, and diversity of outcomes.
d.   effort, performance, adequacy of performance, efficiency, and process are useful categories for determining the success or failure of programs.

Correct Response. You should have selected "d." These are the criteria that Suchman proposed for assessing the success or failure of a program.

Incorrect Responses.

a.   While Suchman emphasized the need to assess programs in relation to their practical settings, he suggested specific criteria for assessing program success, as noted above.
b.   Suchman's view of appropriate criteria obviously was not restricted to intervening variables and immediate outcomes.
c.   Suchman did not identify recidivism and diversity of outcomes among the main categories of criteria he recommended.

Question 12. Which of the following statements most truly reflects Suchman's views concerning administrative influences and the position of the evaluator?

a. Suchman contended that if the results of the evaluation tend to weaken the power of the organization, such a study will be accepted as beneficial because appropriate changes can occur to bolster weaknesses.
b. The evaluator is a judge of success or failure and will determine the continuation or change of a program.
c. Research is subject to social constraints from the organization within which the evaluator is working.
d. Suchman considered that the evaluator and program manager must be wary of unnecessary openness with each other; it is advisable for them to go their own way so that objectivity is maintained.

Correct Response. You should have selected "c." If such constraints are not understood by the evaluator, and allowances made for them in the study design, it is likely that the outcomes of the study will be inaccurate.

Incorrect Responses

a. Organizations tend to be very sensitive and defensive toward adverse criticism.
b. Suchman contended that the responsibility of an evaluator ceases when recommendations as a result of judgment of success or failure of a program are made.
d. Suchman considered that the evaluator and program manager should discuss the objectives and procedures planned for the evaluation in advance of its commencement.

Interpreting the Knowledge Unit. We suggest that you return to those questions you found difficult or perplexing and use them as a basis for reviewing pertinent sections of the unit.

Questions Without Answers

The following questions may be useful for discussion purposes:

1. In which ways did Suchman differentiate between basic research and evaluation research?

2. What are some of the main purposes Suchman saw for evaluation?
3. What are the main aspects of the model proposed by Suchman to show that the intended causal sequence of an evaluation becomes only one of many possible actions and events leading to outcomes?
4. Suchman warned that evaluation research is "fraught with administrative considerations." What are some of these?

References

Fleck, A.C. 1961. Evaluation as a logical process. *Canadian Journal of Public Health, 52* (May), 185-191.

Herzog, E. 1959. *Some guide lines for evaluative research.* Washington, D.C.: U.S. Department of Health, Education, and Welfare.

James, G. 1958. Research by local health departments — Problems, methods, results. *American Journal of Public Health, 48* (March), 354-379.

_____ . 1961. Planning and evaluation of health programs. In *Administration of community health services.* International City Managers' Association, Chicago, pp. 124-134.

Klineberg, O. 1955. The problem of evaluation. *International Social Science Bulletin, 7.3,* 347-362.

Suchman, E.A. 1954. *The principles of research design.* In J.T. Doby et al.,, *An introduction to social research.* Harrisburg, Pa.: The Stackpole Co., pp. 254-267.

_____ . 1963. *Sociology and the field of public health.* New York: Russell Sage Foundation.

_____ . 1966. Medical deprivation. *American Journal of Orthopsychiatry, 36* (July), 665-672.

_____ . 1967. *Evaluative research: Principles and practice in public service and social action programs.* New York: Russell Sage Foundation.

5 CRONBACH'S DESIGNING EVALUATIONS: A SYNOPSIS

During the past 40 years, Lee J. Cronbach has concerned himself with many aspects of evaluation of social science programs. Much of his thinking in these areas has culminated in a book entitled Designing Evaluations of Educational and Social Programs *(Cronbach, 1982), a lengthy and erudite work, the preliminary version of which was completed in April 1978. Containing 374 pages, the book includes some new aspects for the design of educational evaluations, while discussing the pros and cons of some of the design concepts already in use.*

In his introduction to the issues of planning evaluations, Cronbach states that designing an evaluation investigation is an art because each design has to be decided according to its appropriateness to each new undertaking. He

---

This unit is focused on Cronbach's 1982 book *Designing Evaluations of Educational and Social Programs.* A view of evaluation is presented in the 438-page book entitled *Toward Reform of Program Evaluation* (Cronbach and Associates, 1980). Together these books provide an in-depth view of Cronbach's philosophy of evaluation and his practical approach to evaluation design.

points out that the evaluator must be aware of the choices available so that the advantages that accrue from each feature of the design can be balanced against any sacrifices that each choice entails. The design, therefore, becomes very much a matter of planning for allocation of investigative resources, based upon a selection of the most appropriate questions and guided by practical and political considerations.

The strong contrasts between some of the remarks of the adherents of the scientific approach to evaluation and the enthusiasts for the holistic or naturalistic approach suggest a polarization so strong that no reconciliation is possible. However, Cronbach believes that the conflict is exaggerated and that the more an evaluative effort becomes a program of studies (rather than a single study) the more appropriate for a mixture of styles. The need for political awareness, open-mindedness, and good communications by the evaluator in both the design and operational stages of an investigation runs through all that Cronbach writes.

Social institutions learn from evaluative experience, and so do program clients and political constituencies. Evaluation is intended to speed up the learning process by communicating what otherwise might be overlooked or wrongly perceived.

Because of the length of Cronbach's book (Cronbach, 1982), no attempt will be made to cover all its material in this brief unit. If, however, you find the points raised interesting, you may be assured that they are well worthy of further exploration by reference to the complete text. Here we select from Cronbach's work those thoughts that fit into the general context dealing with investigative components and resources for an evaluation, such as the place of various styles in evaluation design, identification of research questions, and the importance of evaluator–decision-maker communications. In addition, we introduce Cronbach's concept of the elements in an evaluation design, namely, units, treatments, and observing operations (*uto*).

By working through this unit, you should be able to gain a grasp of Cronbach's thinking (in general terms) about the influences on program evaluation design. Exercises appear at the end of the unit to test your knowledge. A list of unit objectives now follows. When you have studied them, read the unit and then attempt the knowledge test, checking your answers against the keyed ones.

Objectives

The objectives of the chapter are as follows:

1.   To develop an understanding of some of the general issues involved in the designing of evaluations by considering thoughtful planning for flexibility, the profitable evaluation, conflicting approaches to evaluation, consensus in design elements, and balance in evaluation design (summary).
2.   To introduce Cronbach's concept of the elements in an evaluation design; in particular, units, treatments, and observing operations; *UTOS:* the domain of investigation; definitions of the elements of *uto* and *UTO*; and *UTOS:* the domain of application.
3.   To gain a grasp of ways of identifying the research questions by considering the divergent phase and the convergent phase.
4.   To emphasize the importance of communication in respect to the utility of findings, direct communication, and extrapolating from findings.
5.   To investigate Cronbach's vision of the promise of evaluations, which includes flexibility of design, evaluation and politics (limitations), and other considerations.

Introduction to the Issues

Thoughtful Planning for Flexibility

Cronbach is convinced that a premium should be placed upon planning an evaluation that will withstand certain kinds of challenge because, in Cronbach's opinion, evaluations are intended to serve a political function. The challenges to the information arising from evaluations will often be politically motivated. This is an inescapable statement of any evaluation. To accommodate a wide range of legitimate expectations about the outcome of an evaluation, the planning of the evaluation should be something akin to the planning for a program of investigation. And thus, at its best, the evaluation has the same flexible responsiveness to its own findings as it has to the changing concerns of the political community. When planning (and replanning) a fully professional study, the evaluator strives to make it more likely that voters, managers, operating personnel, and/or policy makers will give serious consideration to the findings. Nothing else justifies the effort vested in both the planning and the actual evaluation.

Evaluations are most often undertaken at the request of an administrator. Possibly, the administrator may wish to reduce the evaluator to a technician, setting forth questions to be answered and asking the evaluator to apply skills of sampling, measurement, and statistical analysis without reflecting on the implications of these tasks. Cronbach, however, envisages an evaluator asking for, and obtaining, much fuller responsibility so that the evaluation may be more worthwhile. While evaluators cannot, and should not, substitute their judgment for that of the sponsoring agency, they should have license to offer views about the agenda for investigation. Administrators, then, should ask competent evaluators to think about the design possibilities before any decision to proceed is made.

Cronbach believes that no one individual has the breadth of qualifications to make all the judgments that go into design and interpretation; almost always, responsibility must be shared by a team. This approach has certain advantages, as it brings in multiple perspectives and promotes healthy professional debate. Planning, therefore, is likely to occur at two levels: general planning to set priorities and allocate responsibility to teams, and detailed in-team planning, which should result in designs based on the experience and interactions of those constituting the team. Thus, evaluation design and studies become thoughtful, evolving processes and not simply mechanically objective, patterns.

To reflect upon events themselves is of greater importance than to rely upon what Cronbach calls "mindless data-processing." Like Carol Weiss (1972), Cronbach believes that evaluation must be viewed as a way of illuminating complex mechanisms as treatment realizations vary, as the process as well as the outcome is to be studied, and as information from a field test is most likely to be used in decisions about actions other than the one tested.

The Profitable Evaluation

Designs are planned on the basis of some conception of what an excellent evaluation is or does. The best design is one that promises to increase the social benefit from the evaluation; the choice of design alternatives is made on the basis of how evaluations can influence social affairs. Social institutions learn from experience, and so do program clients and political constituencies. Evaluation, in Cronbach's terms, is intended to speed up the learning process by communicating what otherwise might be overlooked or wrongly perceived.

To be profitable, an evaluation must have as its core "scientific activities," for if the observations reported are not realistic or the interpretations are poorly reasoned, an evaluation cannot have much value. On the other hand, a study that is technically admirable falls short if what the evaluator learns does not enter the thinking of the relevant political community, such as clients, program staffs, bureaucrats, and interested citizens.

As a result of the scientific approach, evaluators' work may generate insights in others; thus, evaluators are educators whose success is to be judged, at least in part, by their success in communication. Cronbach believes that this teaching begins when the evaluator first sits down with members of the policy-shaping community to elucidate their questions. It then continues in every contact the evaluator makes with program participants or with relevant others. The end report is only one of the means of instruction at the evaluator's disposal: the work as a teacher lies as much in the matter of raising questions as it does in providing answers. Especially in value-laden matters, the evaluator's responsibility (as an educator) is to help others to ask better questions and determine actions appropriate to their aims.

Cronbach stresses that at all stages of an evaluation, from design to reporting, "excellent information" is essential. Like Wilensky (1967), Cronbach believes that excellent information is

clear because it is understandable to those who must use it.

timely because it reaches them when they need it.

reliable because diverse observers (using the same procedure) see it in the same way.

valid because it is cast in the forms of concepts and measures that capture reality.

wide-ranging because major policy alternatives promising a high probability of attaining organizational goals are posed or new goals are suggested.

If the communications from the evaluation are the product that counts, the following questions should be raised regarding the completed evaluation:

Did each section of the audience attend to the message?

Did they understand it?

Did they find it credible?

Were the questions that were significant to them answered as well as possible?

Did the answers alter their preconceptions?

Was the dialog leading to the decisions enriched and elevated as a consequence of the evaluation?

If the communications are such that all these questions can be answered positively, then the evaluation plan and procedures must be judged as good.

One obvious difficulty in making such a judgment is that arising from each consensus, for in a politically lively situation there is a policy-shaping community and not a lone decision maker. All those who play roles in approving the program or in advocating alternatives are part of that community. Moreover, ideally, the evaluator will strive to reach normally silent citizens, whose voices should be raised and questions answered by appropriate communication.

An evaluation should reduce uncertainty regarding alternatives that confront its audience. In addition, it ought to complicate views that are too simple and too certain. Although evaluators may not be able to persuade all segments of the political community to make the fullest use of their findings, they must nevertheless plan in that direction.

An evaluation design should lead to a study that will clarify issues for participants and highlight any ways in which they operate under false assumptions or take action without sufficient understanding. Thus, the highly profitable evaluation is one full of suggestions for future realizations of issues and clarifications of meanings.

Cronbach points out that conventional programs of evaluation center attention on a single agency or technique or intervention. While this strategy is useful and necessary, it may all too easily be shortsighted, as it may not lead toward an understanding of the basic problem. The implication for evaluation seems to be clear. The more difficult it is to sustain optimistic hopes regarding a particular line of intervention, the more important it is for the evaluation to contribute to basic understanding of the phenomenon. When an evaluation achieves this, it can reasonably aspire to advance societal understanding of the problem area.

Conflicting Approaches to Evaluation

The strong contrasts between some of the remarks of the adherents of the scientific approach to evaluation and the enthusiasts for the holistic or naturalistic approach suggest a polarization so strong that no reconciliation is possible. However, Cronbach believes that the conflict is exaggerated and that the more an evaluative effort becomes a program of studies (rather than a single study) the more place there is for a mixture of styles. An evaluation, in other words, is a place for every kind of investigation, and only in this way is it likely that the full truth of a situation may be assessed.

The difficulty for evaluators, however, is that they must decide on the distribution of investigative effort in a particular project at a particular time; so the trade-offs in design must be very much the center of concern for evaluators. A particular study may therefore demand more emphasis upon the experimentalist rather than the naturalistic predilections. For his part, Cronbach has used both approaches according to the nature of the study. On the whole, however, his book gives more weight to the planning of structured evaluations than to the planning of case studies or the illuminative approach. He feels that as yet little cumulative thought has been given about the more naturalistic approaches because there has been no exchange of views comparable to that regarding approximations to experiments. Consequently, issues that divide the various approaches such as the naturalistic and experimentalist remain beneath the surface.

Consensus in Design Elements

Cronbach points out the general agreement that society should innovate. Social institutions and services are seldom what they could be, and even arrangements that once worked well sometimes failed under changing social conditions. Some form of evaluation for improvement is therefore necessary.

There is also agreement that evaluation should be empirical and that events should be examined on sites where the program is being tried. Neither humanistic nor behavioristic/scientific evaluators are likely to argue with this as a general statement of need. The humanist tradition, however, may assert that a program is worthy in its own right. Moreover, any conclusions reached about facts gathered are inferences beyond the data. They are fallible and rest on assumptions, presuppositions, or working hypotheses; thus, conclusions are plausible to a greater or lesser degree. It must always be remembered that statistical estimates are attended by uncertainty.

Nevertheless, unwitting consensus between humanists and behaviorists may be perceived when advocates of experimentation begin to speak of understanding or insight, for it is then that they come much closer to those favoring naturalistic studies. Naturalistic investigators spread resources over the numerous treatment, process, and outcome variables, and comb subsets of data for patterns. They report and interpret many relations that are by no means statistically significant. In other words, they opt for bandwidth at the expense of fidelity, thereby striking a compromise between emphasis upon strong control and parsimony on the one hand and total lack of controls on the other. To sum up, there seems to be some consensus among important writers in the field that circumstances are rare where one may depend wholly upon statistical methods in evaluation and their attendant statistical inferences.

When designing the study, the evaluator must make certain choices. These may include, perhaps, a standard treatment that is unlikely to operate in the absence of the investigator's pressure for reducing variabilities (that is, the traditional experimental method) or a naturalistic approach that will allow for heterogeneous interpretations of the institution under normal operating circumstances. However, Cronbach insists that the evaluator "can choose a plan anywhere in the range from the fully reproducible, fully controlled artificial study, to the opportunistic, wholly unconstrained, naturalistic study."

Balance in Evaluation Design: Summary

Discussion in the last section indicates that some evaluators in the design and practice of their study may plan to use both the scientific and the humanistic approaches. On the other hand, some may insist upon applying a uniform style to a particular study.

Those who favor formal summative tests also favor objectivity in observation and analysis. By contrast, those who call for case studies are likely to advocate impressionistic interpretation. The first group stresses the fixed character of the hypothesis that is under challenge at the moment, the second, the emergent quality of research questions. When the evaluator cannot adequately specify in the planning stage the most significant variables, the study then proceeds in a context of discovery. The discovery grows out of the collected data, which are interpreted in the light of the investigator's prior experience (direct and vicarious). Strong designs, on the other hand, are appropriate if variables can be clearly defined and hypotheses clearly formulated. The whole point of the strong design in basic science is to provide an objective, reproducible, and indisputable challenge to a prediction from theory.

Cronbach states that there is no necessary conflict between experimental control and use of qualitative information or subjective interpretation, or between open-minded exploration and producing objective evidence. This means that even a formal experiment can incorporate interviews of program operators and clients in an open-ended fashion and ultimately apply "blind coding to obtain machine-compatible data." On the other hand, quantitative, highly structured data may be used for case study hypothesis construction. Some writers, moreover, make it clear that they would combine strong design with subjective interpretation. Scriven, in particular, wishes evaluators to report whether the treatment is good or bad and thus bring their own values into play. For their part, naturalistic observers may inject objectivity into the study by documenting incidents as they occur and also by use of additional observers focusing on particular aspects of the program being evaluated.

In planning and carrying out an evaluation, the sophisticated evaluator will emphasize some preferences for the methodology to be employed rather than others in an endeavor to facilitate resolution of a particular political problem at a particular time, and he will "harden his study in some respects and keep it loose in other respects. Seemingly, even the strongest advocate of some one style of evaluative inquiry is prepared to endorse the opposing style as suited to some tasks."

Cronbach summarizes the thinking about the "continuum" between scientific and humanistic designs in evaluation with the following statement: "The rhetoric that makes polar opposites of experiments and naturalistic case studies is useful only to bring critical questions to attention."

In actual planning, it almost always makes sense to introduce some degree of control — in data collection if not in manipulation of treatment — and to make some naturalistic observation of events within the planned structure. The balance between the styles will vary from one subquestion to the next and may well shift (in either direction!) as the evaluative program proceeds.

Cronbach's Concepts of the Elements in an Evaluation Design: *Uto*

The conclusions drawn from an evaluation should indicate what is expected if a certain plan of intervention is adopted in a certain type of situation. These conclusions may be predictions about program delivery, the reaction to clients, behavioral change, institutional change, and so on. The designer of an evaluation should strive to ensure (as far as possible) that the inferences contained in the conclusions are as valid and persuasive as possible. Ultimately, "validation consists of a critical scrutiny of the logic of each interpretation and of the research operations behind it."

Units, Treatments, and Observing Operations

Cronbach presents a theory upon which recommendations for design may be based. His abstract concept characterizes the sample, the domain the sample purports strictly to represent, a domain in which the decision-making community is interested, and the relations among these three. The three abstract concepts are units, treatments, and observing operations. Thus, an evaluator attends to the following:

1. *Units:* either individuals or classes.
2. *Treatments:* a unit is exposed to the realization of a particular treatment; for example, a teacher selects and organizes lessons and proceeds in what may be either a lucid or a confusing style; thus, even with a so-called standard treatment realizations inevitably vary.
3. *Observing operations:* the evaluator obtains data before, during, and/or after the treatment and administers a certain form of test or sends a certain visitor to the class to record particular kinds of impressions. These are observing operations.

When discussing a particular study, Cronbach refers to the units actually in the study, the treatment realizations, and the observations as *uto*, respectively. As each *u* is paired with at least one *t* and *o*, the symbol *uto* is formed, which refers to the study as realized — or to any member of the class of studies that might be realized under a particular specification. Thus, *uto* may refer to data on a single unit or to data on the whole sample.

When units are selected, local settings are inevitably included. For instance, if teachers are being studied, they are observed in a social context and not as isolated individuals. Teachers are influenced by supervisors, by tensions that arise from interpersonal relationships, and by union negotiations (to mention some of many likely influences). In addition, there is a larger setting. The intellectual and political climate of a situation impinges on all units. Moreover, outcomes in one situation at one time are not necessarily to be expected some years later, even within that same unit.

UTOS: *The Domain of Investigation*

Cronbach states that corresponding with *uto* are domains *U, T,* and *O.* These combine with *S* in *UTOS,* a concept that will be explained later. By definition, *UTO* specifies the class of unit-treatment-operation combinations that the investigator purports to describe on the basis of *uto.* For instance, a day-care program may meet certain specifications intended for children from a defined class of families with reference made to evidence of particular kinds such as health ratings by a physician, mother's report on the use of the time the service makes free for her, and acceptance of the service by defined subgroups in the community. This specification of a class of unit-treatment-operation combination is an example of *UTO.* Cronbach defines *UTO* as the "universe of admissible observations." It follows that any observed *uto* is presumed to fall within the domain that interests the investigator.

If the definition is adequate, independent readers will agree as to which instances of units, realizations, or operations fall within *UTO*. Moreover, the range and distribution of *uto* within *UTO* should (ideally) match the interests of the investigator. As Cronbach points out, the domain may be broad or narrow. For instance, one study may investigate independent study methods based on data accepted from any school that purports to offer an individualized learning methodology to students; another study may define a specific kind of individualized learning methodology and confine attention to instances of one particular kind of activity only. It is important to note that when the definition changes, the question under direct investigation also changes.

Cronbach stresses that the ideal design defines a *UTO*, and then plans for selecting a *uto* to represent it. To the extent that the design is logical and is carried out strictly, one can legitimately infer from the findings in *uto* the findings probable in *UTO*.

The *u, t* and *o* are random elements. The evaluator thinks of the *u* as having been sampled from a population and controls the sampling to the degree considered practicable. The evaluator defines the collection of units that are of interest — the population, *U* — and carefully draws a representative sample. The report from observations of a particular occasion, *o*, is taken to represent what would have been reported on all other occasions; ideally (if costs were not a barrier) one would like to have data from every *o* in *O*. A similar point of view applies to *t* and *T*, as the designated treatment defines a class of realizations about which the investigator is concerned, and the realizations are a sample from the domain. The point is that, typically, *U, T,* and *O* in an evaluation are all subject to sampling and to the pitfalls of sampling. It must be clearly borne in mind by an evaluator at the design stage of study that both behavior and variations in responses may contribute to imperfect generalizations resulting from data gathered, however carefully, by the sampling process.

The concept of an inhomogeneous population *U* from which samples are drawn is not unusual. In *UTOS* Cronbach extends that concept. He points out that in most social research, *t* and *o* are thought of as fixed, while in a program evaluation they are not. The data interpreter generalizes, perhaps subconsciously, over treatment realizations just as over schools or students. Similarly, the observing procedure actually carried out is one of many allowable realizations of a plan. The *S* in *UTOS* represents a setting, *S*, which should be regarded as fixed. By this convention, each study has one setting only (although units are associated with sites within that setting).

Definitions of the Elements of uto and UTO

The *unit* is the smallest independent entity within which the influence of the treatment effect is fully operative. The unit may be thought of as a "system." It is sufficiently complete and autonomous that its experiences and responses are not influenced by the experiences and responses of parallel entities.

Very often, the objects under investigation have a nested structure, as, for example, pupils within classes, within schools, within districts, and within states.

> Which level is taken to be the unit depends upon one substantive conception of the mechanism through which the proposed intervention operates and on the level at which the intervention will be installed.

The choice of unit is a subtle design decision. It must be realized that the assumption of independence is weakened by taking the highest level of the hierarchy as the level of the unit. On the other hand, to define the sampling plan at several levels may be advantageous.

For the design of the study, the central issue is to judge what are independent *treatment* units. The choice of units for sampling follow from this, together with the strength of inference from u to U.

In any manipulative study, the evaluator specifies a course of action to influence what happens to the units. The treatment *specified* for the unit is T, while the treatment unit actually experienced is t. The actual treatment events (t) are unlikely to be entirely consistent with the investigator's specifications, as there is bound to be variation on what is planned at the design stage of the study. Cronbach points out that when a set of instructional materials is field tested, a full description of the actual t will include, for example, the pace at which the teachers schedule the work, the exercises designed, the rewards made available to students, and so on. These actual descriptions of t vary from a generalized statement T to include what is generally spoken of as "delivery" — those elements of a planned treatment that unit u actually received. The specification of T may, of course, include directives and guidelines and supervisory procedures, qualifications of personnel delivering the treatment, instructional materials, and details for treatment events; or, on the other hand, it may be no more than a global specification such as "individual progression within classes," with each and every realization that carries this label being admitted.

Observing operations include tests, interviews, classroom visits (in the case of schools), tape recordings of dialogues and procedures for coding the remarks, and use of archival data. There may, in addition, be observation of background characteristics of initial and final status of achievements, of abilities and attitudes, and of various intermediate or processed variables. In the design stage of an evaluation, the ideal is to specify procedures so clearly that another investigator would be able to collect comparable data. Lamentably, this is not normal practice.

In the natural sciences, Cronbach points out that procedures are likely to be so well standardized that the distinction between the class O and the instance o is of little importance. By contrast, behavioral measures cannot be closely standardized. The usual emphasis in "operational definition" is placed on specifying a rather homogeneous class of procedures. It follows that the specific o falling within the class is likely to agree. Those who are to make use of the evaluation report, however, are often more interested in a broadly defined construct. Rather than choosing a single procedure to be applied to all subjects, the evaluator may best represent the interests of the client by defining a domain of diverse activities associated with the concept under investigation. For instance, rather than saying that reading comprehension is to be measured, it may be preferable to specify a number of different forms of reading comprehension; all these tasks become elements in O.

Cronbach emphasizes that the class O is to be specified with as much care as U and T, as a vague label for the variable to be measured is insufficient and possibly misleading.

*UTOS: *The Domain of Application*

A further refinement of $UTOS$, and one that Cronbach considers basic to his argument, is the development of the concept of $^*UTOS$. The asterisk is placed first (thus "star $UTOS$") because an asterisk at the end might suggest UTO in S^*.

Only a small fraction (if any at all) of a report audience is centrally interested in the $UTOS$ that defined the study. More than likely the individual is interested in particular aspects of the report. This particular concern is referred to by Cronbach as $^*UTOS$, a concept that differs from the original in some respect. For this individual the evaluation has value and purpose only as it serves to provide plausible extrapolation from a reported observation to the circumstances of $^*UTOS$, with its individualistic interpretation of observations.

It follows that if an evaluation is to be useful, results should reduce uncertainty about whatever $^*UTOS$ enter policy discussions after data (based on observations) are recorded. It also follows that, in the design of a study, the evaluator has to anticipate, as best as possible, the U^*, T^*, and O^* that clients or audiences for the report will wish to know, and some considerations must also be given (as shown below) to the S^*.

The question Will it work with *our* students? expresses concern for the specificity of a U^*. Cronbach points out that an outcome difference found in a laboratory situation may not hold up in everyday school situations, or a difference found in a representative national sample may not be found either in the wealthiest or the most isolated school districts. The point is made that U and U^* differ, and that the importance of their differences "has to be weighed when actions affecting U^* are taken."

If the original O was narrow, audiences are likely to show an interest in O^* and receive greater satisfaction by the closer definition afforded by O^*. For instance, a mathematics course may well appear to be successful when O is tailored only to the lessons covered. Some critics may well argue, however, that graduates of the mathematics course are deficient in the area of problem solving. A preferred measure of O^* covering such additional questions about the course may well be adopted.

As has been mentioned earlier, the audience for the evaluation is really concerned with whether or not to adopt the experimental T of the original study. As the study progresses, discussions about it will suggest variations to improve on the original plan. Each such variation becomes a T^*. Cronbach suggests an interesting example of this phenomenon:

> When the first returns on compensatory education came in, few discussants confined attention to the conclusion about the UTO on which data were collected. One reaction contemplated a change in treatment: "It is all very well to report negatively on Head Start (T); but does not that show that compensatory treatment needs to continue for a longer time (T^*)?" So Follow Through was mounted as a T^* (and later evaluated directly).

It is interesting to note that the treatment domain can change when considerations move from $UTOS$ to $^*UTOS$ — "even when the operational specification of T remains unaltered." If U changes to U^* or S to S^*, the frequency of realizations changes because the way a treatment is realized depends on the local settings and participants and such factors as organizational and social climates. Thus S^* may be a significant aspect of $^*UTOS$ when the population of realizations changes.

Those who interpret the results of an evaluation have this question on their mind: How much difference does the change from $UTOS$ to such-and-such a $^*UTOS$ make? Possibly, the change is not of great consequence "either because the phenomenon under study is impervious to social change or because the change is too small to matter." Moreover, if a question is to be *directly investigated*, it could be cast in the form of a parameter of a *UTOS* that is to be estimated. Cronbach points out that the parameter may be a mean, a regression coefficient, or a proportion of cases in a category. Where questions are not directly investigated, they could be cast in the form of a parameter of **UTO* in which an estimate is sought. As an example, a person responsible for a program may wish to know the value of a particular indicator of a student motivation (O^*) if a particular ruling regarding multicultural education (a T^*) is issued to all high school districts of one state (U^*).

*UTOS, the domain of application, is a central and basic aspect of the planning of any evaluation that is to offer specific and needed information for audiences.

Identifying the Research Questions

Cronbach states:

> Questions for an evaluation come chiefly from uncertainties of members of the decision-making community, or from disagreements among members, each of whom is certain about his answer. To identify the most pertinent questions is a first step in designing an evaluation; to distribute effort appropriately among them is the second.

The evaluator, Cronbach considers, is not a free agent in choosing questions to investigate because a sponsor may be willing to support certain inquiries and not others. Other constraints pertain. An administrator may be unwilling to conform to an experimental scheme for a number of reasons, or informants may have limited willingness to supply data. On the other hand, communications between the evaluator and the sponsor before the design stage may encourage the latter to accept suggestions for broadening the inquiry.

Two phases of planning are described: the *divergent* phase of listing possible questions and the *convergent* phase of assigning priorities among them. In practice, the two activities go on simultaneously. It would seem wise for an agency proposing to sponsor an evaluation to go through both the divergent and convergent planning processes before it asks an evaluator to work out an operational plan. Consequent exchanges and negotiations between the evaluator-designate and the sponsor will lead to a revised list of questions. The process of amendment will inevitably continue after fieldwork is launched.

The Divergent Phase

This phase opens the minds of both the evaluator and the sponsor to the widest possible range of questions to be entertained, at least briefly, as prospects for investigation.

Sources of Questions.   While planning which individuals or groups should be candidates for questions that are important to a study, the evaluator must plan to seek out a wide variety of informants. As a result of this, omissions will result from informed choice and not from the restricted vision of the sponsor or the administrator or whoever has central responsibility.

Cronbach contends that "the evaluator engages to produce something — information — that has value to consumers and for which they are willing to pay." Thus, the decision about which product to deliver is an economic one to which both sides of the supply-demand factors contribute.

The evaluator has certain advantages over the sponsor in envisaging questions to be answered:

He brings a fresh set of biases.

The evaluator may be in a better position than the sponsor to collect and appreciate the questions current in nonpolitical, as well as political, circles.

From knowledge of past research, the evaluator can recognize the challenges and counterinterpretations to which the study is subject and thus can suggest specific controls needed to bolster the plausibility of its answers.

The evaluator knows the state of *his* art and can inform the sponsor (or manager) how adequately a given question can be answered at any given scale of expenditure.

However, in the end, it is the sponsor's estimate of the political and administrative relevance of the many questions that directs the evaluator. The point to be made is that the sponsor should not have to make these decisions unaided.

Treatments and Processes.   In the social services area, the place where the evaluation is to occur will not likely be subject to modification for purposes of the study. In other instances, the services are open to manipulation; treatments may be arranged to provide a direct test of an innovative proposal. In either case, as Suchman (1967) points out, the evaluator requires a list of treatments that might be worth installing for investigation, or worth locating where they presently exist.

Both the sponsor and the evaluator should be aware of different pressures from partisan groups, who will suggest certain candidates for questions or groups for treatments. Other candidates may be suggested, with profit to the study, by persons further removed from the center of political action. At the stage of listing candidates, friction should not exist. Later, political realities will make some questions far more appropriate and useful than others, but this will be discussed in the convergent stage.

Behind any program proposal are two concepts: one regarding the ways in which existing social conditions and the services already offered combine to produce an unsatisfactory result, and the other regarding the ways in which the alternative service will produce a more satisfactory result. Cronbach, therefore, advocates a sketch for intervention in which the various likely events are laid out in tabular or flowchart form. This, in itself, should surface questions that will be valuable when the process of intervention and its effects are clarified by the evaluation process. It should be noted, however, that the hypothesized process and the particular questions to be raised (for evaluation) will differ with each program variant. This is true whether the variations were planned or were recognized when realizations took form in various sites.

The "intensity" of the intervention must be included in the design. Should a larger team be trained to meet this perceived need? The intensity of intervention may also be centered on questions about intermediate stages of the program being introduced. If the final outcomes are not what the proponent had hoped for or anticipated, evidence of these intermediate stages and processes will be useful. To monitor and record such evidence, most likely a considerable team has to be trained and employed for the study.

Outcomes. The goals stated by the sponsor or by proponents of the intervention are a significant source of questions for the divergent phase. The list should include others' goals, of whom questions are asked in relation to the evaluation, and also intermediate outcomes.

Cronbach warns that even a well-specified list of goals is necessarily incomplete as a source of questions if it does not give attention to unwanted outcomes. The evaluator must therefore direct some attention to side effects as well as goals. It is also important to note that in the educational context, increments of progress are welcome no matter where the student is on the scale. Thus, the global intention that a program is to "achieve its goals" is to be considered circumspectly by the evaluator. At the time when the study is designed, the only reasonable question is, What outcomes should we attend to? Whether the level reached is satisfactory must be judged after the evaluation is completed "through a process of political negotiation." Even though the evaluation staff ought to press for clear statements about the outcome variables that the program planners have in mind, in the divergent stage it is important to keep in mind that hard-to-define and -assess variables, such as affective outcomes, must not be dropped from sight.

Cronbach contends that the divergent list ought to include outcomes that are expected to become observable only after the evaluation has been completed and reported. He says that often it will be appropriate to bank the data so that a later follow-up can give a clearer picture of long-term consequences. It is to be expected that long-run differences between treatments will not match those on the immediate posttest.

An important part of the planning is the evaluator's discussions with persons who have some images of the program, discussions regarding what partisans hope or fear, of how they expect various effects to develop. A wide range of factions within the decision-making community should be approached so that the evaluator may learn to perceive the program through the eyes of the various (biased) sectors of the community, including the professionals who would operate the program if adopted and the citizens to be served. Learning the hopes and fears of these sectors is essential. Moreover, the evaluator has the responsibility to bring into the total picture those values for which there is no effective political voice. Reaching out for divergent sources and those that do not readily press their views should be the aim of the evaluator.

The Convergent Phase

The convergent phase stresses the necessity of questions to be raised by a wide diversity of individuals and groups. Some questions should be dropped for practical reasons. Cronbach points out that there are at least three reasons for reducing the range of variables treated systematically in an evaluation:

1. *Cost:* there will always be a budget limit.
2. *Attention span of the evaluator:* as a study becomes more complicated, it becomes increasingly more difficult to administer, the mass of information becomes too great to consider, and, consequently, much of information is lost in the course of data reduction and synthesis.
3. *The attention span of the decision-making community:* very few persons want to know all there is to know about a program, and, indeed, few have the time to offer the evaluator all their opinions.

The divergent phase, therefore, identifies what could *possibly* be worth investigating. The convergent phase is dedicated to deciding what incompleteness is most acceptable. The evaluator is likely to invest time and effort in the study of a particular question (or plan to do so) when the following conditions exist:

1. Great uncertainty about the answer.
2. A prospective large yield of information.
3. Low cost of the inquiry.
4. A high degree of leverage for the choices the information would bear on (the term *leverage* is discussed next).

When an original list of questions is framed, it is done so in terms of U, T, and O, which are significant to some participants in decision making. In addition, the list may contain questions about artificial conditions that shed indirect light on a practical concern. In the convergent process, however, some of these questions are picked out to become UTO of the field study after they are further specified.

Leverage.   Cronbach defines leverage as referring to the "weight of a particular uncertainty in the decision-making process." In planning an evaluation to have future influence, an evaluator, in conjunction with the sponsor or administrator, may need to judge what leverage information varying on a particular issue is expected to have. After the study has been completed, judgment about leverage may be made from the response of the community to the evidence presented in the report. A matter that receives appreciable attention from the whole community has great leverage. It may also have leverage if it is significant to an interest bloc or to an uncommitted group whose support or opposition would be crucial. An issue influencing large decisions, such as "go-no go" has more leverage than an issue whose resolution would affect minor details of the plan.

Leverage, therefore, has two aspects: the importance of the issue or choice on which the evidence bears and the weight the evidence brings to bear. The evaluator must consider how much influence each of the conceivable answers to a question is expected to have.

Cronbach points out that it is in examining leverage that the evaluator explicitly considers the values of participants. Nothing on the divergent list of questions deserves consideration if the findings are not value laden for at least some of the decision making. Things that would be merely "nice to know" do not qualify for an investment of evaluative resources. Discussing prior uncertainty, Cronbach considers that, with things being equal, attention should be given to the question about which uncertainty is greatest; that is, when two questions seem to be equally open to investigation, greater resources should be invested in the question for which the community's uncertainty is more widespread and intense.

Accordingly, the evaluator is advised to make a priority scale for investigative effort:

1. If a question has high leverage and high uncertainty, it deserves investment to bring down the uncertainty.
2. If leverage is low and uncertainty is high, investment is warranted.
3. If leverage is high and prior uncertainty low, incidental information should be collected.
4. If leverage is low and uncertainty is low, the investigator should do no more than to keep open the channels for incidental information.

Planning for Communication

The Utility of Findings

The usefulness of an evaluation depends on the degree to which members of the decision-making community become aware of its findings and consider them plausible. Cronbach also believes that information is invariably lost in moving from the field observations to the report. Some observations are never communicated by the observer to the rest of the team, some are lost in the process of encoding and statistical summary, and others are lost because not everything can be placed in a report. Once a report is written, the information passes through further filters, as some information may be squeezed out or altered — moreover, the sponsor may suppress some findings. Furthermore, the audience perceives selectively and may tend to oversimplify information or assimilate new information in the light of old beliefs instead of correcting those beliefs.

Cronbach warns that an audience has limited time only and many social issues and programs compete for its attention. It is a rare person who gives an evaluative report on a public question a thorough reading. Moreover, few in the audience can grasp the solid technical account of procedures and analysis.

The point to be emphasized is that the reporting task of the evaluator is different from the task the scientist usually faces. The scientist reports to a select audience that shares his language and style of thought. The evaluator, however, speaks to numerous and scattered audiences, most of whom receive only secondary and watered-down accounts. The evaluator who finds that an audience has misinterpreted a report finds it difficult, or even impossible, to address a reply.

Cronbach addresses two questions:

1. What might be reported that would facilitate the evaluation user's thinking?
2. What does this imply for the earlier field operations of the evaluation?

Direct Communication

The evaluator should consider the possibility of increasing direct communication. Such communication would be comparatively informal because of the audience to be reached and because public knowledge should be as timely as possible. The evaluator points out that perhaps the most potent report is the informal conversation — in the office of the legislator or around the conference table.

The evaluator, Cronbach considers, has a role much like that of a journalist who investigates matters of public interest, judges what merits public attention, and packages it in a form that attracts attention. Persons within the evaluation team have rich experience and reasonable opportunity to exchange views within the team and with informants. They are therefore in a good position to carry out the reporting task of the journalistic function as well as the investigative task. If the team restricts itself to formal reporting, it leaves to outsiders the delivery of its message.

Evaluators are understandably suspicious of constraints on their reporting. This kind of tension can be resolved only when the political system makes clear the role that evaluations play. In Cronbach's view, the public interest will be best served by institutional arrangements that free evaluators to speak directly to all those who will participate in decisions about programs. It is important, therefore, that at least some members of the evaluation team should have skills of informal communication. Cronbach agrees with Stake, who advocates the designing of evaluative reports for a broad community, an approach often employing unconventional forms of communication, such as press releases and speeches and the dramatic reproduction of program events like logs and scrapbooks to bring home the message. The aim is to give the audience a feeling for the program and the experience of participants rather than an abstract summary alone. It is necessary that the evaluator who foresees the need to report vividly should begin early to amass material that will add color and realism to an otherwise bald and un-convincing narrative.

Cronbach has found it profitable for observers to file narrative accounts of revealing incidents seen in classrooms and of remarks of program participants. These memoranda need not be in a polished form, but they should provide sufficient context and continuity. They should be factual rather than interpretative. In Cronbach's opinion, "the anecdotes add wonderfully to the interest and belief the report commands."

Reporting, whether of anecdotal information or formal measurement and statistics, must be highly selective. Shorter and longer reports, with small technical content or perhaps a great deal, can serve various audiences. Even the most complete report can be reasonably synthesized to some brief statements by omitting analyses and data sets that seem unlikely to influence desions. Nevertheless, the complete report may display a few items to illustrate any patterns of differences as well as a few items representative of the no-difference category, thus obviating the proclivity felt by some evaluators to flood the reader with a display of all the differences.

Extrapolating from Findings

Cronbach firmly believes that decision-making audiences have both the right and the need to extrapolate as much as they sensibly can from the results of any study. He states:

> It is emphatically not sufficient to conclude an evaluation report with the standard cautionary warning: "The findings reported apply to the conditions and population we have studied. Further research is required to extend the conclusions to other conditions and populations." The world *must* extend the conclusions to get on with its business, and the evaluator is in a good position to recognize plausible extensions.

The evaluator may therefore offer alternative predictions, consistent with different sets of beliefs. These could lead to a promotion of discussion in which conflicting interpretations could be aired.

The suggestion that the evaluator should carry the interpretation as far as possible, with appropriate caution, suggests the wisdom of keeping comparatively rich descriptive records. Cronbach emphasizes the value of periodically reappraising the study design so that consequent surprises and puzzles can be given close attention. Explaining intermediate unintended outcomes that may possibly affect the future of the program is then possible before continuing research operations about that program.

The Promise of Evaluation

Flexibility of Design

A large section of Cronbach's book (1982) deals with an elaboration of controls used to strengthen inferences and make some conclusions more plausible. In a sense, the listing of available controls in this book is a kind of checklist for the evaluator. He points out that some of the controls that strengthen inference cost very little, either in terms of resources or of relevance. Specifying what *UTO* one intends to study, for example, is nearly cost-free. Arriving at the specification itself brings the evaluator face-to-face with choices that might otherwise be made inadvertently.

Cronbach goes on to say that there may never be a social program for which *all* evaluation resources ought to go into a tightly controlled study to support inferences to a narrow *UTO*. Nevertheless, in many instances, tightly controlled substudies might be useful within an evaluative effort. In other instances, it would be wise to structure an investigation so that a strong inference may be reached, and to make intensive studies of some sites of units within the samples by naturalistic and even impressionistic methods "that enable the investigator to learn about events and processes that were not anticipated." As has been pointed out earlier, it may be possible to combine the statistical comparison of the experimental and control averages with intense studies of individuals or groups of people by naturalistic methods.

Evaluations and Politics: Limitations

Cronbach strikes the word of warning that evaluations will inevitably disappoint if they are expected to *resolve* political conflicts:

> The reasonable aspiration of the evaluator is to produce information that less systematic observation of the program would not have produced, or information that is more plausible, and hence more influential than similar reports from less systematic observations would have been. A narrow-band investigation tries to accomplish this by offering good information on a few of the relevant questions; to the same end, a wide-band investigation produces more comprehensive but somewhat less dependable information. The choice among such options comes down to a judgment about leverage, i.e., about influence of decisions.

In other words, the evaluation plan that is too broad and therefore too thin in one context may be quite appropriate in another. The targeted study that focuses narrowly and obtains information that is strong yet limited in scope may be just right for one context but quite inappropriate for another.

Cronbach looks upon evaluations as short-term inquiries that are expected to illuminate decisions that are on the "current political agenda or just over the horizon." The value of an evaluation is not limited to its contribution to these kinds of decisions alone. Society learns from its experience with the program and learns more clearly from the contribution made by the evaluation. The evaluation contributes to the thinking about problems in a particular social milieu and so generates new ideas and feelings out of which arise the possible areas of change and methods of support. The worth of an evaluation therefore is not confined to its influence on the fate of the program being studied. Cronbach stresses that insofar as the evaluation illuminates the phenomenon, it may have a lasting influence on the way the problem is understood and on the shape of future programs.

Other Considerations

Cronbach considers that evaluation will have greater promise when designs and studies place emphasis upon the value of accounting for successes and failures rather than simply measuring outcomes. Fresh insights are needed, and therefore the investigator must not be restricted to questions identified in advance, important as these are. It is also important for the evaluator not to delay reporting until fully satisfied that all possible answers have been ascertained. On the contrary, the evaluator may need to report to the decision-making community well before the treatment has run its full course. This is one reason why design, planning, observation, and interpretation (to decision makers) should go on simultaneously rather than successively.

Along similar lines, Cronbach suggests that the evaluating plan should free some staff time for reflection at each stage of the work. Such reflection should prohibit, for example, too premature a focus upon controversial social issues or recalcitrant social problems. It may offer to decision makers wiser counsel than otherwise would be possible.

Cronbach believes that a description favoring a particular style of evaluation or emphasizing certain controls is of limited applicability. By his theory, evaluators should be called on to exercise judgments about substantive and political, as well as methodological, matters. They should not make judgments unassisted; rather, they should draw on sponsors, professional colleagues, or politically interested parties:

> Evaluators making use of such advice to locate and properly weight evaluative questions will need a broader training than they have typically received. Political, philosophical, and organizational theory can be as important in planning a potentially influential evaluation as knowledge of statistics and theory of, say, child development.

Like Stufflebeam and Stake earlier, Cronbach asserts that when evaluation is divided among members of a team, the team must work as a single unit if insight is to flourish. While members of the team must be fully conversant with all major aspects of the study, those at the center of the project must assume the greatest responsibility for setting priorities, making sense of observations and gleaning first-hand experiences from clients and course participants. In this way, the team as a whole will gain the correct perspective and interpret properly computer printouts and other reports. Necessarily, then, some members of the team must have first-hand field observations and communicate these to other members of the team.

Finally, Cronbach states that evaluation could be dangerous if society were to curtail programs that evaluators condemn and to expand those they praise. Evaluators have a valuable and satisfying contribution to make because they can discover facts and relations that casual observers would miss. It is Cronbach's belief that evaluators will have greater influence in future years with the improvement of the art and with society coming to rely on "systematic studies for the enlightenment they offer."

Knowledge Test for Unit 5

This knowledge test contains nine multiple-choice questions. The purpose of these questions is to determine whether you have a sufficient grasp of the knowledge objectives of this unit. In each instance, circle the letter for what you consider to be the most reasonable response or responses. A comparison may then be made with the keyed response provided after each question. When all nine knowledge questions have been completed, we recommend that you assess your performance and use this as a basis for further study of the unit.

Question 1. Evaluations, according to Cronbach,

a. should rely entirely on well-established and standardized methods.
b. inevitably cause change within social institutions.
c. serve a political function.
d. should be planned only in general terms.

Correct Response. You should have circled "c." Cronbach considers it an inescapable fact of evaluations that political motivations influence the commission of an evaluation and will challenge the information arising from it.

Incorrect Responses

a. Incorrect because Cronbach believes that an evaluation must be viewed as a way of illuminating complex issues and may incorporate various approaches to gathering information — some defying normal processing methods.
b. Incorrect because sometimes political considerations will be more influential than the information arising from the study and not infrequently will contribute to maintaining the status quo.
d. Incorrect because Cronbach stresses the necessity for a carefully worked out design for the study; nevertheless, it must make allowances for flexibility of procedures once the investigation has commenced.

Question 2. Cronbach considers that the choice of a design should be made on the basis of

a. the wishes of the client.
b. maximizing objectivity, controls, standardization, and stability of the information-collection process.
c. promoting healthy professional debate about the findings of the study.
d. maximizing the evaluation's potential influence on social affairs.

Correct Response. You should have responded with "d." Cronbach believes that the best design is that which promises to increase the social benefit from the evaluation.

Incorrect Responses

a. Incorrect because while the client commissioned the evaluation, the design task is the responsibility of the evaluator, who may well call on the expertise of team members and address the information needs of a broad audience.
b. Incorrect because Cronbach believes that designs should be "thoughtful, evolving processes" and not, therefore, bound to set patterns.
c. Incorrect because although such debate may occur, and indeed is very useful, the prime purpose of the design (and the study which follows) is to influence social affairs.

Question 3. If communications from the evaluation are the product that counts, which of the following questions should *not* be raised regarding the completed evaluation?

a. Did each section of the audience respond to the evaluation?
b. Did they find it credible?
c. Were the questions significant to them answered as well as possible?
d. Was consensus about the findings assured?

Correct Response. You should have circled "d." There is often justifiable difficulty (if not impossibility) in reaching consensus because there is a decision-making community and not a lone decision maker.

Incorrect Responses. 'a', 'b' and 'c' are incorrect responses, as all are essential to a successful evaluation.

Question 4. With which of the following statements would Cronbach most likely agree?

a. Only true experiments, and approximations of true experiments, are acceptable modes of evaluation.
b. An evaluation uses various styles of investigation according to the circumstances.
c. The naturalistic style of evaluation is the most valuable.
d. Generally, the experimentalist, rather than the naturalistic, approach to evaluation should be used.

Correct Response. You should have circled "b." The evaluation design, according to Cronbach, may derive insights from anecdotal evidence and from case studies before progressing to summative tests based on the analysis of gathered data. He stresses that a mixture of evaluative styles may be employed within one study.

Incorrect Responses

a. and c. Incorrect for the reasons given above for the correct response.
d. Incorrect; although Cronbach's monograph tends to give more weight to the planning of experiments than to case studies or the naturalistic approach, he nevertheless makes it clear that the circumstances of a program to be evaluated will determine both the evaluative styles to be used, as well as their weighting.

Question 5. Both humanistic and behavioristic/scientific evaluators are likely to agree on which two of the following statements?

a. Social services and institutions should be evaluated because they seldom function as well as they could.
b. The evaluator should invent controlled situations for the purposes of testing.
c. Summative tests are essential.
d. Evaluations should be empirical.

Correct Responses. You should have marked "a" and "d." Response "a" indicates consensus opinion that some form of evaluation is necessary to all institutions and services, since even the best of them sometimes fail under changing social conditions. Response "d" indicates that events should be examined on sites where the program is being tried.

Incorrect Responses. "b" and "c" are incorrect because both statements refer only to the stances adopted by evaluators favoring the behavioristic/scientific schools.

Question 6. The relationship between Cronbach's concepts of *UTO* and *uto* is such that

a. any observed *uto* is presumed to fall within the domain (*UTO* of interest to the evaluator.
b. The range of distribution of *uto* within *UTO* is of little concern to the investigator.
c. *U, T,* and *O* and *u, t,* and *o* are random elements.
d. *UTO* is always fully represented by any of its *uto*.

Correct Response. You should have marked "a." As the *UTO* is the universe of admissible observations, it follows that accurately defined and selected *u, t,* and *o* will be encompassed by that *UTO*.

Incorrect Responses

b. Incorrect because the range and distribution of *uto* within *UTO* match (as closely as possible) the interests of the investigator.
c. Incorrect because *u, t,* and *o* only are random elements; *UTO* is the universe.

d. Incorrect because any *uto* may never fully represent a *UTO*, although through representative sampling an evaluation may nevertheless legitimately infer from the findings in *uto* the findings possible in *UTO*.

Question 7. While an evaluator contemplates what people say as part of the situation to be investigated, which of the following sources, according to Cronbach, is best for identifying the questions to be addressed by the study?

a. The instructions of the client or the administrator of the program.
b. Those who are most closely involved in the program (e.g., teachers and students in a school situation).
c. Uncertainties of members of the decision-making community or from disagreements among members.
d. The evaluator's experience and contemplation of the situation.

Correct Response. You should have answered "c." According to Cronbach, these groups, or circumstances, will generate the most pertinent questions — the decision makers because they have to decide the fate of the program, and those arising from disagreements because the polarization of opinions will give rise to problems that need elucidation and examination.

Incorrect Responses

a. Not the most appropriate response; while the clients' and administrators' opinions may be sought, their perspectives, taken alone, may limit and bias the study.
b. Not the best response; the opinion of those most closely involved in the operation of the study, while necessary and possibly very valuable, again may display a particular perspective or bias.
d. Incorrect because the evaluator must seek questions (at the design stage) from the personnel on site; while it is his task to generate questions, he is exceeding his professional authority if the only questions for study are of his invention.

Question 8. Which of the following is *most* consistent with Cronbach's definition of the evaluator's role during the divergent phase of gathering questions?

a. The evaluator contacts a wide range of potentially interested persons asking them to assess the importance of the client's specified information requirements.

b. The evaluator seeks the widest possible range of questions to be entertained, however briefly, as foci for the investigation.

c. The evaluator strives to identify all the relevant audiences and to stimulate their interest in evaluation.

d. The evaluator has certain advantages over the client(s) for envisaging questions to be answered and thus relies mainly on his own professional judgment.

Correct Response. You should have selected "b." During the divergent phase, the evaluator must open both his mind, and his client's, to all possible sources of questions that may prove important to the problems and uncertainties which the evaluative study will endeavor to clarify for decision makers.

Incorrect Responses

a. Incorrect because Cronbach emphasizes that in the divergent phase as many as possible relevant personnel should be asked to nominate questions, not merely to assess the client's questions.

c. Not the best response; the statement is accurate but incomplete, as it does not specify that a wide range of questions should be entertained.

d. Incorrect; while the evaluator may have certain advantages over the client(s), they should be used to strengthen the divergent phase, but these advantages are not a definition for that divergent phase.

Question 9. According to Cronbach, the usefulness of information depends most on

a. the degree to which members of the decision-making community become aware of the findings and consider them plausible.

b. the extent to which the evaluator increases the possibility of direct communication with decision makers.

c. the extent to which the final reporting is free from technical content.

d. the amount of validated extrapolation entirely distinct from plausible extrapolation which decision makers are able to make from the findings.

Correct Response. You should have marked "a." This statement stresses the two factors that Cronbach considers to be essential if an evaluation is useful, namely, good communications of the findings and their credibility in the eyes of the decision-making community.

Incorrect Responses

b. Not the best response, as this is only one facet of the usefulness of an evaluation.
c. Incorrect; although Cronbach states that often too much technical jargon may spoil the usefulness of a final report, some technical content may be appropriate particularly if various forms of reporting are presented.
d. Not the best response; although Cronbach considers that plausible extensions from conclusions should be recognized by evaluators (and decision makers), the possibility of such extrapolation will depend upon the nature of a particular evaluation's procedures and findings.

Scoring of the Knowledge Test. Having completed the knowledge test, total the number of correct responses. A score of 8 or 9 indicates a good grasp of the material. A score of 6 or less is inadequate; you are advised to reread the unit, concentrating on areas of weakness.

Application Exercises

This section contains two essay questions, which should further determine your understanding of Cronbach's various stances about evaluation. You may, if you wish, relate Cronbach's advice and theory to actual situations in which an evaluation could take place. Or you may wish to relate Cronbach's concepts to a hypothetical situation or, as a final alternative, merely to outline Cronbach's thinking in relation to the various essay topics.

Following each exercise is a list of points that we see as contributing to an appropriate response. A review of these points should help you assess your work. You may wish to reread the relevant parts of this chapter when you have completed an exercise to gain a more complete assessment of your answer.

Exercise 1. Write an essay entitled "The Profitable Evaluation." Your answer should include these main elements:

a. The aim of the "best design," including "scientific activities."
b. The evaluator as an educator.
c. The nature of excellent information.

   d. Questions to be answered at the conclusion of the study, including alternatives for the decision-making community to consider.

   e. Further realizations of issues — the contribution to basic understanding of a problem area.

Response to Exercise 1 could appropriately include the following:

   a. The aim of the "best design," including "scientific activities"
1. Gives rise to social benefits, influences social affairs.
2. Leads to institutions' and individuals' learning from the experience.
3. Is the core of "scientific activities," based on real observations and well-reasoned interpretations.

   b. The evaluator as an educator
1. What evaluators learn must enter the thinking of the relevant political community.
2. Thus, insights in others are generated.
3. The success of the evaluator as an educator is judged by his success in communications.
4. Teaching begins when the evaluator elucidates questions with those involved.
5. In value-laden matters, the evaluator's responsibility is to help others ask better questions.

   c. The nature of excellent information
1. Clear, understandable to those who use it.
2. Timely, reaches audience when needed.
3. Reliable, diverse observers (using the same procedures) see it similarly.
4. Valid, cast in a form that captures reality.
5. Wide-ranging, offers various alternatives for attaining organizational goals, or new goals are suggested.

   d. Questions to be answered at the conclusion of the study, including alternatives for the decision-making commmunity to consider
1. Did each section of the audience attend to the message, understand it, and find it credible?
2. Were the questions significant to them answered as well as possible?
3. Did the answers alter their preconceptions?
4. Was consensus attained to the degree possible in a politically lively decision-making community?
5. Were the normally silent citizens reached by the evaluator, and were their questions answered?

e. Further realizations of issues — the contribution to basic understanding of a problem area
    1. The evaluator must reach all sections of the decision-making community to make fullest warranted use of the findings.
    2. The study must clarify issues and false assumptions, then suggest future realizations and clarifications of issues.
    3. The evaluation must aspire to advancing societal understanding of the problem area.

Exercise 2. Write an essay entitled "Identifying the Research Questions — The Divergent Phase." In your answer, include these main points:

a. How questions arise.
b. Constraints placed on the evaluator.
c. The divergent phase — sources of questions.
d. The divergent phase — treatments and processes.
e. The divergent phase — outcomes.

Response to Exercise 2 should include the following:

a. How questions arise
    1. Uncertainties of the decision-making community.
    2. Disagreements among members (who are nevertheless certain of their particular stance).
    3. Certification of the most pertinent questions is the first step in the design of an evaluation.
b. Constraints placed on the evaluator
    1. The sponsor may be willing to support certain inquiries and reject others.
    2. The administrator may be unwilling to accept an experimental approach.
    3. Informants may be unwilling to supply data.
    4. Nevertheless, correct communication may lead to the sponsor's accepting a broadening of the inquiry.
c. The divergent phase — sources of questions
    1. Widest possible range of questions must be entertained.
    2. Also, a wide variety of candidates for nominating questions, including those persons normally silent on issues must be approached.
    3. Evaluator has certain advantages over the sponsor (e.g., fresh set of biases and knowledge of past research).
d. The divergent phase — treatments and processes

    1. Unlikely that the place where evaluation is to occur will be subject to modification.

    2. Therefore, consideration must be given to the most appropriate treatments to produce the most relevant data.

    3. Evaluator needs to be aware of different pressures of partisan groups offering candidates for questions or groups for treatments.

    4. A sketch for intervention, in tabular form, should bring questions to surface for the evaluative process.

    5. The design should indicate the "intensity" of the intervention planned for various stages of the study.

e. The divergent phase — outcomes

    1. Questions must also include those that may uncover unwanted outcomes.

    2. Attention of the evaluator is directed to side effects.

    3. Need to be cautious about the global intention that a program is to "achieve its goals."

    4. Hard-to-define and -assess variables, such as affective outcomes, cannot be ignored.

    5. Divergent list also to include outcomes that may become discernible only after the completion of the study.

    6. To consult many sources is the essence of the divergent phase.

Questions Without Answers

Five questions are offered in this section, but answers are not provided.

The questions may be used as subjects for group discussions or as individual assignments. You may prefer to gain deeper insights into Cronbach's thinking about evaluation designs by reading his complete text or other books recommended in the reference section. However, questions may be answered on the basis of material contained in this unit and throughout the book.

1. "Political realities make some questions far more appropriate than others." Discuss this statement in relation to Cronbach's convergent phase of question considerations.

2. In what ways does Cronbach's scheme for the raising, and consideration, of questions differ from (a) Stake (particularly in relation to his Countenance Approach)? (b) Wolf (the Adversary Model)? (c) Scriven (Goal-Free Evaluation)? What are the comparative merits of each method?

3. Cronbach states that the "usefulness of an evaluation depends on the degree to which members of the decision-making community become aware of its findings and consider them plausible." Discuss the particular emphasis that Cronbach places on communications in evaluation. Do other evaluators place the same importance on communications?

4. In what manner does Cronbach's delineation, definition, and explanation of the elements in an evaluation design (i.e., *uto*) help in the logical planning and development of an evaluative study?

5. What are the significant differences between *UTOS* — the domain of investigation — and **UTOS* — the domain of application? Why does Cronbach consider **UTOS* to be basic to an understanding of his approach to the design of educational evaluations?

References

Campbell, D. T. 1957. Factors relevant to the validity of experiments in social settings. *Psychological Bulletin, 54,* 297–312.

_____. 1973. The social scientist as methodological servant of the experimenting society. *Policy Studies Journal, 2,* 72–75.

_____. 1975. Assessing the impact of planned social change. In G. M. Lyonds (ed.) *Social research and public policies.* Hanover, N.H.: Public Affairs Center, Dartmouth College.

Cronbach, L. J. 1963. Course improvement through evaluation. *Teachers College Record, 64,* 672–683.

_____. 1982. *Designing evaluations of educational and social programs.* San Francisco: Jossey-Bass.

Cronbach, L. J., et al. 1976. Research on classrooms and schools: Formulation of questions, design, and analysis. Occasional paper, Stanford Evaluation Consortium, Stanford University, Calif.

Cronbach, L. J., and Associates. 1980. *Toward reform of program evaluation.* San Francisco: Jossey-Bass.

House, E. R. 1976. Justice in evaluation. In G. C. Glass (ed.), *Evaluation studies review annual,* Vol. 1. Beverly Hills, Calif.: Sage, pp. 75–99.

MacDonald, B. 1976. Evaluation and the control of education. In D. Tawney (ed.), *Curriculum evaluation today: Trends and implications.* London: Macmillan Education, pp. 125–136.

Riecken, H. W., and Boruch, R. F. (eds.), 1974. *Social experimentation,* New York: Academic Press.

Rossi, P. H., and Williams, W. 1972. *Evaluating social programs: Theory, practice and politics.* New York: Seminar Press.

Scriven, M. 1967. The methodology of evaluation. In R. W. Stake, et al., *Perspectives on curriculum evaluation. AERA Monograph Series on Curriculum Evaluation*, No. 1. Chicago: Rand McNally, pp. 39–83.

_____. 1974. Pros and cons about goal-free evaluation. *Evaluation Comment, 3* 1–4.

Stake, R. E. 1967. The countenance of educational evaluation. *Teachers College Record, 68* (April), 523–540, 63, 146.

Suchman, E. A. 1970. Action for what? A critique of evaluative research. In R. O'Toole (ed.), *The organization, management, and tactics of social research.* Cambridge, Mass.: Schenkman.

_____. 1967. *Evaluative research.* New York: Russell Sage.

Weiss, C. H. (ed.) 1972. *Evaluating action programs: Readings in social action and education.* Boston: Allyn and Bacon.

Wilensky, H. 1967. *Organizational intelligence: Knowledge and policy in government and industry.* New York: Basic Books.

6 STUFFLEBEAM'S IMPROVEMENT-ORIENTED EVALUATION

This unit argues that evaluations should foster improvement, provide accountability records, and promote increased understanding of the phenomena under review; it argues further that the first of these is paramount. The module explicates the CIPP model for evaluation by describing its development, contrasting it to other approaches, depicting its role in improving programs, explicating its main concepts, and outlining the requirements of a sound evaluation design. Finally, it emphasizes the importance of subjecting one's evaluation work to evaluation through metaevaluation.

The most important purpose of evaluation is not to prove but to improve. . . . We cannot be sure that our goals are worthy unless we can match them to the needs of the people they are intended to serve.

This unit presents an improvement orientation to program evaluation. Because historical context is useful in understanding any conceptualization of a field of professional practice and because I am aware that my professional background and experiences greatly influenced my own views, I have personalized the presentation. I traced the development of the CIPP model, contrasted it to other approaches, characterized its systems and program-improvement orientation, and described each of its four main types of

151

evaluation. I also explained my view of what is involved in designing particular evaluations and, in concluding, discussed metaevaluation.

In working through this unit, I suggest that you study its objectives to discern what you can learn from it; then read through the material, complete the knowledge test and application exercises, and check your answers against the keyed ones. Finally, you should find it instructive to address the "Questions Without Answers." I suggest that you discuss them with other students of evaluation and review relevant literature. Pertinent books and articles are listed at the back of the unit.

Objectives

The following are the objectives of this unit.

1. To identify the order in which the author arrived at the concepts of context, input, process, and product evaluation, and explain how this developmental sequence was a response to field-based needs for evaluation.
2. To identify the conditions identified by the PDK Committee as symptomatic of the illness of educational evaluation.
3. To characterize the PDK Committee's objections to definitions that equate evaluation to experimental design, measurement, professional judgments, and comparing outcomes to objectives.
4. To discuss the five problems identified by the PDK Committee as underlying the failure of educational evaluation.
5. To identify and explain the definition of evaluation that is embodied in CIPP evaluation.
6. To identify key similarities and differences between the CIPP model and views of evaluation advanced by Stake and Scriven.
7. To characterize the potential contributions of CIPP evaluations to meeting requirements for accountability.
8. To explain the CIPP model's orientation toward improvement.
9. To characterize the role of CIPP evaluation in the context of an institution's efforts to improve its program.
10. To describe the purpose, methods, and uses, respectively, of context, input, process, and product evaluation.
11. To explain the purpose and procedures of the advocacy-team technique.
12. To describe the author's concept of evaluation design.
13. To define the concept of metaevaluation.

Some Personal History

My entry into program evaluation was quite accidental. Along with numerous other persons who had some acquaintance with research methods, I was drawn into the massive effort to meet the federal requirements for evaluating projects funded by America's Elementary and Secondary Education Act (ESEA) of 1965. Initially, I responded in much the same way that many of my colleagues were responding: by recommending the use of validated tests and accepted research designs. But in the course of trying to apply these recommendations, I drastically changed my view of the applicability of experimentation and objective tests to field evaluation studies and began to search for a more relevant and feasible approach. A main result of this search and attendant developmental effort has been the so-called CIPP Evaluation Model, which is the main topic of this unit.

The Elementary and Secondary Education Act of 1965 provided billions of dollars to school districts throughout the United States for the purpose of improving the education of disadvantaged students and, more generally, for upgrading the total system of elementary and secondary education. The act also required educators to evaluate their funded projects. This requirement created a crisis, since educators generally were not qualified by training or experience to design and conduct evaluations and since school districts could not receive ESEA funds until they presented an acceptable plan for evaluating each proposed ESEA project.

A number of universities and service agencies set up programs designed to assist the school districts to meet the ESEA evaluation requirements. I was assigned to head such a program at Ohio State University and, more generally, to organize and direct a center that would advance the theory and practice of evaluation. The new center was directed to address six goals: (1) to provide evaluation services to educational agencies, (2) to study these service experiences, (3) to conceptualize improved ways of doing evaluation, (4) to devise tools and strategies to carry out new ideas about evaluation, (5) to train educators to use the new tools and strategies, and (6) to disseminate information about the work and achievements of the center.

Development of the CIPP Model

As one means of pursuing these goals, the center contracted with the Columbus, Ohio, public schools to evaluate their ESEA projects. These three-year projects included a prekindergarten project, mathematics and reading improvement projects, an after-school study center, a health services project, and several others; the projects were supported by a $6.6 million federal grant. The Columbus district subcontracted about 8 percent of this amount to the Evaluation Center to sponsor their work in evaluating the eight projects and in helping the district to develop its own evaluation system.

The center staff set about their evaluation task in a traditional way. They sought to determine whether the eight projects were achieving their objectives. According to this approach, we were to identify the behavioral objectives for each project, select or develop appropriate instruments for measuring student performance, administer these instruments after instruction, and then compare student performance with project objectives. You will recognize this as the Tylerian evaluation rationale (unit 3), which has been a mainstay of American educational evaluation theory for over 30 years.

We soon found that this approach was not adequate for evaluating the Columbus projects. The assumption that educators knew or could easily determine what student behaviors should result from the projects was far from realistic. The original objectives contained in the funding proposal were general and did not reflect data about the functioning of the students to be served. In fact, the objectives usually had been written by consultants and administrators who had little or no direct experience with these students. What's more, the project staff could not agree, even after the project had started, on which specific objectives should be adopted. In retrospect, they and we wasted valuable time in trying to do so, since the needs of the students were highly variable and had not been the subject of serious study and since no common set of objectives could have been responsive to their varied developmental levels and needs. A related technical problem was the fact that existing tests were not geared to the language patterns and functional levels of disadvantaged students; and developing such tests in time to use them in evaluating the ESEA projects presented great problems of feasibility. Also, and more seriously, our employment of the Tylerian approach promised to yield reports only at the end of each project year, too late to help the project staff to identify and address their problems.

The irrelevance of our approach became apparent to me when I visited project staff members and observed their project activities. While I expected to find the projects being implemented across schools and classrooms with some degree of consistency, I found nothing of the sort. Instead there was widespread confusion on the part of the teachers concerning what they were supposed to be doing. Most of them had not had an opportunity to read the proposal that they were supposed to be implementing. Many of those who had seen the proposal were in disagreement with it or confused by it. Not surprisingly, the activities within a given project were not consistent across classrooms, and these activities bore little resemblance to those described in the funding proposal. As I considered this situation, the outcome data that my staff and I were planning to collect seemed of low importance.

I concluded that educators needed a broader definition of evaluation than one constrained to determining whether objectives had been achieved. The needed definition should lead to evaluations that would aid in managing and improving programs. I believed that the best hope of doing this would be to supply the school administrators, project directors, and school staff with information they could use to decide on and bring about needed changes in the projects. As an alternative to the Tylerian definition, I proposed, at a meeting on ESEA evaluation and in a journal article, that evaluation be redefined as a process of providing useful information for decision making (Stufflebeam, 1966). This proposal received widespread support, especially from the U.S. Office of Education, several large school districts and research and development agencies, and many educational administrators.

Since I thought evaluation should be geared to serve the information requirements of decision makers, it seemed appropriate to identify the main types of decisions that typically confronted them, then to derive appropriate evaluation strategies. Based on the experience with the Columbus ESEA projects, decisions of immediate concern seemed to be those associated with implementing the project designs, that is, how to bring teachers "up to speed" in carrying out the projects, how to allocate resources, how to assign and remodel facilities, how to obtain and sustain community support, how to schedule the needed transportation of students, how to adapt instructional materials, and how to foster communication among those participating in the project. To service these and other *implementation* decisions, I instructed my staff to start interacting with and observing the activities of project staff on a continuous basis and at least once each two weeks to report *process* results to project staff so that operational problems could be detected or highlighted and solved. The other main type of decision, especially in view of the government's annual funding cycle, quite apparently included decisions related to continuing or terminating a project, increasing or decreasing funding, merging the project with another one, institutionalizing the project, and so forth. I called these *recycling* decisions and suggested that they should be supported by information about what a project had *produced.* Accordingly, my staff and I continued our efforts with project staff to clarify which evidence of project outcomes would be appropriate, and we developed and administered quite a few tailor-made performance tests and rating scales. To summarize, at this point this reconceptualization of evaluation included *process evaluation* to guide *implementation* and *product evaluation* to serve *recycling decisions.* Process evaluation was a relatively new entry in the lore of educational evaluation; product evaluation, of course, was akin to what Tyler had meant by evaluation per se.

Shortly after developing this scheme, I was invited to describe it at an Ohio State faculty-student colloquium. One key reaction was that the proposed conceptualization was a decided improvement over classical ideas about educational evaluation, since it evidenced a concern for process as well as product. However, three members of the group charged that the approach ignored the fundamental concern for assessing goals.

They were correct. The selection of goals places constraints on what is hoped for and attempted in a project and thus is a key decision. I had neither included the choice of goals as a decision to be served by evaluation nor proposed any evaluation strategies that would assist evaluators in choosing or assessing goals. Also, I knew that the choice of goals to guide the Columbus projects had been based more on a review of the literature concerning disadvantaged children and educational innovations, in general, than on a systematic study of the needs of the students in Columbus. I suspected that the goals of the eight ESEA projects were only generally reflective of the needs of the students in Columbus, and there was no evidence to the contrary. To address this type of deficiency, I proposed that evaluators assess and report on student needs and system problems as a means of aiding educators to choose sound goals. The language that was added to the emerging CIPP framework advised educators to conduct *context evaluation* as a means of servicing *planning decisions.* However, this insight came too late to enable us to conduct and report a context evaluation as a basis for selecting and shaping project goals in the Columbus program.

There was an obvious gap in the emerging evaluation scheme, since it did not consider decisions necessary to specify which *means* are required to achieve a given set of goals or a set of assessed needs. These decisions are illustrated by the procedures, schedules, staffing plans, and budgets that appear in proposals that are sent to school boards and funding agencies, and, in general, by the choice of one plan over other possibilities. I called these decisions *structuring decisions* and proposed that they be serviced by *input evaluations,* which are studies that identify and assess the relative merits of alternative project designs.

At this point, the basic framework of the CIPP was complete (context evaluation to help develop goals, input evaluation to help shape proposals, process evaluation to guide implementation, and product evaluation to serve recycling decisions). Howard Merriman, who was a student in the Evaluation Center at the time and who later became the director of the Columbus school's new Department of Evaluation (which our project developed), observed that the first letters of the labels for the four evaluation concepts would provide a convenient acronym to help people remember them. Thus, the label CIPP was affixed to the scheme.

The PDK Study Committee's Elaboration of CIPP Evaluation

In 1969, Phi Delta Kappa set up a national study committee on evaluation. It included Walter Foley, Bill Gephart, Egon Guba, Robert Hammond, Howard Merriman, Malcolm Provus, and myself as chairman. We were charged to assess the state-of-the-art in educational evaluation and to provide generalized advice for conducting sound evaluations. Our report appeared in Stufflebeam et al. (1971).

We opened the report by arguing that evaluation was seized with a great illness. We said this illness was recognizable by symptoms exhibited by administrators, staff, and evaluators at all levels of education and by the dismal quality of their evaluation work:

Avoidance of efforts to evaluate their programs.

Anxiety over the prospects of having their programs evaluated because they perceived the evaluation process to be ambiguous, cursory, inadequate, subject to error, and often biased.

Immobilization regarding efforts to move forward to confront the problems of evaluation.

Skepticism that the "experts" could ever agree on what constitutes sound evaluation, let alone conduct studies that would help educators to do their jobs.

Lack of guidelines (especially from funding agencies) for meeting evaluation requirements even when evaluations are required.

Poor advice (from experts and in the literature) about how to conduct evaluations in field settings.

The *no-significant-difference syndrome,* in which study after study report, in effect, that the particular instructional approach followed makes no difference as regards study outcomes.

The *missing elements* symptom, that is, lack of pertinent theory; of clear conceptions of information requirements; of appropriate instruments and designs; of mechanisms for organizing, processing, and reporting evaluative information; of and trained personnel.

We further noted that the dominant approaches to evaluation, individually and collectively, were inadequate. We advised our audience not to equate evaluation to measurement, to professional judgment, to experimental research, or to congruence of outcomes and objectives. While each of these approaches was acknowledged to provide certain advantages for use in evaluation, each approach was also judged to have serious limitations. The advantages and limitations of these four approaches as we saw them are summarized in table 6–1.

While the PDK Committee acknowledged that each of the classic approaches to evaluation has desirable qualities, they concluded that none was adequate to respond to the evaluation requirements of the ESEA. They selected the CIPP model as a general framework within which to develop a sounder approach. And they defined five problems that needed to be addressed in improving the conceptual base for evaluation work:

1. *Definition.* Existing definitions were judged either to be too vague, too erroneous in their underlying assumptions, and/or too flawed in their methodological orientation.
2. *Decision making.* The committee saw evaluation as integrally related to decision making, but it thought that decisions needing to be serviced in change efforts were poorly understood. In addition, the committee saw a need for a clearer view of the process by which evaluators could project and respond to decision problems and associated information requirements.
3. *Values.* The committee believed that many evaluations erroneously reflected a value-free orientation. Also, they charged that there was a dearth of enlightening literature on the crucial subjects of how to recognize and deal with multiple value perspectives, how to derive appropriate criteria and associated instrumentation, and how to assign value meanings to obtained information.
4. *Levels.* The committee believed that evaluators largely had failed to recognize that different audiences at different organizational levels have different information requirements. An evaluation designed to meet the requirements of a particular audience — for example, a school project staff — would not be likely to meet the requirements of other audiences — for example, the U.S. Department of Education. Therefore, the committee saw the need for a process in designing evaluations by which to guide evaluators in identifying audiences, assessing their unique and common information needs, and planning data collection and reporting activities so as to accommodate the needs of the different audiences.
5. *Research design.* The committee advanced the position that research and evaluation have different purposes that require different pro-

cedures, and research and evaluation designs should be judged by different standards. Serious problems were encountered in ESEA evaluations when classic research designs intended to develop generalizable truth were used to evaluate innovative projects, where the need was not for generalizable knowledge but for timely guidance to serve particular decision problems.

We devoted a chapter to analyzing each of these problems, then presented and elaborated the CIPP model. An updated version of the formal definition we proposed and expanded upon is as follows:

> Evaluation is the process of delineating, obtaining, and providing descriptive and judgmental information about the worth and merit of some object's goals, design, implementation, and impacts in order to guide decision making, serve needs for accountability, and promote understanding of the involved phenomena.

This definition summarizes the key concepts in the CIPP model. It posits three purposes for evaluation: guiding decision making, providing records for accountability, and promoting understanding of the involved phenomena (consistent with the model's improvement orientation, the first of these purposes is viewed as most important). It presents evaluation not as an event but as a process, and defines that process to include the three steps of delineating, obtaining, and providing information (hence, evaluators need to be trained in both technical and communication areas). Both descriptive and judgmental information are viewed as appropriate for assessing and helping to improve the object of interest. The key aspects of the object that, according to the definition, should be assessed include its goals, design, implementation, and impacts (respectively, these are assessed by context, input, process, and product evaluation). The fundamental criteria to be involved include its worth (its response to assessed needs) and its merit (its quality).

The book that explicated this definition had considerable influence in promoting decision-oriented evaluations, especially in large school districts. The remainder of this unit is largely an update of the key concepts and recommendations that appeared in the PDK book.

CIPP Compared to Other Recent Evaluation Proposals

While my colleagues and I were developing the CIPP framework, Robert Stake was developing the "countenance of evaluation" approach, which he has since incorporated in his "responsive approach" (see unit 7). We exchanged drafts of our working papers in 1966, and I was interested to see whether we had independently been developing similar or different approaches.

Table 6-1. Advantages and Disadvantages Accruing from Different Traditional Approaches to Evaluation (adapted from Stufflebeam et al., 1971, p. 15)

Approach	Advantages	Disadvantages
1. Norm-Referenced Measurement	Based on psychological theory Employs standardized technology Designed to assure reliability and validity Availability of published tests and scoring services Supported by professional standards Standards come from norms	Focused only on available instruments Inflexible because of time and cost required to produce new instruments Trades off content validity in favor of reliability of individual difference scores Emphasizes knowledges and abilities that can easily be measured by paper and pencil tests Elevates the norm as the standard for all students
2. Professional Judgment	Easy to implement Potentially brings all variables into consideration Exploits available expertise and experience No time lag while waiting for data analysis	Dictated mainly by expediency Questionable reliability and objectivity Both data and criteria are ambiguous Not susceptible to checks on validity Generalization very difficult
3. Experimental Design	High scientific respectability Potentially yields data about cause and effect Arranged to yield high levels of reliability, validity, and objectivity	Imposes controls that are unattainable in educational contexts or inimical to the purposes of the evaluation Interferes with the normal operations of the projects under study

	Potentially rank orders the decision maker's options Supported by inferential statistics	Requires inapplicable assumptions — limits study to a few variables Services restricted decision rules Yields results only at the end
4. Congruence of Outcomes and Objectives (Tylerian)	Integration with instructional design Yields data on both students and curriculum Possibility of periodic feedback Defines standards of success Possibility of process and product data	Places evaluator in technical role Focuses narrowly on objectives Elevates behavior as the ultimate criterion of every educational action Fails to evaluate the objectives Focuses on evaluation as a terminal process

The consistency between the CIPP and countenance frameworks was considerable, but there were also some notable differences. Both approaches called for assessment of outcomes, but Stake emphasized the need to search for side effects as well as intended effects. This was an excellent recommendation, which I later incorporated in my view of product evaluation. His provision for observing and analyzing "transactions within a project" was similar to process evaluation. While Stake provided no analogue for input evaluation, both it and context evaluation could be assumed to be covered in his provision for identifying and assessing "antecedent conditions" (those that existed before the project started and before the evaluator entered the scene). Clearly, the use of either approach called for a more comprehensive assessment of a project than was embodied in the outcomes-oriented Tylerian rationale. One difference concerned how the two approaches dealt with the so-called "point of entry" problem. By relegating concerns for assessing needs and project plans to the category of antecedents, Stake seemed to assume that the evaluator would enter during the implementation stage when it would be most appropriate to look at ongoing transactions. CIPP provided for entry either before or during a project and allowed for the possibility of conducting a single type of evaluation only (context, input, process, or product) or some combination depending upon the needs of the audiences.

Neither approach gave much credence to initiating an evaluation after a project had been completed in order to perform a postmortem (or motivate a celebration), since both emphasized the improvement function of an evaluation. While both approaches were geared to helping particular audiences to use evaluation to carry out their assignments, the Stake approach was geared most directly to serving the involved project staff and teachers, and the CIPP approach was oriented more to the needs of those charged with planning and administering the projects. Another difference concerned the bases used by the two approaches to form conclusions about the success of projects. In the Stake approach such conclusions were to be derived by collecting and analyzing judgments from all persons and groups with an interest in the project, whereas the CIPP approach looked more to whether assessed needs had been met. Both approaches evidenced a tension — and I believe a healthy one — between obtaining a comprehensive view of a project and tailoring the evaluation to address the most important information needs of the relevant audiences.

Michael Scriven's "formative-summative" approach offered a fairly sharp contrast to both the countenance and CIPP approaches (for an updated version of his approach see unit 10). He defined evaluation as the systematic and objective determination of the worth or merit of an object, and said this definition could best be implemented by engaging an independent evaluator to render a judgment of an object based on the accumulated evidence about how it compared with similar objects in meeting the needs of consumers. He called this approach summative evaluation and said it was fundamentally more important than formative evaluation, in which an evaluator collects and reports data and judgments to assist the development of an object. Based on this rationale, Scriven (1970) charged that the CIPP approach was flawed because it almost totally ignored the fundamental role of summative evaluation due to its preoccupation with fostering improvement.

At a meeting of the May 12 Group on Evaluation, Michael Scriven and I debated the relative merits of an improvment orientation versus a summative-judgment orientation. Later, AERA put this debate on the road, so to speak, and we were commissioned to codirect and team teach four traveling training institutes. Subsequently, NIE commissioned us to chair teams that designed competing plans for the evaluation of regional educational laboratories and research and development centers. Through these contacts I became convinced that our different views of evaluation were more apparent than real and that they mainly reflected different perspectives and experiences. In my work with the Columbus schools an orientation toward a final, externally based judgment of worth would have been stifling and nonresponsive to the staff's need for guidance toward "shaking down" and improving their ESEA projects. Likewise, given that Scriven had been extensively involved in advising groups concerned with evaluating competing national curriculum packages, it is easy to see why he was placing emphasis on comparative summative evaluations. His main audience included the potential purchasers of these packages and they obviously were interested not in data by which to improve the packages but in recommendations about which of the alternatives would serve them best. Finally, the compatibility of our views was confirmed when our two teams' designs for the NIE evaluation work were found to be highly similar, even though they had been independently developed (Reinhard, 1972).

Nevertheless, these experiences pointed up the need to clarify and extend the CIPP model to ensure that it would serve needs for summative as well as formative evaluation. Accordingly, I issued an article on the applicability of the CIPP approach to accountability (Stufflebeam, 1971). In this article, I characterized evaluation for decision making as formative or proactive in nature, and evaluation for accountability mainly as summative or retroactive. In the main, this article was written to explain a version of the chart presented in table 6-2. This chart shows that context, input, process, and product evaluations may be used both to guide decision making, the formative role, and to supply information for accountability, the summative role. Based on

Table 6-2. The Relevance of Four Evaluation Types to Decision Making and Accountability

	Context	Input	Process	Product
Decision making (formative orientation)	Guidance for choice of objectives and assignment of priorities	Guidance for choice of program strategy Input for specification of procedural design	Guidance for implementation	Guidance for termination, continuation, modification, or installation
Accountability (summative orientation)	Record of objectives and bases for their choice along with a record of needs, opportunities, and problems	Record of chosen strategy and design and reasons for their choice over other alternatives	Record of the actual process	Record of attainments and recycling decisions

this scheme, the evaluators would design and conduct evaluation so as to assist a staff to plan and implement its program. Regardless of how narrow or broad the information requirements of the developers, they would also keep in mind and try to address the full range of information needs of external audiences that someday would want to form conclusions about the worth and merit of the improvement effort. Moreover, they would maintain a record of the information collected and evidence of the extent that the developers used it to guide their work. While such information would not answer all the questions of an external summative evaluator, it would certainly help in answering some of them. Especially, a full implementation of the CIPP approach would yield information of use in addressing the following questions:

1. What needs were addressed, how pervasive and important were they, and to what extent were the project's objectives reflective of assessed needs (addressed by context information)?
2. What procedural, staffing, and budgeting plan was adopted to address the needs, what alternatives were considered, why was it chosen over them, and to what extent was it a reasonable, potentially successful, and cost-effective proposal for meeting the assessed needs (addressed by input information)?
3. To what extent was the project plan implemented, and how and for what reasons did it have to be modified (addressed by process information)?
4. What results — positive and negative as well as intended and unintended — were observed, how did the various stakeholders judge the worth and merit of the outcomes, and to what extent were the needs of the target population met (product information)?

CIPP as a Strategy for Improving Systems

Compared to the Stake and Scriven orientations, CIPP is more in line with a systems view of education and human services. It is concentrated not so much on guiding the conduct of an individual study but on providing ongoing evaluation services to the decision makers in an institution. Especially, it is based on the view that the most important purpose of evaluation is not to prove but to improve. It is a move against the view that evaluations should be "witch-hunts" or merely instruments of accountability. Instead, it sees evaluation as a tool by which to help make progrms work better for the people they are intended to serve. This position is consistent with those recently presented by Patton (1978) and Cronbach and Associates (1980) (see unit 5). However, the CIPP orientation is not intended to discount the likelihood that some programs are unworthy of efforts to improve them and thus should be terminated. By promoting the demise of unneeded or hopelessly flawed programs, evaluations also serve an improvement function by helping to free resources for allocation to more worthy efforts. Fundamentally, the use of the CIPP model is intended to promote growth and to help the responsible leadership and staff of an institution to obtain and use feedback systematically so as to excel in meeting important needs, or at least, to do the best they can with the available resources.

The orientation toward helping to maintain and improve the quality of institutional operations is illustrated in the flowchart in figure 6-1. Starting in the left-hand corner, it acknowledges that the operations of a school, or some other institution, include various and perhaps uncoordinated evaluation efforts, but that periodically the institution needs to undergo a special context evaluation. Such an evaluation would examine the needs of the institution's clients; expose opportunities such as funding programs, advanced educational technologies, or industries with a willingness and capacity to aid the institution; collect and examine perceptions about problems in the institution that warrant change; and assess the efficacy of institutional goals and priorities. Such a context evaluation might be motivated from inside the institution as a regular "state of the institution" assessment or as a response to indications from some sector of dissatisfaction about the institution's performance. A context evaluation might also be motivated from outside the institution, as when an accrediting agency requires a self-study or a funding agency requires a "needs assessment" as a basis for justifying a funding request. Such studies may be targeted on specified areas of concern or focused more generally on a wide range of institutional functions. In general, such studies aid in system renewal and promotion of better and more efficient service, in diagnosis of particular problems and targeting of improvement efforts, and in communication about the institution's strengths and weaknesses with its constituency.

The results of the context evaluation, ideally, would lead to a decision about whether to introduce some kind of a change in the system. If decided in the negative, then the institution's staff would continue with their program operations as usual. However, if a decision to change the institution in some way were made, then the program staff would clarify the problem(s) to be solved and formulate their objectives. Next, they would consider whether some appropriate solution strategy is apparent and readily adaptable to their situation. If so, they would install it and redirect their attentions to using it and evaluating it in the ongoing program of the institution.

If no satisfactory solution were apparent, then the staff, according to the flowchart, would conduct an input evaluation. Such an evaluation would

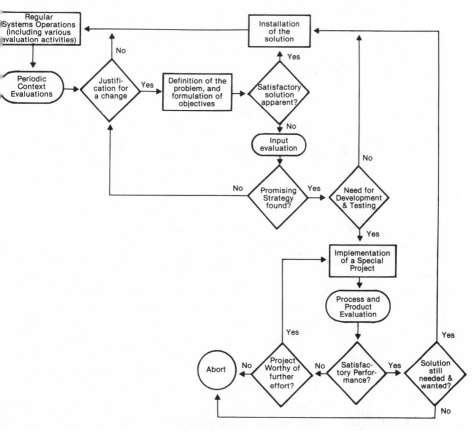

Figure 6-1. A Flowchart Depicting the Role of CIPP Evaluation in Effecting System Improvement

search the relevant literature, question personnel in other institutions that may have dealt successfully with a similar problem, draw on the ingenuity and creativity of the institution's staff and constituent groups, and possibly would involve outside experts. Subsequently, one or more teams would be assigned to write up one or more proposed solution strategies. The resulting proposal(s) would then be assessed against such criteria as responsiveness to the defined needs, problems, and objectives; theoretical soundness; and feasibility.

The results of the input evaluation would be used to decide whether a sufficiently promising solution strategy had been found to warrant going ahead with its further development. If not, the staff would reconsider whether the desired change is sufficiently important to warrant further search and if so, would recycle through the search for a solution strategy. If a promising strategy had been found, then the staff would decide whether the strategy could justifiably be installed without further testing. If much was known about the strategy and there was little concern about being able to install it, the staff would likely turn their attention directly to incorporating the change into their regular ongoing activities, without any further specialized evaluation support.

However, if they decided to test it further, they would direct their attention to a field test of the strategy and would subject it to process and product evaluation over whatever time period would be required to shake down and debug the procedure and reach the desired level of performance and readiness for installation. At some point, however, if the project has not performed satisfactorily or is viewed as too costly, the leadership of the institution might conclude that no further effort is warranted and, in accordance with this conclusion, decide to abort the effort. Such decisions have frequently been made at the conclusion of federally supported projects, when the grantee had to decide whether to allocate local funds for the institutionalization of a project. As shown in the bottom right-hand corner of the flowchart, even if a project had succeeded, the institution's leadership might determine that conditions in the institution had changed sufficiently that the previously desired change was no longer needed and, accordingly, terminate the effort. Under the assumption that the project was a success and the solution it afforded was still needed and wanted, the institution would install the proven project and return to regular operations, including regularized evaluation of the ongoing program.

The preceding analysis of evaluation in the context of an institution's change process points up a number of important features of a systems approach to evaluation:

1. Evaluation is an integral part of an institution's regular program and not merely a specialized activity involved in innovative projects, and the implementation of CIPP or any other specialized approach is only a part of the total mosaic of informal and formal evaluation in the institution.
2. Evaluations have a vital role in stimulating and planning changes.
3. The employment of each type of evaluation in the CIPP model is indicated only if information beyond what already exists is needed, not by the inherent value in doing each kind of evaluation. In other words, context, input, process, and product evaluations are only a part of a

larger milieu of evaluation in any institution, and the most important function of those commissioned studies is in serving the institution's marginal needs for evaluative information.

4. The development of new programs should include the provision for their ongoing employment and use of evaluation once they have been installed through something akin to curriculum-embedded evaluation (wherein evaluation is built in to the implementation of a curriculum and, as a matter of course, yields feedback of use in diagnosing, prescribing, and checking progress).

5. Evaluation information not only provides guidance for institutional problem solving, but if recorded and made available for public review, it also provides a basis for judging whether decisions either to abort or institutionalize a special project were made on defensible grounds.

6. Decisions to commence, sustain, install, or abort programs and program improvement efforts almost always will reflect dynamic forces — irrational and rational — that extend far beyond the evaluator's sphere of study and influence.

An Overview of the CIPP Categories

In addition to viewing the CIPP approach in an institutional or systems context, it is instructive to examine each type of study more closely. The matrix in table 6–3 is presented as a convenient overview of the essential meanings of context, input, process, and product evaluation. These four types of studies are defined in relation to their objectives, methods, and uses.

Context Evaluation

The primary orientation of a context evaluation is to identify the strengths and weaknesses of some object, such as an institution, a program, a target population, or a person, and to provide direction for improvement. The main objectives of this type of study are to assess the object's overall status, to identify its deficiencies, to identify the strengths at hand that could be used to remedy the deficiencies, to diagnose problems whose solution would improve the object's well-being, and, in general, to characterize the program's environment. A context evaluation also is aimed at examining whether existing goals and priorities are attuned to the needs of whoever is supposed to

Table 6-3. Four Types of Evaluation

	Context Evaluation	Input Evaluation	Process Evaluation	Product Evaluation
Objective	To define the institutional context, to identify the target population and assess their needs, to identify opportunities for addressing the needs, to diagnose *problems* underlying the *needs*, and to judge whether proposed objectives are sufficiently responsive to the assessed needs.	To identify and assess *system capabilities*, alternative program *strategies*, procedural *designs* for implementing the strategies, budgets, and schedules.	To identify or predict in process, *defects* in the procedural design or its implementation, to provide information for the preprogrammed decisions, and to record and judge procedural events and activities.	To collect descriptions and judgments of outcomes and to relate them to objectives and to context, input, and process information, and to interpret their worth and merit.
Method	By using such methods as system analysis, survey, document review, hearings, interviews, diagnostic tests, and the Delphi technique.	By inventorying and analyzing available human and material resources, solution strategies, and procedural designs for relevance, feasibility and economy. And by using such methods	By monitoring the activity's potential procedural barriers and remaining alert to unanticipated ones, by obtaining specified information for programmed decisions, by describing the actual process,	By defining operationally and measuring outcome criteria, by collecting judgments of outcomes from stakeholders, and by performing both qualitative and quantitative analyses.

| Relation to decision making in the change process | For deciding upon the *setting* to be served, the *goals* associated with meeting needs or using opportunities, and the *objectives* associated with solving problems, i.e., for *planning* needed changes. And to provide a basis for judging outcomes. | For selecting *sources of support*, solution *strategies*, and procedural *designs*, i.e., for *structuring* change activities. And to provide a basis for judging implementation. | For *implementing and refining the program design and procedure*, i.e., for effecting *process control*. And to provide a log of the actual process for later use in interpreting outcomes. | For deciding to *continue, terminate, modify,* or *refocus* a change activity. And to present a clear record of effects (intended and unintended, positive and negative). |

be served. Whatever the focal object, the results of a context evaluation should provide a sound basis for adjusting (or establishing) goals and priorities and targeting needed changes.

The methodology of a context evaluation may involve a variety of measurements of the object of interest and various types of analysis. A usual starting point is to interview the clients of the study in order to obtain their perceptions of strengths, weaknesses, and problems. Hearings, community forums, and further interviews may be conducted to generate additional hypotheses about what changes are needed. These hypotheses may be used to construct a survey instrument, which may be administered to a carefully defined sample of stakeholders and made available more generally to anyone who wishes to provide input, with the analyses of the two sets of responses kept separate. Existing records should also be examined to identify performance patterns and background information. Special diagnostic tests might be administered. An expert review panel might be engaged to visit, closely observe, and judge the worth and merit of a program. Throughout the study, an advisory committee representative of the various stakeholder groups might be involved in clarifying the evaluative questions and interpreting the findings. A consensus-building technique, such as Delphi, might be used to secure agreements about priority needs. And a workshop might be conducted to help the clients to study and apply the findings.

A context evaluation may have a number of constructive uses. It may provide a means by which a school district communicates with its public to gain a shared conception of the district's strengths and weaknesses, needs and opportunities, and priority problems. It may be used to convince a funding agency that a proposed project is directed at an area of urgent need or to convince an electorate of the need to pass a tax issue. It might be used to formulate objectives for staff development and/or curriculum revision. It could be used to select particular schools for priority assistance. Of course, it would often be used to help students and their parents or advisers to focus their attention on developmental areas requiring more progress. Also, it could be used to help decide how to cut programs, hopefully to help the institution get stronger while getting smaller. I see these as important examples of how a context evaluation could assist individuals and groups to set priorities for improvement efforts. Another use comes later when there is a need to assess what has been accomplished through an improvement project. One basis for judging outcomes is by assessing whether they are adequately responsive to the needs that were identified through the context evaluation. Finally, context evaluation records are a pertinent means by which to defend the efficacy of one's goals and priorities.

Input Evaluation

The main orientation of an input evaluation is to help prescribe a program by which to bring about needed changes. It does this by searching out and critically examining potentially relevant approaches. It is a precursor of the success, failure, and efficiency of a change effort. Change projects are constrained by initial decisions about how resources will be allocated, and a potentially effective solution to a problem will have no possibility of impact if a planning group does not at least identify it and assess its merits when it is planning its change project.

Essentially, an input evaluation should identify and rate relevant approaches (including the one(s) already operating in the main program of interest) and assist in explicating and "shaking down" the one chosen for installation or continuation. It should also search the clients' environment for barriers, constraints, and potentially available resources that ought to be considered in the process of activating the program. The overall intent of an input evaluation is to help the clients consider alternative program strategies in the context of their needs and environmental circumstances and to evolve a plan that will work for them; another important function is to help clients avoid the wasteful practice of pursuing proposed innovations that predictably would fail or at least waste resources.

The methods involved may be described in a series of stages, although there is no set sequence of steps for conducting an input evaluation. One might begin by reviewing the state of practice with respect to meeting the specified needs; this could be done by reviewing relevant literature, visiting exemplary programs, consulting experts and representatives of government querying pertinent information services, and inviting proposals from involved staff. This information might be organized in a special planning room and subjected to in-depth investigation by a special study group. Its investigation might be conducted over a period of time through a special decision seminar. This group might use the information to assess whether potentially acceptable solution strategies exist. In addition, it might rate promising approaches for potential effectiveness and feasibility and advise staff and faculty about whether to seek a novel solution. If an innovation is to be sought, the client and evaluators might next define criteria to be met by the innovation, structure a request for proposal, obtain competing proposals, and rate them for potential effectiveness and feasibility. Subsequently, the evaluators might analyze and rank the potentially acceptable proposals and suggest how their best features could be combined. In addition, the evaluators might conduct a type of hearing in which staff and administrators are invited to express concerns and give their realistic appraisal of resources and barriers that, in some way, need to be dealt with in the process of installing the solution.

The advocacy team technique is a relatively new procedure for conducting input evaluations and deserves special mention. This technique is especially applicable in situations where appropriate effective means to meet specified needs are not available. Two or more teams of experts are convened, given the objectives for which a program is needed, provided with specifications for designing a program proposal, and oriented to the criteria by which the competing responses will be judged. The advocacy team reports are rated by a panel of experts and/or pilot tested in accordance with the pre-established criteria. Subsequent steps involve members of the user system in operationalizing the winning strategy or combining and operationalizing the best features of the *two* or more competing strategies. Advantages of the advocacy team technique are that it provides (1) an explicit procedure for generating and assessing competing program strategies; (2) an explicit accountability record of why a particular solution strategy was selected; (3) a forum that exploits bias and competition in a constructive search for alternatives; and (4) a means of involving personnel from the adopting system, either as advocacy team members or as members of the team that performs the convergence and operationalization activities following the ranking of the competing strategies. Additional information, including a technical manual and the results of five field tests of the technique, is available in a doctoral dissertation by Diane Reinhard (1972).

Input evaluations have a number of applications. A chief one is in preparing a proposal for submission to a funding agency or an institution's policy board. Another is to assess one's existing program, whether or not it seems to be working against what is being done elsewhere and proposed in the literature. Input evaluation has also been used in the Dallas Independent school district as a device for screening out locally generated proposals for innovation whose projected costs could be shown to exceed the projected benefits. Another use is to provide a structure and forum by which historically antagonistic groups can reach agreement on some course of action. In addition, the records from an input evaluation study help those in authority account for their choice of one course of action above other possibilities.

Process Evaluation

In essence, a process evaluation is an ongoing check on the implementation of a plan. One objective is to provide feedback to managers and staff about the extent to which the program activities are on schedule, being carried out as planned, and using the available resources in an efficient manner. Another is to provide guidance for modifying or explicating the plan as needed, since not all aspects of a plan can be determined in advance and since some of the initial decisions may later prove to be unsound. Still another objective is to assess periodically the extent to which program participants accept and are able to carry out their roles. Finally, a process evaluation should provide an extensive record of the program that was actually implemented, how it compared to what was intended, a full account of the various costs incurred in carrying it out, and overall how observers and participants judged the quality of the effort.

The linchpin of a sound process evaluation is the process evaluator. More often than not, a program staff's failure to obtain guidance for implementation and to document their activities is due to a failure to assign anyone to do this work. Erroneously, it is too often assumed that the managers and staff can and will do an adequate job of process evaluation as a normal part of their assignments. While some review and documentation can be done through routine activities such as staff meetings, these means are not sufficient to meet the requirements of a sound process evaluation. In my experience, these requirements can be met well only by assigning one or more persons to provide ongoing review, feedback, and documentation.

There is much work for a process evaluator to do in a program. The following scenario is provided as an illustration of what might be done. Initially, the process evaluator could review the program plan and any prior evaluation on which it is based to identify important aspects of the program that should be monitored. Some examples that might be identified are staff development sessions, development and implementation of materials centers, counseling of students, liaison with parents, tutoring services, staff planning sessions, skill grouping of students, classroom instruction, field trips, homework assignments, and the use of diagnostic tests. As another means of identifying what should be looked at, the evaluator might form an advisory group, broadly representative of program participants, and periodically ask them to identify concerns and questions that should be addressed. Other questions of relevance will occur to the evaluator in the observance of program activities.

With questions and concerns such as those mentioned above in mind, the process evaluator could develop a general schedule of data collection activities and begin carrying them out. Initially, these probably should be as unobtrusive as possible so as not to threaten program staff or get in their way. Subsequently, as rapport is developed the process evaluator can use a more structured approach. At the outset, the process evaluator might try to get an overview of how the program is operating by visiting and observing centers of activity, reviewing program documents, attending staff meetings, and interviewing key participants. The process evaluator then could prepare a brief report that summarizes the data collection plan, reviews what was learned, and points up the key issues. The report could then be presented at a staff meeting and the staff director invited to lead a discussion of it and to use it for program revision as he and the staff see fit. Later in the meeting, the process evaluator could review with the staff his plans for further data collection and a subsequent report. He could ask for their reactions about what feedback would be most useful at a subsequent meeting, as well as their suggestions about how best to obtain certain items of information, such as observations, staff-kept diaries, interviews, or questionnaires. On the basis of feedback from the staff, the evaluator would schedule future feedback sessions, modify the data collection plan as appropriate, and proceed accordingly. He should continually demonstrate that the main purpose of process evaluation is to assist the staff in carrying out its program, through a kind of quality assurance process. Throughout this interactive process, the evaluator should periodically prepare and file reports on his perception of the extent that the program plan has been implemented. He should describe main deviations from the plan, and should make special note of variation within the program concerning how different persons and subgroups are carrying out the plan. He should also characterize the ongoing planning activity and trace the evolution of the basic plan on which the program is based.

The main use of process evaluation is to obtain feedback that can aid staff to carry out a program as it was planned or if the plan is found to be inadequate, to modify it as needed. Some managers see regularly scheduled process evaluation feedback sessions as a means of keeping staff "on their toes" and abreast of their responsibilities. Process evaluation records are also useful for accountability, since funding agencies, policy boards, and constituents typically want to know whether grantees did what they had proposed. Process evaluations can also help external audiences to learn what was done in the program in case they want to conduct a similar one. And a process evaluation is a vital source of information for interpreting product evaluation results, since in considering why program outcomes turned out as they did, one would want to know what was actually done in carrying out the program plan.

Product Evaluation

The purpose of a product evaluation is to measure, interpret, and judge the attainments of a program. Feedback about achievements is important both during a program cycle and at its conclusion, and product evaluation often should be extended to assess long-term effects. The main objective of a product evaluation is to ascertain the extent to which the program has met the needs of the group it is intended to serve. In addition, a product evaluation should look broadly at the effects of the program, including intended and unintended effects and positive and negative outcomes.

A product evaluation should gather and analyze judgments of the program's success from a broad range of people associated with the program. Sometimes it should compare the outcomes of the program under study with those of alternative programs. Frequently, the client wants to know how the attainments compare to previously stated objectives and the extent the outcomes are worth more than the cost of attaining them. Usually, it is quite important to offer interpretations of the extent that failure to achieve objectives or meet needs was correlated with a failure to implement the program plan. Finally, a product evaluation usually should view outcomes from several vantage points: in the aggregate, by subgroupings of program recipients who might be differentiated by needs and services received, and sometimes by individuals. An outcome associated with an individual may be classified as a success or failure depending on whether it has satisfied a diagnosed need of the individual; such product evaluation at the level of individuals also allows aggregation across individuals to get an overall index of the extent to which the program has succeeded in meeting the collective and differential needs of individuals.

There is no set algorithm for conducting a product evaluation, but there are many applicable methods. In general, a combination of techniques should be used to obtain a comprehensive view of effects and to provide crosschecks on the various findings. The following scenario is intended to illustrate the range of techniques that might be employed.

The product evaluators might begin by assessing performance in relation to some previously chosen standard. Such assessments might be made based on test performance compared to a profile of previously assessed needs, pretest performance, selected norms, specified performance standards, or the performance of a comparison group. The tests used might be published objective tests, specially made criterion-referenced tests, or applied performance tests (see Sanders, 1977). Performance assessments might also be based on ratings of performance by observers, employers, and/or the program recipients themselves. And experts might assess work products and compare them to previously developed needs profiles for the program recipients who produced them.

In order to assess performance beyond that related to intended outcomes, evaluators need to make an extensive search for unanticipated outcomes, both positive and negative. They might conduct hearings or group interviews to generate hypotheses about the full range of outcomes and follow these up with clinical investigations intended to confirm or disconfirm the hypotheses. They might conduct case studies of the experiences of a carefully selected sample of participants in order to obtain an in-depth view of the program's effects. They might survey, via telephone or mail, a sample of participants to obtain their judgments of the project and their views of both positive and negative findings. They might ask the participants to submit concrete examples, such as pieces they have written, of how the project has influenced their work. They might engage observers to view the performance of program and comparison groups in regular settings and to develop and validate tests that distinguish between their performances, thus giving a view of the unique contributions of the program, pro and con (see Brickell, 1976). They might search out and examine program outcomes in relation to a comprehensive checklist of outcomes that have been observed for similar programs. As a final example, they might conduct a "jury trial" by which to introduce and examine all available evidence that reflects on the success or failure of the program (see Wolf, 1974).

Reporting of product evaluation findings may occur at different stages. Interim reports may be submitted during each program cycle to indicate the extent the targeted needs are being addressed and met. End-of-cycle reports may sum up the results achieved and interpret them in the light of pre-assessed needs, costs incurred, and the extent the plan was carried out. Follow-up reports may also be submitted to indicate what if any long-term impacts can be found. In such reports, the results might be analyzed in the aggregate, for subgroups, and for individuals.

The basic use of a product evaluation is to determine whether a given program is worth continuing, repeating, and/or extending into other settings. It also should provide direction for modifying the program so that it better serves the needs of all members of the target audience and becomes more cost effective. Of course, it should help potential adopters of the program to decide whether it merits their serious consideration. Product evaluations have psychological implications, since by showing signs of growth and/or superiority to competing efforts, they reinforce the efforts of both staff and program recipients; likewise they may dampen enthusiasm when the results are poor. Product evaluation information is an essential component of an accountability report, and when significant achievement is evidenced it can aid in securing additional financial and political support from the community and funding agencies. When this information reveals that no important gains warrant the associated costs, product evaluation can help avoid continued wasteful investments in the program. Moreover, a record of the results obtained, especially in consideration of the program approach used and the costs involved, can assist other developers to decide on the wisdom of pursuing a similar course of action.

The preceding discussion indicates that context, input, process, and product evaluation serve unique functions, but that a symbiotic relationship exists among them. It further shows that a variety of methods are applicable to each type of evaluation. But it doesn't deal with the evaluator's practical problem in deciding which methods to employ in a particular study. This problem is treated in the next section of this unit.

Designing Evaluations

To guide the implementation of an evaluation — whether context, input, process, or product evaluation (or some combination) — the evaluator obviously needs to design the work to be done. This involves preparing the preliminary plans and subsequently modifying and explicating them as the study proceeds. These plans must deal with a wide range of choices pertaining to the conduct of the evaluation, such as the key audiences and questions; the object to be assessed; whether a context, input, process, and/or product evaluation is indicated; the timing and location of the study; the extent and nature of controls to be imposed; the contrasts to be made; the sources of needed information; the methods, instruments, and schedule for data collection; the formats and procedures for labeling, storing, and retrieving information; the methods of analysis and interpretation; provisions for communicating findings; and criteria and arrangements for assessing the evaluation results. Decisions about such evaluation activities form the basis for contracting and financing the evaluation work, working out protocol with the involved institutions, staffing the study, and scheduling and guiding staff activities.

We might wish that evaluators could finalize design decisions at the outset and then follow them precisely. However, the dynamic and interactive qualities of many evaluations plus their service orientation make difficult, if not impossible, the accurate, long-range projection of specific information needs. Consequently, technical plans for data collection and analysis, made prior to the start of a study, often are based on erroneous assumptions and found later to be inappropriate or incomplete. Rigid adherence to the original evaluation design — especially if it had been defined in specific terms — often would detract greatly from the utility of the study by directing it to the wrong questions, using erroneous assumptions to guide it, and/or convincing members of the audience that the evaluator has an ivory-tower orientation.

Hence, evaluators are faced with a dilemma. On the one hand, they need to plan their evaluation activities carefully so that they can carry them out efficiently and with an acceptable amount of rigor and convince their clients that they know what they are doing. On the other hand, they need to approach the design of evaluation studies flexibly and provide for the design's periodic review and modification so that the evaluation remains responsive to the needs of the audiences. This dilemma is especially troublesome to evaluators, since clients often expect or demand up-front technical designs and later become disenchanted when rigid adherence to the original design yields much information that is no longer perceived as useful. Clients often perceive that somehow evaluators should have been smarter in projecting information needs and more skilled in planning the data collection activities.

To address this dilemma evaluators must view design as a process, not a product, and they need to get their clients to do likewise. Evaluation goals and procedures should be sketched in advance, but periodically reviewed, revised, expanded, and operationalized. Fundamentally, this process should be guided by a defensible view of what constitutes sound evaluation, by a sensitivity to factors in the real world that often interfere with evaluation work, and by ongoing communication between the evaluators and their audiences about the pertinence and adequacy of the design.

At the outset of the process, I believe it is important to listen and probe. Who are the primary clients? What do they want from the evaluation? Why? What type(s) of evaluation (context, input, process, product) would be most responsive? How do the clients think the evaluation should be conducted? What timeline do they have in mind? Who do they see as the main audience? Who might "get hurt" as a consequence of the evaluation? Why? Whose cooperation will be essential? What information already exists? What's the relevant history? Realistically, what positive benefits from the evaluation could be expected? What deleterious effects are real possibilities, and how could they be avoided? What qualifications are required to do the job? And so on. Whenever a choice is available, evaluators should pursue questions like these before agreeing that an evaluation should be done or that they are the right ones to do it.

Assuming a positive decision to go ahead, the evaluator should sketch an overall plan. This plan should take into account what the evaluator has learned about the setting and particular needs for the evaluation, and it should conform to generally accepted standards of sound evaluation. In addition, it should speak, at least in a general way, to the full range of tasks to be done.

Table 6–4 provides a general outline of the points to be addressed in an evaluation design. These points are applicable when developing the initial design or later when revising or explicating it. Of course, they serve only as general indications of the detailed information that eventually must be provided to flesh out and operationalize the design.

Table 6-4. Outline for Documenting Evaluation Designs

Review of the Charge
    Definition of the object of the evaluation
    Identification of the client and audiences
    Purpose(s) of the evaluation (i.e., program improvement, accountability,
        and/or understanding)
    Type of evaluation (e.g., context, input, process, or product) to be
        employed
    Principles of sound evaluation (e.g., utility, feasibility, propriety, and
        accuracy) to be observed

Plan for Obtaining Information
    The general strategy (e.g., survey, case study, advocacy teams, or field
        experiment)
    Working assumptions to guide measurement, analysis, and interpretation
    Collection of information (i.e., sampling, instrumentation, and data
        collection)
    Organization of information (i.e., coding, filing, and retrieving)
    Analysis of information (both qualitative and quantitative)
    Interpretation of findings (i.e., identification of standards and processing of
        judgments)

Plan for Reporting the Results
    Preparation of reports
    Dissemination of reports
    Provision for follow-up activities to promote impact of the evaluation

Plan for Administering the Study
    Summarization of the evaluation schedule
    Plan for meeting staff and resource requirements
    Provision for metaevaluation
    Provision for periodical updating of the evaluation design
    Budget
    Memorandum of agreement or contract

The formulation of the design requires that the client and evaluators collaborate, from the outset, when they must agree on a charge. The client
needs to identify the object, for example, the program to be evaluated, and
the evaluator can help by guiding the client to define clear and realistic
boundaries around what will be looked at. The client is a prime source for
identifying the various groups with potential interest in the study, but the
evaluator also needs to touch base with the potential audiences and think
about the evaluation within the relevant social context in order to identify
the full range of legitimate audiences. The client and other audiences need

to identify the purpose of the study — that is, indicate what information they need and how they plan to use it — and the evaluator needs to pursue clarifying questions in order to sort out different (perhaps conflicting) purposes and to get the client to assign priorities. The evaluator needs to indicate what general type(s) of study (context, input, process, and/or product) seems needed, and the client should confirm this general choice or help to modify it. In rounding out the charge, the evaluator needs to make clear that the evaluation will be conditioned to meet a certain set of standards, and the client should be asked to help select and assign priorities to the applicable standards.

Basically, the plan for obtaining information should be worked out by the evaluator, but it should be subjected to careful review by the client and modified accordingly. The evaluator should provide an overview of the general strategy to be employed (e.g., survey, case study, site visitation, advocacy teams, goal-free search for effects, adversary hearings, or field experiment) and technical plans for collecting, organizing, and analyzing the needed information. While the clients should at least react to the technical plans, they should exert a major influence in deciding how the findings will be interpreted (e.g., against objectives, against the results of prior needs assessments, based on the evaluator's professional judgment, or through some type of formal group process). The evaluator and client should anticipate that the plan for obtaining information will likely change and expand during the course of the evaluation, as new audiences are identified and information requirements change.

The part of the evaluation design devoted to reporting results should be geared to promote utilization. The client and audience should be involved in projecting the contents and timing of needed reports. They should also assist in planning how the results will be disseminated (organized, displayed, delivered, reviewed, revised, and documented for later use). Moreover, the client and evaluator should seriously consider whether the evaluator might play an important role, beyond the delivery of the final report, in helping the client and audience to apply the findings to their work. Overall, the plan for reporting should be directed to promote impact through whatever means seem appropriate (for example, oral reports and hearings, multiple reports targeted to specified audiences, press releases, sociodramas to portray and explore the findings, and workshops aimed at applying the findings).

The final part of the design, the plan for administering the study, is oriented toward operationalizing the conceptual and technical plans. The evaluator needs to identify and schedule the evaluation tasks, consistent with the client's needs and in consideration of the relevant practical constraints. Staff who will carry out the evaluation work and special resources (such as office space and data-processing facilities) need to be identified; and the client needs to assure that the proposed personnel have the necessary level of credibility as viewed by the audiences. The evaluator and client need to agree on how the evaluation plans, processes, and reports will be assessed against the agreed-upon standards. They also should agree on a mechanism by which periodically to review, update, and document the evolving evaluation design. They need to lay out a realistic budget. And, in my view, they should summarize and formalize their general agreements about the form and function of the evaluation in a memorandum of agreement or a contract.

The foregoing discussion of table 6–4 has been necessarily general, but it indicates that designing an evaluation is a complex and ongoing task. It recommends continued collaboration between evaluator and client and emphasizes the importance of evolving the evaluation design in order to serve emerging information requirements. Also, it emphasizes the need to maintain professional integrity in the evaluation work.

Metaevaluation and Standards

This latter point leads to a consideration of the need to evaluate evaluations. If evaluations are to provide proper guidance, the evaluations themselves must be sound. Among other considerations, they must be focused on the right questions, accurate in their portrayals, free from bias, understandable, and fair to those whose work is under examination. Assessing evaluations against such considerations is addressed in the literature under the topic of metaevaluation (Scriven, 1972; Stufflebeam, 1975), which encompasses the criteria, process, and techniques used to evaluate evaluations.

If evaluators and their clients are to employ and use the results of metaevaluations effectively, they must be in accord about the criteria for assessing the evaluations. Until recently, the determination of such criteria depended on the personal views and negotiations of the various evaluators and their clients. Recently, however, a major resource for identifying widely shared principles of sound evaluation was developed. This is the *Standards for Evaluations of Education Program, Projects, and Materials* (Joint Committee, 1981), referred to in unit 1. Over a period of five years, a committee that I was privileged to chair, representing 12 professional organizations, developed these *Standards*.

Metaevaluations carried out both in this country and others using the *Standards* as criteria for judgments indicate that the contents of the *Standards* form a very substantial basis for metaevaluations. If an evaluator (or evaluation team) makes sensible use of the *Standards* in conjunction with clients both before and after an evaluation study, a sound and convincing evaluation should result. Such an application of the *Standards* helps to ensure that the final evaluation report is useful, feasible, proper, and valid.

Conclusion

Michael Scriven once said that "evaluation is nervous making," and it is. I have often been reminded of the Biblical warning "Judge not, lest ye be judged."

But evaluation is also a necessary concomitant of improvement. We cannot make our programs better unless we know where they are weak and strong and unless we become aware of better means. We cannot be sure that our goals are worthy unless we can match them to the needs of the people they are intended to serve. We cannot plan effectively if we are unaware of options and their relative merits. And we cannot convince our constituents that we have done good work and deserve continued support unless we can show them evidence that we have done what we promised and have produced beneficial results. For these and other reasons public servants must subject their work to competent evaluation. It must help them sort out the good from the bad, point the way to needed improvements, be accountable to their sponsors and clients, and gain a better understanding of their field.

This unit has stressed the improvement function of evaluation. It has updated the CIPP model, shown how it was developed, contrasted it to other approaches, shown how it can be used to guide improvement efforts and serve accountability needs, and explained its main concepts. It has provided general guidelines for designing evaluation studies. Moreover, by referencing the *Standards for Evaluations of Educational Programs, Projects, and Materials* (Joint Committee, 1981), the module has cast the CIPP model within what appears to be an emerging consensus about what constitutes good and beneficial evaluation.

Knowledge Test for Unit 6

This knowledge test contains sixteen multiple-choice questions. The purpose of these questions is to help you determine whether you have achieved the knowledge objectives of this unit. For each question, select the response you consider best. And then compare your choice with the explanation for the correct and incorrect choices that follow.

When all knowledge questions have been completed, you will be instructed to score and interpret (and, if indicated, advised to remediate) your overall performance. Then you will be directed to attempt a number of application questions. The unit concludes with a list of "questions without answers" and a list of recommended readings.

Question 1.   In what sequence and on what basis did Stufflebeam arrive at the concepts of context, input, process, and product evaluation?

a.   Context, input, process, product. The development was totally conceptual, with Stufflebeam identifying a sequence of evaluation studies that would be needed to plan and conduct an innovative project.
b.   Product, process, context, input. Stufflebeam started with the Tylerian provision for comparing outcomes to objectives (product evaluation); then proceeded to add process evaluation in response to managers' needs for assistance in implementing their projects; then added context evaluation in response to a criticism that his approach failed to provide for judging goals; and finally added input evaluation since the other three types omitted any concern for evaluating proposals.
c.   Process, context, input, product. Stufflebeam started with Cronbach's suggestion that evaluations should be geared to curriculum improvement and should thus concentrate on process; then he added context evaluation to accommodate his research interests; then he added input evaluation to reflect his experience in helping the Columbus schools' staff to write proposals; and finally he added product evaluation to stimulate the government to increase their interest in evaluation of outcomes.
d.   Actually, Stufflebeam developed these concepts simultaneously after reflecting on his three-year experience in helping the Columbus schools to evaluate their ESEA projects.

Correct Response.   You should have selected "b." This description is consistent with the account provided in the text.

Incorrect Responses

a.   Incorrect both because the sequence is wrong and because the four concepts were developed in response to Tyler's previous conceptual development, practical experience in Columbus, critical feedback from colleagues, and logic.
c.   Incorrect both because the sequence is wrong and because the four reasons given are inconsistent with the text.

d. Incorrect because Stufflebeam did identify the sequence in which he arrived at the four concepts.

Question 2. Which of the following was *not* seen by the PDK Committee as symptomatic of evaluation's "illness"?

a. Educators exhibited considerable anxiety over the prospects of having their programs evaluated.
b. Educators were overly confident in the ability of experts to conduct sound evaluations.
c. Study after study had failed to turn up any significant information.
d. Although grantees were required to evaluate their projects, the government sponsors had failed to provide clear guidelines for conducting the needed evaluations.

Correct Response. You should have selected "b." Actually, the PDK Committee observed that educators were skeptical that the "experts" could ever agree on what constitutes sound evaluation, let alone conduct studies that would help educators to do their jobs.

Incorrect Responses. "a," "c," and "d" were all among the symptoms listed by the PDK Committee as indicative of the illness of evaluation.

Question 3. Which of the following, according to the PDK Committee, is a likely consequence of equating evaluation to experimental design?

a. Projects being evaluated will be modified and refined frequently, based on continual feedback from the evaluation.
b. Evaluation will provide explicitly for the assessment of project goals.
c. Evaluation will provide in-depth case study findings concerning the operation of a single project design.
d. Evaluation will provide relatively unequivocal findings concerning the relative performance of competing project designs.

Correct Response. You should have selected "d." This is the only one of the four options that the PDK Committee cited as an advantage of the experimental approach.

Incorrect Responses

a. Incorrect because experimental design typically requires that treatments be held constant during the period of the experiment and because experiments typically provide findings only at the end of a project cycle.

b. Incorrect because experimental design does not provide for performing needs assessments or in any other way judging goals.
c. Incorrect because experimental design focuses on more than one treatment and assesses product as opposed to process.

Question 4. Which of the following, according to the PDK Committee, *best* characterizes the *limitations* of the Tylerian rationale vis-à-vis evaluating ESEA projects?

a. It offers little guidance for explicitly defining standards of success.
b. It sharply separates evaluation from the process of improving instruction.
c. It generates anxiety through its insistence on evaluating the validity of the developer's objectives.
d. It concentrates effort on assessing postproject outcomes.

Correct Response. You should have selected "d." Essentially, Tylerian evaluation calls for assessing the congruence between outcomes and objectives, as illustrated by Stufflebeam's account of his attempt to use this approach in evaluating ESEA projects in Columbus. Tylerian evaluation often fails to provide the continuous feedback needed to guide developmental projects.

Incorrect Responses

a. Incorrect because this approach provides specific advice for defining desired outcomes of a project.
b. Incorrect because the approach portrays evaluation as an integral part of the curriculum development process.
c. Incorrect because, on the contrary, the Tylerian approach does not "second guess" the validity of the developer's objectives.

Question 5. Which of the following *best* characterizes the levels problem?

a. Evaluators do not properly aggregate data gathered at a system's microlevel so that these same data can be applied to assist decision making at the macrolevel of the system.
b. Evaluators do not determine what information is needed at each level of the system before designing their data gathering and analysis activities.
c. Evaluators do not control their evaluation reports for appropriate levels of readability.

d. Evaluators do not properly disaggregate data gathered at a system's macrolevel so that these same data can be used to answer specific questions at microlevels of the same system.

Correct Response. You should have selected "b." The "levels problem" is that evaluators fail to determine what information is needed by different audiences before designing data gathering, analysis, and reporting activities. Since information requirements vary significantly across system levels, evaluations designed to serve one level will not likely meet the needs of other levels.

Incorrect Responses

a. Incorrect because it assumes incorrectly that data gathered to serve the needs of the microlevel of a system, if properly aggregated, will be sufficient to serve the needs of higher levels of the same system.
c. Incorrect because it denotes a different problem from what has been termed the levels problem.
d. Incorrect for two reasons. It assumes incorrectly that data gathered to serve one level of questions can be disaggregated to serve more specific questions. It also assumes incorrectly that the information requirements of a macrolevel encompass those of lower levels of the system.

Question 6. Which of the following is *most* consistent with Stufflebeam's proposed definition of evaluation?

a. An evaluation is a judgment of worth or merit, that is, an event.
b. The basic criteria for determining the success or failure of a program are to be found in the program's objectives.
c. The primary purpose of educational evaluation work is to promote increased insights into the teaching-learning process.
d. The scope of information that is potentially useful in an evaluation is broad.

Correct Response. You should have selected "d." Stufflebeam's definition provides for both descriptive and judgmental information pertaining to a program's goals, design, implementation, and impacts; this encompasses a very wide range of information.

Incorrect Responses

a. Incorrect because the definition depicts evaluation not as an event but as process of delineating, obtaining, and applying information.

b. Incorrect because the definition calls for description and judgment of a program's goals, design, implementation, and impacts and because it implies that the basic judgmental criteria are to be derived from concepts of worth and merit.
c. Incorrect because while the definition identifies the promotion of increased understanding as a legitimate purpose of evaluation, the discussion related to this definition repeatedly emphasizes the primacy of the improvement orientation.

Question 7. Which of the following *most* accurately contrasts the CIPP model with Stake's countenance of evaluation approach?

a. Both approaches called for the assessment of outcomes, but Stake was the first to emphasize the need to search for side effects as well as unintended effects.
b. The Stake approach is geared most directly to serving the needs of top administrative officials, whereas CIPP is oriented more to the information needs of project staff, especially teachers.
c. In the Stake approach conclusions are based mainly on whether objectives have been achieved, whereas CIPP looks more to whether assessed needs have been met.
d. Both approaches emphasize the accountability function of evaluation.

Correct Response. You should have selected "a." Stufflebeam agreed with Stake's emphasis on the need to search broadly for outcomes, including those intended and unintended.

Incorrect Responses

b. Incorrect because the converse is a more accurate statement.
c. Incorrect because Stake's approach calls for deriving conclusions based not on a determination of whether the developer's objectives have been achieved but on a careful examination of the judgments offered by a wide range of stakeholders.
d. Incorrect because, on the contrary, both approaches emphasize the improvement function of evaluation.

Question 8. In response to his exchange with Scriven, Stufflebeam extended his presentation of CIPP to show how it could be used to serve accountability (the summative role) as well as decision making (the formative role). Which of the following statements illustrates the use of the CIPP model to serve accountability?

a. The model provides information on the needs, problems, and opportunities of a system from which goals and objectives can be derived.
b. The model provides a record of the objectives chosen and the bases for their choice.
c. The model provides information on whether to terminate, continue, or modify a program.
d. The model provides for the monitoring of project activities so that it can be improved as it is implemented.

Correct Response. You should have selected "b." Accountability is the ability to describe and defend past decisions and actions. Hence, providing a record of what objectives were chosen, which were rejected, and why is a use of context evaluation to serve accountability.

Incorrect Responses

a. Incorrect because it denotes not an instance of accountability but a use of context evaluation to assist in choosing objectives.
c. Incorrect because it denotes a use of product evaluation to serve a recycling decision as opposed to serving an accountability need.
d. Incorrect because it denotes a use of process evaluation to assist in implementing a design instead of assisting in retrospectively describing and judging the completed process.

Question 9. Which of the following is *not* consistent with the improvement orientation that is embodied in CIPP evaluation?

a. Evaluation services should be designed so as to provide a steady supply of useful information to the decision makers in an institution.
b. Evaluations should be used mainly to help ensure that programs continually improve their services.
c. In order to be accepted and used evaluations must begin with the assumption that the program to be looked at is basically worthy and, at worst, is in need of improvement.
d. In order to help with the improvement of services, evaluations should help decision makers to allocate available resources to those programs that will best serve the needs of the institution's clients.

Correct Response. You should have selected "c." On the contrary, the CIPP orientation assumes that an institution's improvement efforts will be enhanced by identifying and promoting the demise of unneeded or hopelessly flawed programs, since such practice frees resources for allocation to more worthy efforts.

Incorrect Responses

a. Consistent with CIPP because CIPP is centered not so much on conducting individual studies but on providing ongoing evaluation services in the context of an institution's full array of needs and programs.
b. Consistent with CIPP because while Stufflebeam identified accountability and promoting increased understanding of the involved phenomena as appropriate purposes of evaluation, he emphasized that the main purpose of evaluation work should be to help improve services to clients.
d. Consistent with CIPP because Stufflebeam defined the improvement function as involving both the improvement of services and allocation of resources to the most worthy and meritorious programs.

Question 10.   Which of the following is *not* consistent with Stufflebeam's characterization of context, input, process, and product evaluation within the context of an institution's efforts to improve its services (see figure 6–1)?

a. CIPP evaluation is properly seen as a problem-solving device.
b. To ensure that the full range of information needs in an institution are met, all programs should be subjected to context, input, process, and product evaluation on some cyclical basis.
c. The conduct of any particular evaluation study can be justified only if it would add needed information beyond what already exists.
d. Evaluators should assume that while their efforts may promote more rationality in institutional decision making, decisions to commence, continue, and/or abort improvement efforts necessarily will be influenced by a wide range of rational and irrational concerns that extend far beyond their purview and control.

Correct Response.   You should have selected "b." In his discussion of figure 6–1, Stufflebeam emphasized that context, input, process, and/or product evaluation should be conducted only when they would contribute to serving an institution's marginal needs for evaluation.

Incorrect Responses

a. Consistent with Stufflebeam's characterization of CIPP, since figure 6–1 and the associated discussion mainly analyze how context, input, process, and product evaluations can be used to identify and address problems.

c.   Consistent with Stufflebeam's view because he assumed that evaluation is pervasive in institutional programs and that specialized evaluation services are best directed to help their clients to meet their marginal needs for evaluative information.
d.   Consistent with Stufflebeam's view because figure 6-1 allows for aborting programs and program evaluation efforts at any point, irrespective of need or results.

Question 11.   Assume that a board of education has decided to develop a new middle school facility and has defined the specifications for this building. According to the CIPP model, what type of evaluation should be conducted to assist in selecting an appropriate architectural design?

a.   Context evaluation.
b.   Input evaluation.
c.   Process evaluation.
d.   Product evaluation.

Correct Response.   You should have selected "b." Input evaluations identify and assess the relative merits of alternative plans for bringing about some desired change.

Incorrect Responses

a.   Incorrect because context evaluation appropriately would have been involved in determining the need and specifications for the new building.
c.   Incorrect because process evaluation appropriately would be applied to monitoring and judging the implementation of the selected architectural plan as opposed to choosing it in the first place.
d.   Incorrect because product evaluation does not assist in the initial choice of a plan, but assesses its effects once it has been chosen and implemented.

Question 12.   Which of the following is *most* consistent with Stufflebeam's recommended uses of process evaluation?

a.   To assess progress in carrying out a program of work and also to consider why the project's outcomes turn out as they do.
b.   To identify and compare competing plans for achieving a given set of objectives and also to be accountable for choosing one course of action over other possibilities.
c.   To reformulate goals and priorities and also to select schools and/or programs for priority attention.

d. To decide whether an improvement effort is worth continuing or extending into other settings.

Correct Response.   You should have selected "a." The main use of process evaluation, according to Stufflebeam, is to aid staff to carry out a program; one of several other uses is to help interpret product evaluation findings.

Incorrect Responses

b. Incorrect because these are proposed uses of input evaluations.
c. Incorrect because these are proposed uses of context evaluations.
d. Incorrect because these are proposed uses of product evaluations.

Question 13.   Which of the following is *most* consistent with Stufflebeam's methodological recommendations for conducting context evaluations?

a. The process should involve continued interaction between evaluator and client. Their communications should be focused on identifying and reviewing the implementation of key program activities.
b. This type of study may appropriately involve comparison of the outcomes of a project (as assessed by tests, rating scales, or judgment of work products) to certain standards (such as assessed needs, defined competencies, or specified objectives).
c. This type of study may appropriately employ special teams that are charged to prepare competing plans by which to address a specified set of needs.
d. This type of study may start with interviews and hearings focused on hypothesizing strengths, weaknesses, and problems, followed by surveys and case studies directed at diagnosing needs and problems.

Correct Response.   You should have selected "d." These are among the unique suggestions offered for focusing and conducting context evaluation studies.

Incorrect Responses

a. Incorrect because these suggestions are associated mainly with process evaluations.
b. Incorrect because the focus on the outcomes of a given project identifies these suggestions as applying most closely to product evaluations.
c. Incorrect because the advocacy team technique applies uniquely to input evaluations.

Question 14. Which of the following is *not* consistent with Stufflebeam's description of the advocacy team technique?

a. It is mainly applicable when several solutions to a given problem have been developed, packaged, and made available for purchase.
b. It provides a forum in which representatives of historically antagonistic groups can compete in a constructive search for and a fair assessment of competing program proposals.
c. It has a constructive orientation since advocacy teams are charged to create novel solutions to specified problems as opposed to attacking some existing or proposed strategy.
d. The reports delivered by advocacy teams are subjected to some type of independent assessment.

Correct Response. You should have selected "a." On the contrary, this technique was designed specifically for situations in which existing solution strategies are judged to be inadequate.

Incorrect Responses

b. Consistent with the discussion because the technique does provide a forum that exploits bias and competition in a constructive search for alternatives.
c. Consistent because the teams are directed not to attack each other's proposals but to create and flesh out the best alternative proposals they can.
d. Consistent because the advocacy team reports are rated by a special panel against prespecified criteria and, sometimes, subjected to comparative field tests.

Question 15. Which of the following is *most* consistent with Stufflebeam's conception of evaluation design?

a. Designing evaluations involves a process of preliminary planning and subsequent modification and fleshing out of the evaluation procedures.
b. The choices to be made in formulating an evaluation design may be subsumed under sample selection, instrumentation, and analysis.
c. When first planning an evaluation, the evaluator should suggest an optimal design, then negotiate only those deviations that are deemed essential given time and resource constraints.
d. The evaluator should emphasize early on in negotiations with the client that the evaluation design, once determined, should be implemented as

precisely as possible so as to ensure that findings can be unambiguously interpreted.

Correct Response.   You should have selected "a." Stufflebeam identified the evaluator's dilemma in needing both to project procedures, work schedules, and resource requirements in advance and periodically to revise the evaluation plan so as to respond to emergent information requirements. To address this dilemma, he said, evaluators must view evaluation design as an ongoing process.

Incorrect Responses

b. Incorrect because these labels would cover only the technical aspects of an evaluation design and would omit other choices that Stufflebeam viewed as important, namely, clarification of the charge, plan for reporting the results, and the management plan.
c. Incorrect because following this suggestion would negate Stufflebeam's insistence on keeping the evaluation responsive to audience needs.
d. Incorrect because Stufflebeam said that rigid adherence to an initial design would usually lead to serving clients' information needs poorly.

Question 16.   Which of the following is *not* consistent with Stufflebeam's discussion of metaevaluation and evaluation standards?

a. Metaevaluation means evaluating evaluation.
b. Metaevaluation provides a useful means of helping to ensure that evaluations offer sound guidance.
c. The Joint Committee's *Standards* are offered as widely shared principles about what constitutes a good educational program.
d. The Joint Committee's *Standards* were developed to clarify four basic conditions for a sound evaluation.

Correct Response.   You should have selected "c." The Joint Committee's *Standards* were offered not as a basis for judging educational programs but as principles to be invoked in evaluating evaluations.

Incorrect Responses

a. Essentially this is how Stufflebeam defined metaevaluation.
b. Consistent with Stufflebeam's view that evaluations themselves must be evaluated to ensure that they will provide sound and useful information.

d. Consistent with the discussion since the 30 standards are grouped in terms of utility, feasibility, propriety, and accuracy.

Scoring of the Knowledge Test. Having completed the knowledge test, total the number of correct responses. We would evaluate your initial performance as follows: 15-16 excellent, 13-14 very good, 11-12 good, 8-10 fair, 0-7 poor. Mainly, though, we suggest that you use the record of your initial performance to improve your understanding of this module. By reviewing the text material you should be able to correct any misunderstandings that are revealed in your score. For each question you missed, we suggest that you reread the question, then review the text to strengthen your understanding of the involved concepts.

Application Exercises

This section contains essay questions designed to help you assess whether you have understood the basic premises and concepts presented in this unit. We suggest that you answer the questions on separate sheets of paper. Following each question is a sample response or a list of pertinent points that might have been included in your response. Reviewing these will help you assess your response.

Exercise 1. The CIPP conceptualization of evaluation identified four types of evaluation for use in serving four types of decisions. Below is a brief description of a hypothetical improvement effort. Analyze this example to identify what instances of context, input, process, and product evaluation were involved in helping to formulate goals, design an improvement project, implement it, and decide whether to continue it.

A school district obtained funds to upgrade the teaching of instrumental music. A citizens committee had charged at a school board meeting that poor children in the district rarely received opportunities to develop their musical interests and abilities. The board of education directed the superintendent to investigate the charge and to report the results. A committee, appointed by the superintendent, ascertained that compared to neighboring districts, their district evidenced a general weakness in music education, but especially in instrumental music at the elementary level. Further they noted that a disproportionately low percentage of disadvantaged students had been involved with the few music opportunities that were offered. As a consequence, the superintendent and the committee decided to start a music improvement project and to place highest priority on upgrading instrumental music offerings in the elementary schools and on intensifying their efforts to involve disadvantaged children. The superintendent reported the results of the study to the board and received their concurrence in the decision to launch an appropriate project.

The committee next developed a proposal for external funding of the project. They first created two planning committees and charged them to develop independently plans for the desired project. One plan concentrated on upgrading the music teaching skills of the district's elementary school teachers; the other called for the purchase of musical instruments for loan to poor children, employing three instrumental music teachers who would work full-time in the elementary schools, and instituting a volunteer program for talented musicians in the community to assist in the program. The committee compared these plans for their feasibility and their potentials in improving instrumental music offerings, and increasing the involvement of disadvantaged students. They consistently ranked the second plan higher than the first and submitted their findings to discussion at a faculty meeting. In general, the faculty endorsed the committee's recommendation, and the second plan was subsequently fleshed out and submitted to a private foundation. With slight modifications, the proposal was funded.

The superintendent employed two instrumental music teachers (a third qualified candidate could not immediately be located) and directed them to purchase the needed instruments, assign the instruments to interested disadvantaged students, and recruit and involve interested community members. She charged the original planning committee to monitor and evaluate both the implementation and the effectiveness of the project.

In their first report to the superintendent and the new music teachers, the committee noted that it was likely fortunate that the third music teacher had not been employed. They thought the additional money would be better spent on more musical instruments. The music teachers agreed, and with the concurrence of the funding agency the plan and budget were modified accordingly. This is but one example of how the committee's periodic reports influenced the conduct of the project.

At the end of the three-year project, the committee reported that the project had been largely successful. Each elementary school now had a band. Group instrumental music lessons were now available to all students beginning at the fourth-grade level. Participation of both disadvantaged and advantaged students was deemed good. Two of the three elementary schools now had active band boosters clubs. And a few community members had become involved in offering free music lessons as a part of the school program. Based on this report, the board of education endorsed the continuation of the program, and they appropriated regular funds to pay the salaries of the two music teachers.

Responses to Exercise 1 might appropriately include the following:

a. Context evaluation was involved in determining that poor children rarely received opportunities to develop their musical interests and abilities. More context evaluation was involved in discovering that the district was especially weak in instrumental music offerings at the elementary school level.
b. Input evaluation was used to identify and assess two plans for improving the districts' instrumental music offerings.
c. Process evaluation was useful in determining that two instead of three new teachers could carry out the project and that more money than originally allocated was needed to purchase instruments.
d. Product evaluation indicated that the project, in a number of important respects, had succeeded and was worthy of continuation.

Exercise 2.   Assume that you direct an evaluation service agency. Based on the CIPP model, develop a brief proposal in response to the following letter.

Dear Director:

Presently, Valley Foundation is implementing a three-phase program to assist private or independent colleges in our region. The program primarily attempts to assist colleges to improve their enrollments and retention rates, the efficiency of the teaching-learning process, and the exploitation of an area unfamiliar to most colleges at this time, deferred giving. It is assumed that the foundation will designate several million dollars to participant colleges to apply some of the innovative programs to their own situations for the specific reasons of increasing college revenue, decreasing the rate of expenditure, and increasing and maintaining the quality of the educational product.

Given this brief summary of the foundation's program, I would like to indicate to you that we are deeply interested in developing an evaluation program that will tell us, rather precisely, how effective our grants have been. If you feel that your center could be of some service, I would encourage you to explain your ideas and outline a specific proposal explaining how you might tackle this very challenging problem-opportunity.

Sincerely,

Phil Anthropy

Responses to Exercise 2 might appropriately present and develop the following points:

a. The approach we recommend would respond to your main concern of determining the effectiveness of your grants. Moreover, it would reflect a quality assurance or improvement orientation. Our primary concern is to ensure that our reports would both be useful and used.
b. The approach would provide feedback about each project and the overall program in order to meet the most important evaluative needs.
c. The approach would examine and provide guidance for improving goals, design, implementation, and outcomes.
d. The design of the evaluation would be evolved in response to ongoing communications between us, your group, and representatives of each project.
e. We would collect and report both descriptions and judgments of the projects and the overall program.
f. Basically, we would assess your program and the individual projects for their response to assessed needs (worth) and for quality of efforts and results (merit).
g. We would design and conduct our work so as to take account of reasonable resource and time constraints and in order to ensure that our work is as unobtrusive as we can make it.
h. We would work with your group to ensure that the evaluation is conducted on a fair and impartial basis.
i. Overall, we would have our plans and reports assessed for their utility, feasibility, propriety, and accuracy.

Exercise 3. Assume that you and two associates have been commissioned to conduct a three-day workshop in your area of expertise for about 60 persons, and that you plan to employ evaluation to guide and assess the workshop. Assume further that you plan to use the CIPP model and that at most you will have $300 to support the evaluation work. The workshop is to occur in a motel about six weeks from the present time.

List any assumptions that you feel are necessary. Then identify what you believe are essential classes of data for any employment of context, input, process, and product evaluation. Subsequently, give examples of the data you would collect for each type of information and identify the means of data collection. Finally, describe the overall evaluation plan, and in so doing, place special emphasis on how you would analyze and report the findings. Record your response on separate sheets of paper. You might find the format shown in figure 6–2 useful as a guide to the completion of this exercise.

Working Assumptions

	General data requirements	Data to be collected in this evaluation	Means of data collection
Context Evaluation			
Input Evaluation			
Process Evaluation			
Product Evaluation			

Narrative description
of the evalution plan
with emphasis on
analysis and reporting.

Figure 6-2.   Suggested Format to Exercise 3

Responses to Exercise 3 might appropriately approximate the following sample response:

Working assumptions:

1. The workshop will be offered to high school principals to help them learn about demonstrably effective approaches to improving the reading capabilities and attitudes of high school students.
2. The workshop will be funded jointly by the state department of education and the workshop participants.
3. The audience for the evaluation, in priority order, includes the workshop staff, the funding agency, and the participants.
4. The workshop staff will be primarily responsible for the evaluation, but they will engage a graduate student who has had some coursework in

evaluation to assist by collecting and analyzing data and submitting a
final report.
5. In order to lend an independent perspective, a representative of the
    funding agency has agreed to audit the evaluation work by comparing it
    to the *Standards,* and he has agreed to respond to certain requests for
    information based on his knowledge of reading programs in the state.
6. A graduate student in need of evaluation internship experience has
    agreed to conduct and report a comprehensive evaluation of the work-
    shop without any fee.

Given the preceding assumptions, the general plan shown in figure 6–3 is offered to guide the evaluation work. The narrative description to accompany
this plan also follows.

Narrative Description to Accompany Figure 6-3:

The workshop staff would coordinate the context evaluation. Basically,
they would incorporate the context evaluation questions in their workshop
application form; they would read and discuss each application as a means
of reviewing and revising their tentative objectives. In addition, they would
meet with one or more representatives of the funding agency to get a better
grasp on statewide needs and resources and obtain critical reactions to their
plans. They would telephone and send written requests to state officials and
school districts to obtain documents pertaining to high school reading programs, and would charge their graduate assistant to read and report on
these documents vis-à-vis workshop objectives. Finally, they would instruct
the graduate student to prepare a background report, which would focus on
general characteristics and needs of the selected participants and pertinent
needs and developments in the state and elsewhere, and would provide an
assessment of the workshop's objectives. This report would be shared during the workshop with the participants and would be used later in preparing
a final report on the workshop.

The workshop staff would develop a tentative plan for the workshop and
ask the graduate assistant to evaluate it. The assistant would contact directors of similar workshops, describe the proposed plan to them, and invite
them to offer criticisms and suggestions. He would also request that they
mail in copies of the plans for their workshops. He would prepare a report
summarizing, comparing, and contrasting what he saw as the main alternative workshop strategies and summarizing the criticisms and suggestions
that had been offered in relation to his superiors' plan. The project staff
would then meet with the assistant and funding agency representative to review the evaluation results and to discuss how their plan might be improved.

	General data requirements	Data to be collected in this evaluation	Means of data collection
Context Evaluation	Needs	1. Reports by prospective participants of their reasons for applying to participate in the workshop, and of their experiences with reading programs	Workshop application form (1, 3, 4) Meeting with funding agency representative (2, 3, 4)
	Problems	2. Description of statewide needs, problems, and opportunities by the representative of the funding agency	Telephone and letter requests (4)
	Opportunities	3. Rating of potential outcomes of the workshop by prospective participants and by the representative of the funding agency	
	Proposed Objectives	4. Pertinent state and local school district reports	
Input Evaluation	Alternative plans	1. Plans and reports of similar workshops	Telephone survey of directors of similar workshops (1, 3)
	Activities, staffing, schedule, facilities, budget, etc.	2. The staff's plan	Meeting to discuss the staff's plan vis a vis the results of the telephone survey (2, 3)
		3. Review of the preliminary plan by the representative of the funding agency, by	

			selected prospective participants, and by directors of similar workshops
Process Evaluation	Implementation of the plan, level of participation by subjects, level of satisfaction	1. Record of activities and deviations from the plan	Daily meetings with a panel of participants (3, 4)
		3. Attendance and involvement	Observer (1, 2, 3, 4)
		3. Ratings of the process	Daily rating form (3, 4)
		4. Suggestions for improvements	Daily feedback session (1, 3, 4)
Product Evaluation	Effects (intended & unintended, positive & negative, immediate & longer term)	1. Ratings of proficiency vis a vis each objective	Pre and post self rating scale (1)
		2. Judged quality of each work product in the workship	Staff session to review and judge work products for selected participants (2, 3)
	Judgments of outcomes	3. Post workshop applications of knowledge gained	Telephone survey (3)
		4. Ratings of the workshop	Workshop ratings form (4)
			Summary judgment by representative of funding agency (4)

Figure 6-3. Completed Format Plan to Accompany Exercise 3

The assistant would be asked subsequently to add a postscript to his input evaluation report indicating how the workshop plan had been affected by the prior evaluation of it and overall how defensible the plan seemed to be, given the identified alternatives and the criticisms and suggestions that had been obtained. This report would be filed for incorporation in the final evaluation report.

Basically, the graduate assistant would carry out the process evaluation. He would use the context evaluation data as a basis for recruiting a small panel of participants, which would be as representative of the total group as possible, and would meet with them during the late afternoons of all three days to obtain their reactions and suggestions. He would observe workshop activities and record main deviations from the plan, and at the end of each day would administer a form on which the participants could rate the process. During the evening of the first and second days, he would meet with the workshop staff to offer feedback and to assist in improving the plan for the following day's work. Each morning the workshop staff would review the previous day's process evaluation feedback with the participants, identify any resulting modifications in the workshop plan, and, within a limited time period, invite further comments and suggestions. At the end of the workshop, the graduate assistant would write a case report summarizing the actual process, noting deviations from the original plan, and, in general, assessing the quality of the effort. This report would be filed for incorporation in the final report.

The graduate assistant would coordinate the product evaluation. He would develop a scale on which each participant could rate his or her capability with regard to knowledges and skills related to each workshop objective and would administer the form anonymously at the beginning and end of the workshop. He would record profiles of pretest and posttest means and analyze the differences using a t-test for correlated observations. He would administer a form on which each participant would rate various aspects of the workshop and later would tabulate and summarize the ratings. Immediately following the workshop, he would convene the staff and ask them to exchange views about what work products had been produced by each participant; the proceedings of this meeting would be tape recorded for later transcription and content analysis. He would conduct a series of telephone interviews following the workshop and, to the extent possible, would obtain examples of work done by the participants that reflected their involvement in the workshop. He would obtain a summary assessment by the representative of the funding agency. He would draft a tentative product evaluation report and send it for review to the funding agency representative, the panel of participants who had helped with the process evaluation, and the workshop staff. Subsequently, he would revise the product evaluation to take account of the feedback.

Finally, the evaluation would be concluded by obtaining the funding agency representative's metaevaluation and by generating the final summative reports. The graduate assistant would first summarize his ratings and arguments regarding the extent that the evaluation had adhered to each of the Joint Committee's 30 *Standards* and would send this assessment to the funding agency representative, asking this person to finalize and submit his metaevaluation report. Then the graduate assistant would draft a two-volume report, the first to include the context, input, process, product, and metaevaluation findings, and the second to include a technical appendix. This report would be sent for review to the panel of participants previously recruited to assist with the evaluation. The graduate assistant would then call a meeting of the funding agency representative and the workshop staff to review the draft reports and feedback from the participant panel. They would collaborate in finalizing the reports and developing plans for dissemination. The funding agency representative and the workshop staff would then thank the tired-out but wiser graduate assistant and take over final production and dissemination activities.

Questions Without Answers

Four questions have been provided in this section, but answers have not been given. The questions may be used as subjects for group discussions, as individual assignments, or as guides to exploring Stufflebeam's writings.

1. React to the criticism that CIPP is ideologically biased toward an already powerful group, namely, the decision makers. The argument briefly is that CIPP serves decision makers and thus makes the powerful more powerful. Since evaluations cost money, only the powerful can afford them. Who protects the subordinates?
2. Stufflebeam developed the CIPP model and coordinated the development of the *Standards for Evaluations of Educational Programs, Projects, and Materials.* Are the *Standards,* therefore, biased in favor of the CIPP model as opposed to other approaches? If not, are there basic inconsistencies between the two sets of recommendations?
3. Scriven (1970) claimed that in the CIPP model, context, process, and some input evaluations are mainly descriptive and, thus, should not be called evaluative activities. What is your reaction?

4.   Guba has charged that the CIPP model is mainly useful for programs of large scope and is applicable only in situations where there is a high level of administrative commitment, much money to support the evaluation work, and a high level of technical expertise. How do you react?

References

Adams, J. A. 1971. *A study of the status, scope and nature of educational evaluation in Michigan's public K-12 school districts.* Unpublished doctoral dissertation, Ohio State University.

Brickell, H. M. 1976. Needed: Instruments as good as our eyes. Evaluation Center, Western Michigan University, *Occasional Paper Series,* Number 7, Kalamazoo, Michigan, July.

Cronbach, L. J., and Associates. 1980. *Toward reform of program evaluation,* San Francisco: Jossey-Bass.

Findlay, D. 1979. Working paper for planning an evaluation system. Unpublished, The Center for Vocational and Technical Education, Ohio State University.

Guba, E. G. 1969. The failure of educational evaluation. *Educational Technology, 9,* 29-38.

Joint Committee on Standards for Educational Evaluation. 1981. *Standards for Evaluations of Educational Programs, Projects, and Materials.* New York: McGraw-Hill.

Nevo, D. 1974. *Evaluation priorities of students, teachers, and principals.* Unpublished doctoral dissertation, Ohio State University.

Patton, M. Q. 1978. *Utilization-focused evaluation.* Beverly Hills/London: Sage Publications.

Reinhard, D. L. 1972. *Methodology development for input evaluation using advocate and design teams.* Unpublished doctoral dissertation, Ohio State University.

Root, D. 1971. *The evaluation training needs of superintendents of schools.* Doctoral dissertation, Ohio State University.

Sanders, J. R., and Sachse, T. P. 1977. Applied performance testing in the classroom. *Journal of Research and Development in Education* (Spring), *10,* 92-104.

Scriven, M. 1966. The methodology of evaluation. Publication #110 of the Social Science Education Consortium, Irving Norrissett, Executive Director, Purdue University, Lafayette, Indiana.

_____ . 1970. Critique of the PDK Book, *Educational Evaluation and Decision Making.* Presentation at the annual meeting of the American Educational Research Association, New York City.

_____ . 1972. An introduction to metaevaluation. In P. A. Taylor and D. M. Cowley (eds.), *Readings in curriculum evaluation.* Dubuque, Iowa: W. C. Brown.

Stake, R. 1967. The countenance of educational evaluation. *Teachers College Record, 68,* 7 (April).

Stufflebeam, D. L. 1966. A depth study of the evaluation requirement. *Theory Into Practice, 5,* No. 3, 121–133.

———— . 1969. Evaluation as enlightenment for decision making. In A. Walcott (ed.), *Improving educational assessment and an inventory of measures of affective behavior.* Washington, D.C.: ASCD.

———— . 1971. The relevance of the CIPP evaluation model for educational accountability. *Journal of Research and Development in Education* (Fall).

———— . 1975. Metaevaluation. *Occasional Paper Series.* Kalamazoo, Michigan: The Evaluation Center, Western Michigan University, *3.*

Stufflebeam, D. L. et al. 1971. *Educational evaluation and decision making.* Itasca, Ill.: Peacock.

Tyler. R. W. 1942. General statement on evaluation. *Journal of Educational Research, 35,* 492–501.

Webster, W. J. 1975. The organization and functions of research and evaluation in large urban school districts. Paper presented at the annual meeting of the American Educational Research Association, Washington, D.C., March.

Wolf, R. L. 1974. The application of select legal concepts to educational evaluation. Unpublished doctoral dissertation, University of Illinois.

7 STAKE'S CLIENT-CENTERED APPROACH TO EVALUATION

The sweeping federal requirements for evaluation that were imposed on American education in the 1960s stimulated the development of a number of new approaches to evaluation. One such approach was introduced by Robert Stake in 1967 in what was to become known as the "countenance model for educational evaluation." This approach built on Tyler's notion that evaluators should compare intended and observed outcomes, but it broadened the concept of evaluation by calling for examination of background, process, standards, and judgments, as well as outcomes. Stake further developed his philosophy of evaluation during the late 1960s and early 1970s, and in 1975 presented his extended view under the label of "responsive evaluation." This presentation retained the countenance approaches's emphasis on examining the "full countenance of a program," but it broke sharply from the Tylerian tradition of gathering data to discuss whether

Dr. Stake's assistance in correcting and clarifying a prior draft and in providing study exercises is gratefully acknowledged. Any distortions or ambiguities regarding his views of evaluation that remain in this version are, of course, the responsibility of the writers.

209

intentions had been realized. Instead, responsive evaluation assumed that intentions would change and called for continuing communication between evaluator and audience for the purposes of discovering, investigating, and addressing issues. In general, Stake is the leader of an emergent "school of evaluation," which calls for a pluralistic, flexible, interactive, holistic, subjective, and service-oriented approach.

Rational judgment in educational evaluation is a decision as to how much attention to pay to the standards of each reference group in deciding whether to take some administrative action.

Robert Stake has contributed uniquely to the philosophical and theoretical development of educational evaluation. In 1967 he issued a landmark article entitled "The Countenance of Educational Evaluation," which attracted great interest in education. Based on people's reaction to the approach embodied in this article and his work with it, Stake, in 1975, published his expanded view of evaluation under the label of "responsive evaluation." In general, Stake has been developing a particular philosophy of evaluation, along with supportive methodology, that we have chosen to discuss under the label of "client-centered evaluation."

We chose this label because one pervasive theme of Stake's writing is that the evaluator must work with and for the support of those educators who develop and deliver primary education services. Potentially, he sees the evaluator serving a wide range of clients, including teachers, administrators, curriculum developers, taxpayers, legislators, financial sponsors, and the public in general. Different clients get different priorities, and program staff will often get the largest attention. But others always get some, even when principal clients object to attending them. He charged evaluators to interact continuously with and respond to the evaluative needs of the various audiences. They are the clients in the sense that they support, administer, or directly operate the programs under study and seek evaluators' counsel and advice in understanding and improving them.

To understand Stake's contributions, it is useful to consider his professional background and experiences. In the 1950s he taught mathematics at the U.S. Naval Academy Preparatory School and later completed his Ph.D. program in psychometrics at Princeton University. In 1963, he joined the faculty at the University of Illinois, where he taught in the educational psychology department and served as associate director of the Center for Instructional Research and Curriculum Evaluation (CIRCE) under Thomas Hastings. Hastings had brought him to Illinois to do research on instruction, but Stake's interest was soon captured by the new work Hastings and Cronbach were doing in curriculum evaluation. When Dr. Hastings retired in 1978, Stake became director of CIRCE and held that position when this unit was written.

His thinking seems to have been influenced by several noteworthy factors. His early training and experiences in mathematics, statistics, and measurement made him conversant about the application of concepts and methods in these areas to the practice of educational evaluation. As he became increasingly skeptical about the classical conception of measurement and its employment in evaluation, his status as a trained expert in these areas gave credibility to his attacks and counterproposals and influenced his audiences to consider his views seriously.

In the mid 1960s (Stake, 1967), he attacked the classical view of evaluation as narrow, mechanistic, and not helpful. His disenchantment seems to have been aided and abetted by Lee Cronbach, who until 1964 was a professor at the University of Illinois. Cronbach (1963) had argued that evaluation's basic function in education should be to guide curriculum improvement, not to judge completed, packaged curriculums; he had argued further that comparative evaluations of curriculum alternatives based on posttest average scores were neither informative nor helpful. Stake later built on these claims when he argued against comparative experiments, called for full descriptions of programs, and emphasized the importance of subjective information.

The influence of Ralph Tyler, who had defined evaluation as determining the extent that valued objectives had been achieved, was also evident in Stake's early writing. In his "countenance" paper, he advocated comparing intended and actual outcomes, but also recommended that evaluators assess antecedent conditions and ongoing transactions, intended and actual. In other words, he expanded on the thinking of Tyler. This link between Stake's and Tyler's work seems understandable, since Tyler's conceptualization (1942) had been the dominant view of evaluation since the 1940s (and may still be so today). Also, both Lee Cronbach and Tom Hastings, who were highly influential on Stake's professional development, had studied under Ralph Tyler. Particularly, Hastings's research demonstrated to Stake that teachers had little use for the measurements and measurement concepts championed by the professional testers.

Stake also was obviously influenced by Michael Scriven's argument (1967) that evaluators must judge. Stake agreed that judgments must be included in evaluations, but he argued, for a number of reasons, that evaluators should collect, process, and report other persons' judgments and withhold their own.

Another main factor, which obviously influenced Stake's views about evaluation, was CIRCE's involvement in the late 1960s with projects, most of which were housed at universities. The projects were developmental in nature, and while they were open to study, observation, and feedback for improvement by evaluators, they were neither stabilized nor available for controlled, variable-manipulative investigation by researchers. Many of these projects were education for the gifted or curriculum development institutes for teachers. Stake and his colleagues felt that available published tests were largely inappropriate for evaluating such projects. The federal evaluation requirements were in essence Tylerian, calling for evidence that sponsored projects had achieved their objectives as measured by appropriate achievement tests. In his countenance papaer Stake wanted to help projects meet the federal requirements in a manner both acceptable to the government and useful to the staff and other constituencies. His countenance approach reflects an attempt to adapt Tylerian evaluation to meet needs current at that time, and it presents a broad view of the many data that can be used to answer the questions of various clients. Its main purpose was to help the reader see the wide range of data that might be used in an evaluation.

Following its publication in 1967, the countenance paper was widely referenced in discussions of educational evaluation. In presenting this paper, Stake did not intend to offer a model (although many readers perceived his recommendations to constitute one), hence the frequently used label "countenance model." Instead, he intended to provide an overview of evaluation. By countenance, he meant "the face of evaluation, the whole picture, an overlay." He thought that different models (or persuasions) would fit here or there and the countenance was a grid or map on which to locate them.

Major points attributed to Stake were the following:

Evaluations should help audiences to see and improve what they are doing (hence our label of client-centered evaluations).

Evaluators should describe programs in relation to antecedents and transactions as well as outcomes.

Side effects and incidental gains as well as intended outcomes should be studied.

Evaluators should avoid rendering final summative conclusions, but instead should collect, analyze, and reflect the judgments of a wide range of people having interest in the object of the evaluation.

Experiments and standardized tests are often inappropriate or insufficient to meet the purposes of an evaluation and should frequently be replaced or supplemented with a variety of methods, including "soft," subjective approaches.

In the early 1970s Stake further developed these views and published them (1975b) in his paper entitled "Program Evaluation, Particularly Responsive Evaluation." "Responsive evaluation" subsequently replaced "countenance evaluation" as the popular label for Stake's approach. However his new formulation retained much of what he had included in his countenance article. The major departure was that he turned sharply away from the objectives orientation of Tyler. In fact, he presented responsive evaluation as much in terms of its differences from Tylerian evaluation (which he labeled "preordinate evaluation") as in terms of its own unity, wholeness, and integrity. In essence then, the countenance paper had served as a bridge between Tylerian, or preordinate, evaluation and a new and relatively distinct view of evaluation called responsive evaluation. Actually, this view reflects the longstanding practice of informal, intuitive evaluation, formalized somewhat.

Stake has other noteworthy contributions to his credit. To help in the implementation of his approach, he helped develop the adversary technique (Stake and Gjerde, 1971) wherein opposing teams contrive and present the most positive and most damaging cases for and against a program. With Tom Hastings, he served as doctoral adviser and mentor to Robert Wolf, who, in response to Stake's call for new methods of collecting and processing judgments, adapted judicial procedures for use in educational evaluation (Wolf, 1973). He also worked extensively to incorporate case study methodology into his responsive evaluation approach. He edited the well-known AERA Monograph Series on curriculum evaluation. He, Len Cahen, and Garley Forehand started the "May 12th Group on Evaluation," which has survived as an important forum for discussions and debates among evaluation theoreticians, methodologists, and practitioners. And he helped establish communication channels and collaborative relationships among evaluators in Sweden, England, Australia, OECD, EEC, and the United States. The productiveness of this international exchange is evident in the book *Beyond the Numbers Game* (Hamilton et al., 1977).

The preceding material has been provided as background information to assist you in studying selected contributions of Robert Stake. In the remainder of this unit, you will be provided further information about the countenance paper, responsive evaluation, and Stake's general philosophy of evaluation. The instructional objectives, around which the unit was developed, are listed below. Review these, read the subsequent material, then complete the knowledge test and application exercise that appear at the end of the unit. Assess your answers against the keyed ones, and if any of your responses are incorrect, review pertinent sections of the text. You may want to conduct further independent investigation by attempting the "Questions Without Answers" (or discussing them with other persons), and consulting other sources of information about Robert Stake's work listed in the references at the back of the unit.

Objectives

The objectives of this chapter are as follows:

1. To identify key factors that influenced Robert Stake's thinking about evaluation.
2. To identify the main ways in which Stake's conceptualizations of evaluation both borrowed and departed from the Tylerian view of evaluation.
3. To identify Stake's objections to traditional views and uses of standardized tests.
4. To define the purpose of the countenance approach.
5. To identify meanings and applications of the following concepts identified in the countenance paper: rationale, antecedents, transactions, outcomes, absolute standards, relative standards, side effects, contingency analysis, congruence analysis, and judgment.
6. To describe Stake's view of the evaluator's role.
7. To analyze Stake's view of the role of judgment in evaluation.
8. To identify basic assumptions that underly responsive evaluation.
9. To identify essential characteristics of responsive evaluation.
10. To identify important differences between preordinate evaluation and responsive evaluation.
11. To identify what Stake considers to be the relative utilities of preordinate evaluation and responsive evaluation.
12. To review Stake's estimates of how responsive evaluators would distribute their time across evaluation tasks as compared to preordinate evaluators.
13. To identify Stake's recommendations concerning how evaluators should choose purposes, questions, and criteria for their evaluations.
14. To provide the authors' characterization of Stake's view of the evaluator's ethical and social responsibilities.
15. To present the authors' view of Stake's philosophy of education.
16. To describe and illustrate each task in the evaluation clock.
17. To identify Stake's general recommendations for using the "evaluation clock."
18. To present the author's comments about Stake's epistemological orientation.
19. To identify and illustrate the main parts of the substantive structure of responsive evaluation.

The Countenance Statement of Evaluation

Stake's 1967 article, entitled "The Countenance of Educational Evaluation" was offered not as a specific guide for designing an evaluation but as general background reading for those facing such a task. In this article Stake roughed out his emerging philosophy of evaluation.

He chose the title of his article to convey a particular message to evaluation specialists and educators in general. He said that few educators see education "in the round." In particular, he noted that formal evaluations often focus narrowly on a few variables in a program (such as outcomes associated with objectives) and that informal evaluations often reflect a few people's opinions (but not carefully collected empirical data). He urged educators and evaluators alike to recognize the shortcomings of their usual evaluation practices and forthwith to pay attention to the full countenance of evaluation.

This countenance, he said, includes (1) description and judgment of a program, (2) a variety of data sources, (3) analyses of congruence and contingencies, (4) identification of pertinent, often conflicting standards, and (5) multiple uses of evaluation. Fundamentally, he noted that evaluating a program requires that it be fully described and judged, and he dealt in some detail with these concepts before presenting his overall approach.

Description

In considering description as a basic act of evaluation, he referenced the prior works of Tyler and Cronbach. The proponents of Tyler's approach had focused their descriptive efforts on discerning the extent that objectives are achieved. They had further narrowed their purview by using mainly standardized tests to collect their data. Stake criticized this narrowness and supported Cronbach's suggestion that educators should broaden their concept of achievements and ways of measuring them. Stake (1967) advised educators to "implore measurement specialists to develop a methodology that reflects the fullness, the complexity, and the importance of their programs." More specifically, he charged that "the traditional concern of educational measurement specialists for reliability of individual student scores and predictive validity is a questionable resource. For evaluation of curricula, attention to individual differences among students should give way to attention to the contingencies among background conditions, classroom activities, and scholastic outcomes." As will be discussed later in this unit, Stake charged educators to fully describe intended and actual *antecedent* conditions, instructional *transactions*, and *outcomes* and to examine the congruences and contingencies among them.

Judgment

In taking up the matter of judgment, Stake agreed with Scriven's position (1967) that an evaluation has not taken place until a judgment has been made. On the other hand, he questioned the wisdom of assigning the responsibility of judgment solely (or sometimes even partially) to evaluation specialists.

Such a practice, he said, would be unrealistic for a number of reasons. Educators, perceiving that evaluators would be the sole judges of their programs, would be unlikely to cooperate with their data-collection efforts. Moreover, evaluators might be censored or criticized by those among their colleagues who believe that evaluators acting as judges — as opposed to objective inquirers — will make social science and behavioral research suspect. Also, Stake suggested that few evaluators would feel qualified to discuss what is best for a briefly known school and community.

To respond to this dilemma, Stake suggested a compromise position. While he doubted that evaluators could or should act as sole or final judges of most programs they evaluate, he thought they were uniquely qualified to collect and process objectively the opinions and judgments of other people. He recommended that evaluations of school programs should portray the merit and fault perceived by well-identified groups, and he mentioned five groups as having important opinions about education: spokespersons for society at large, subject-matter experts, teachers, parents, and students.

This compromise recommendation satisfied Stake's worry about Scriven's advice that evaluators must render the final judgments. Especially, Stake claimed that his recommendation obviated what he believed to be two questionable assumptions underlying Scriven's advice: (1) that a program judged best would be best for all students, and (2) that local option is invalid if it is at odds with the common good. Evaluators would not have to make either assumption if they gathered, processed, and reported judgments from a wide range of reference groups.

Format for Data Collection

Given this background about Stake's views of description and judgment, we turn to a broader view of his overall approach. This view is represented in figure 7-1. The figure was included to denote the main kinds of information to be collected in implementing any evaluation of programs. Note that Stake did not expect these boxes to be filled in. The boxes merely represented a classification of data that might or might not be useful.

Of central importance are the concepts of antecedents, transactions, and outcomes. Stake commented that if evaluators would gather, analyze, and report information about all of these from a variety of sources, they would more successfully approach the objective of dealing with the full[1] countenance of evaluation than they would by persisting in their attempts to determine whether objectives had been achieved. Each of these three concepts is complex and requires explanation.

Antecedents refer to relevant background information. In particular, Stake saw this type of information as including any condition existing prior to teaching and learning that may relate to outcomes — for example, whether a student had eaten a good breakfast before coming to school, whether he had completed his homework assignment, or whether he had a good night's sleep; also, whether the teacher's union opposed required in-service training participation. In order to fully describe and judge a program or a learning episode, Stake argued that evaluators must identify and analyze the pertinent antecedent conditions.

Stake's second class of information, the *instructional transactions,* includes the countless encounters of students with other persons, such as teachers, parents, counselors, tutors, and other students. Stake advised evaluators to conduct a kind of ongoing process evaluation in order to discern the actual workings of the program.

Outcomes pertain to what is achieved through a program. These include abilities, achievements, attitudes, and aspirations. They include impacts on all participants — teachers, parents, administrators, custodians, students, and others. They include results that are evident and obscure, intended and unintended, short range, and long range.

Stake used antecedents, transactions, and outcomes as core concepts to structure his view of what should be done in describing and judging a

---

[1]In a personal correspondence, Stake indicated that he has been puzzled about the "fullness" business. He acknowledged that "countenance" appeals to fullness of description and judgment, not to make reports longer, but to shift attention away from something being done (to be less full there) and to increase coverage of other aspects of the object. He recognized the need to delimit, to focus. In responsive evaluation, he has addressed the needs for broad coverage and delimitation by advising the evaluator to search out and address key "issues."

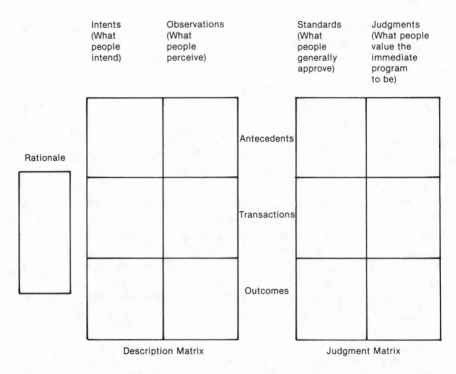

Figure 7-1.   Stake's Format for Collecting Data to be used in evaluating an Educational Program.
Source: Stake, Robert E. 1967. "The Countenance of Educational Evaluation." *Teachers College Record*, 68:523-40.

program. This structuring is seen in the description and judgment matrices in figure 7-1. Antecedents, transactions, and outcomes are the vertical dimension of both matrices.

The horizontal dimension of the *description matrix* is intents and observations. By *intents* Stake referred to all that is planned for, including antecedent conditions, teaching and learning activities, and desired outcomes; he advised evaluators to study what educators exclude as well as what they include under the rubric of "intents" and to express educators' intents in language that is meaningful to them (not necessarily in the form of behavioral objectives). *Observations* refers to what antecedents, transactions, and outcomes are observed and recorded, and these may be collected from a variety of sources and data-collection instruments. Stake advised evaluators to search broadly for the existence of both intended and unintended occurrences.

The following list illustrates the kinds of information that an evaluator might collect as viewed from the perspective of Stake's description matrix:

1. The teacher said that students would enroll in the music appreciation class because they wanted to be there (intended antecdent).
2. However, 40 percent of the students complained that their parents had coerced them to enroll (observed antecedent).
3. The music appreciation curriculum guide specified that students were to spend 40 minutes a week listening to music and 20 minutes discussing it (intended transactions).
4. On the average the students were observed to spend 19 minutes a week listening to music, 3 minutes discussing it, 20 minutes in study-hall activity, and the remainder of the time doing a variety of other things (observed transactions).
5. At the end of the course the students were expected, among other things, to be able to name the composers of selected musical pieces played for them (intended outcome).
6. On the average, the students correctly named the composers of two out of the ten pieces that were played for them; also, unexpectedly, a parent of one of the students contributed a sizable sum of money to help expand the schools' music library (observed outcomes).

While the preceding example is simplistic, it illustrates one basic message Stake was conveying: through studying intended and actual antecedents, transactions, and outcomes, evaluators should be stimulated to describe programs more fully than if they zeroed in on outcomes related to objectives. Stake acknowledged that the boundaries between the cells in his description matrix are vague. But, he said, this situation is unimportant, since the main intent is to stimulate evaluators to think broadly and to give them a heuristic for doing so.

In addition to describing the program of interest in relation to the description matrix, Stake directed evaluators to investigate the program's *rationale* carefully. In effect, what is the program's philosophical background and purposes? Once informed of the program's rationale, the evaluator can use it as a basis for judging program intents. For example, does the planned program constitute a logical step in implementing basic purposes? Stake also observed that the rationale is of use in choosing reference groups who later would be called on to identify standards and pass judgment.

In concluding his discussion of rationale, Stake cautioned evaluators not to overrationalize a program. They should avoid imposing their philosophy and logic on the program. Evaluators should characterize whatever rationale is found in the language of the program staff, not necessarily their own. Although he did not say so, we presume further that Stake would advise evaluators to call attention to problems they perceive in a program's rationale — such as ambiguity, inconsistency, illegality, or immorality.

Following his explanations of the description matrix and rationale, Stake turned to a discussion of ways descriptive information is analyzed. He identified *congruence analysis* and *contingency analysis* as the two basic classes of analysis. He represented these in the paradigm shown in figure 7-2.

Congruence analysis asks whether what was intended occurred. Were the observed antecedent conditions congruent with those that were expected? Did the teachers carry out the directions of the curriculum guide? Were the intended outcomes achieved, and were there additional effects? Congruence analysis essentially is identical to Malcolm Provus's (1971) recommendation that evaluators should search for *discrepancies* between what was intended and what occurred.

In citing *contingency analysis,* Stake argued that "since evaluation is the search for relationships that permit improvement of education, the evaluator's task is one of identifying outcomes that are contingent upon particular antecedent conditions and instructional transactions." He explained further that it is important to investigate contingencies among both intentions and among observations.[2]

As denoted in figure 7-2, the appropriate criterion for identifying and assessing contingencies between intended antecedents and transactions and intended transactions and outcomes is logic. Is it reasonable to assume that the expected background circumstances would permit exercise of the intended instruction? And that the latter would lead to the intended outcomes? Stake observed that in conducting logical analyses evaluators must rely on their previous experience with similar populations and programs and that they might obtain useful insights by studying relevant research literature and, we infer, reports of evaluations of similar programs. Logical analysis of contingencies among intentions is important, as Provus (1971) observed, in guiding judgments about a program's theoretical soundness and structural adequacy.

Contingency analyses of observed conditions, according to Stake, are to be based on the criterion of empirical evidence. Are there correlations

---

[2]In his critique of the prior draft, Stake indicated that these analysis concepts didn't prove productive and thus should not be stressed. We have reviewed them because we think they provide a convenient overview of the approaches to analysis that evaluators usually attempt to carry out, even though these attempts are often unsuccessful.

Descriptive Data

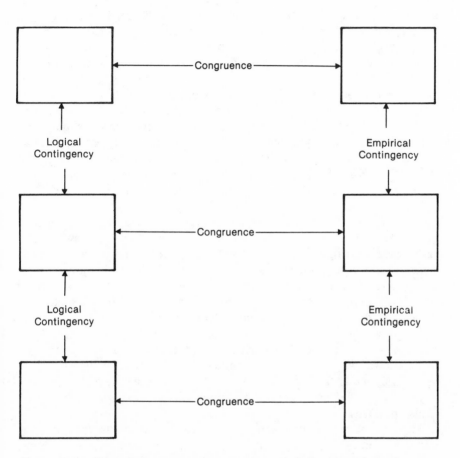

Figure 7-2.   Stake's Representation of the Processing of Descriptive Data.
Source: Stake, Robert E. 1967 "The Countenance of Educational Evaluation."
Teachers College Record, 68:523-40.

between actual background circumstances and observed instructional activities, and between the latter and certain outcomes (unintended and
undesired as well as intended and desired)? Can any of the correlations be
defended as causal? Stake noted that contingency analyses require data
from within the program under investigation and might involve review of
data reported in relevant research reports.

Stake also concluded that the requirements associated with contingency analysis imply special qualifications for the evaluators of given programs. These include familiarity with the relevant theoretical and research literature and prior experience in studying similar programs. Since a single evaluator is unlikely to have these specific qualifications as well as all the analytical, technical, communication, political, and administrative skills required in evaluation, Stake argued that sound evaluation usually requires a team approach.

The collection and analysis of descriptive information and the description of the program's rationale provide the basis for the third major feature of the countenance approach: identifying standards and formulating judgments about the merit of the program. This part appears as the judgment matrix in figure 7–1. Its vertical dimension includes the three core concepts called antecedents, transactions, and outcomes. The horizontal dimension of the matrix is divided into standards and judgments.

Stake defined standards as explicit criteria for assessing the excellence of an educational offering. He observed that school grades, standardized test scores, and opinions of teachers are not good indicators of the excellence of students; and, in general, he said that the evaluations then in vogue did not have wide reference value. He cautioned that in a healthy society different parties should be expected to have different standards. He also cited and supported the claim by Clark and Guba (1965) that different stages in curriculum development involve different criteria. In regard to the complexity of the criterion problem, he advised evaluators to make known, with as much scope and clarity as possible, which standards are held by whom and to take into account both general, pervasive standards and the judgments made by individuals and groups about a particular program.

Stake's concept of judgments is inextricably tied to his view of standards. He said: "Rational judgment in educational evaluation is a decision as to how much attention to pay to the standards of each reference group (point of view) in deciding whether or not to take some administrative action." Moreover, he identified two types of standards to serve as bases for judgments: *absolute standards* (personal convictions about what is good and desirable in a program) and *relative standards* (characteristics of alternative programs that are deemed to be satisfactory).

His representation of operations involved in reaching judgments in an evaluation appears in figure 7–3. While Stake has not seen evaluation as any kind of orderly process, the following task is more or less inherent in the process depicted in figure 7-3.[3]

1. The evaluator collects and analyzes the descriptive information (and describes the program's rationale).
2. The evaluator identifies the *absolute standards* (those formal and informal convictions held by relevant reference groups of what standards of excellence should obtain).
3. The evaluator gathers descriptive data from other programs and derives *relative standards* against which to compare the program of interest.
4. The evaluator assesses the extent that the program of interest meets the absolute and relative standards.
5. Singly or in collaboration with others, the evaluator judges the program, that is, decides which standards to heed. More specifically, he assigns a weight, an importance, to each set of standards.

In contrasting relative and absolute standards, Stake cited a pertinent disagreement between Scriven and Cronbach. Cronbach (1963) had charged that curriculum-comparing studies are poor investments because they do not generalize well to the local situation and because alternate programs have evolved to serve the needs of different groups and have different purposes. In general, he had advised evaluators not to conduct comparative studies, but instead to perform in-depth process studies aimed at helping to improve individual programs. Scriven (1967), on the other hand, had called for direct comparison of a program with its "critical competitors" as the best basis for judging the program's merit. He acknowledged the need for process studies of the type called for by Cronbach (Scriven labeled these "formative evaluations"), but he said they were (at least then) of secondary importance compared to the comparative studies aimed at judging a program's relative merit (he called these "summative evaluations").

Stake saw a need for both types of studies and observed that their relative importance would vary according to the purpose of the evaluation to be

---

[3]In a personal correspondence, Stake indicated that the arrows do not indicate a time passage. The double arrows suggest that the different activities are interactive, and he sees the process as largely unconscious, simultaneous, and not necessarily rational.

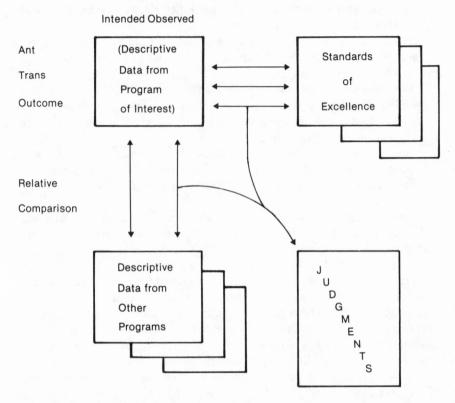

Figure 7-3.   Stake's Representation of the Process of Judging the Merit of an Educational Program.
Source: Stake, Robert E. "The Countenance of Educational Evaluation." *Teachers College Record*, 1967, 68:523-540.

undertaken. That is, he argued that the full countenance of evaluation involves different uses of evaluation reports. He saw comparative summative evaluations as needed by an educator faced with a decision of which program to adopt, but not by the curriculum specialist faced with the task of designing and developing a new program or with the responsibility to improve an existing program. The latter's need for evaluation service would be served better by the formative type of study advocated by Cronbach.

In concluding the countenance paper, Stake acknowledged the difficulty of using it literally. He said that a team approach would usually be required. Specializations to be reflected by the team might include instructional technology, psychometric testing and scaling, research design and analysis, dissemination of information, social anthropology, economics, philosophy, and so forth. He also called for the development of new and better ways of processing judgments and for ways of making evaluations less intrusive. In regard to the last point, he said that the countenance of evaluation should be one of data gathering that leads to decision making, not to troublemaking.

In spite of the difficulties of implementing this approach, Stake urged educators to make their evaluations more deliberate and formal. He suggested they clarify their responsibilities regarding individual evaluations by answering five questions:

1. Is the evaluation to be descriptive, judgmental, or both?
2. Is the evaluation to emphasize antecedents, transactions, outcomes, or their functional contingencies?
3. Is the evaluation to emphasize congruence?
4. Is the evaluation to focus on a single program or to be comparative?
5. Is the evaluation intended to guide development or to choose among available curricula?

Finally, Stake looked to the future and urged that evaluations should be used to develop the knowledge base about education. He urged educators to develop data banks that document causes and effects, congruence of intent and accomplishment, and a panorama of judgments of those concerned with the programs evaluated.

Responsive Evaluation

We turn now to Stake's extension of his philosophy of evaluation under the label of "responsive evaluation." This extension appeared in the paper entitled "Program Evaluation: Particularly Responsive Evaluation," which Stake (1975b) presented at the Conference on New Trends in Evaluation in Gotenborg, Sweden, in 1973.

In introducing responsive evaluation, he noted that his attention was on evaluation of programs, which might be strictly or loosely defined, big or small, and, we infer, ongoing or ad hoc. In considering his approach, he asked his audience to assume that someone had been commissioned to evaluate a program and that the program most likely was underway. He noted that there would be specific clients or audiences to be served and that usually they would include those responsible for carrying out the program. The evaluator, Stake observed, would be responsible for communicating with these specific audiences. These guiding assumptions clearly are consistent with tenets of the countenance paper: namely, that the evaluator's point of entry usually comes sometime after a program has started, and that the evaluator's main role usually will be to provide useful evaluative information to those persons who are operating the program.

Stake identified responsive evaluation as an alternative to eight other evaluation approaches. They include (1) the pretest-posttest model (preferred by most researchers); (2) the accreditation model involving a self-study and visit by outside experts (liked by educators, according to Stake, if they can choose the visitors, but disliked by researchers, since it relies on secondhand information); (3) the applied research on instruction model (advocated by Cronbach, 1963, 1980); (4) consumer-oriented evaluation (recommended by Scriven, 1967, 1974); (5) decision-oriented evaluation (proposed by Stufflebeam, 1966, 1971); (6) metaevaluation (introduced by Scriven, 1976); (7) goal-free evaluation (developed by Scriven, 1974); and (8) adversarial evaluation (advocated by Owens, 1973, and Wolf, 1973). Stake saw the first two of these as the primary models of program evaluation and chose specifically to present responsive evaluation as a clear-cut alternative to the pretest-posttest model, which he labeled preordinate evaluation.

Stake identified responsive evaluation as an approach being advocated by Parlett and Hamilton (1972), MacDonald (1975), Smith and Pahland (1974), and Rippey (1973). Fundamentally, he said, the approach emphasizes settings where learning occurs, teaching transactions, judgment data, holistic reporting, and giving assistance to educators.

In grounding the approach, he subscribed to a generalized definition of evaluation that he attributed to Scriven. According to this definition, Evaluation is an *observed value* compared to some *standard*. Stake characterized this definition in the following ratio:

$$\text{Evaluation} = \frac{\text{Whole constellation of values held for a program}}{\text{Complex of expectations and criteria that different people have for the program}}.$$

Stake noted that the evaluator's basic task is neither to solve the equation numerically nor, as he said Scriven had advocated, to obtain a descriptive summary grade for the program. Instead, Stake advised the evaluator to make a comprehensive statement of what the program is observed to be and to reference the satisfaction and dissatisfaction that appropriately selected people feel toward the program. This advice is clearly reminiscent of the countenance paper, in which Stake said the two main tasks in evaluation are describing and judging a program. In discussing responsive evaluation, Stake did not see the evaluator as formally gathering standards, rating them for importance, and reducing the ratings to an overall judgment. Instead, the evaluator would merely reference — not adjudicate, rank, or synthesize — people's feelings about a program.

The dominant theme in responsive evaluation is providing a service to specific persons (clients). Stake emphasized that evaluations probably won't be useful if evaluators don't know the language and interests of their audience and if they don't couch their reports in this language.

Responsive versus Preordinate Evaluation

Throughout his presentation, Stake repeatedly contrasted responsive evaluation with preordinate evaluation. Our attempt to depict Stake's main distinctions is summarized in table 7-1. As noted we inferred 11 key distinctions. The first and perhaps most telling distinction concerns the *purpose* of the inquiry. The purpose of a preordinate evaluation is seen usually to be focused narrowly on answering a standard question: To what extent were the preestablished objectives achieved? On the other side, a responsive evaluation is aimed at helping the client understand problems and uncover strengths and weaknesses in the program (as seen by various groups).

The second distinction concerns the *scope* of services that the evaluator would provide. In a preordinate evaluation the evaluator would collect, analyze, and report findings in accordance with a strict prespecified plan. The responsive evaluator, on the other hand, would search for pertinent issues and questions throughout the study and would attempt to respond in a timely manner by collecting and reporting useful information, even if the need for such information hadn't been anticipated at the start of the study. In general, the scope of preordinate evaluations is narrow compared to the broad range of issues that might be considered in a responsive evaluation.

Another distinction is in the *formality and specificity of the written agreements* to govern the evaluation. Often, formal obligations of the main parties to the evaluation would be agreed to in writing at the outset of the study in either type of evaluation. However, contracts for preordinate evaluations are likely to be formal, specific, comprehensive, and binding, whereas those for responsive evaluations are likely to be general, flexible, and open-ended.

Table 7-1. Main Distinctions Between Preordinate and Responsive Evaluation

	Distinction	Preordinate Evaluation	Responsive Evaluation
1.	Purpose	To determine the extent that goals were achieved	To help the client discern and address strengths and weaknesses
2.	Scope of services	Meets information requirements as agreed upon at the outset of the study	Responds to audience requirements for information throughout the study
3.	Contracts	Obligations of the formal parties to the evaluation are negotiated and defined as specifically as possible at the beginning of the study	Purpose and procedures are outlined very generally at the outset and evolved during the study
4.	Main orientation	Program intents, indicator variables	Program issues, events
5.	Designs	Prespecified	Emergent
6.	Methodology	Reflective of the "Research Model": intervene and observe	Reflective of what people do "naturally": observe and interpret, particularize
7.	Preferred techniques	Experimental design, behavioral objectives, hypotheses, random sampling, objective tests, summary statistics, and research type reports	Case study, expressive objectives, purposive sampling, observation, adversarial hearings, and expressive reports

	Formal and infrequent	Informal and continuous
8. Communications between evaluator and client	Formal and infrequent	Informal and continuous
9. Bases for valuational interpretation	Refers to the prestated objectives, a norm group, or a competitive program	Refers to different value perspectives of people at hand
10. Key trade-offs	Sacrifices direct service to those in the program in order to produce objective research reports	Sacrifices some precision in measurement in order to increase usefulness
11. Provisions for reducing bias	Use of objective procedures and independent perspective	Replication and operational definition of ambiguous terms

A fourth difference between the two types of evaluations is in their *orientation*. Preordinate evaluators would examine program intents — including especially the objectives, procedures, and timeline laid out in the program proposal — in order to decide what information to gather. In effect they would be predisposed to gather those data required to ascertain whether its objectives had been achieved and sometimes whether the program had been carried out as designed. Responsive evaluators would not let the rhetoric of the proposal be so determining. Guided by certain expectations of what will be important, they would examine program activities and problems but remain free to settle on certain events or questions as most important. They would see preoccupation with program proposals akin to putting on "blinders."

The two types of studies would be guided by *designs* of considerably different types. Designs for preordinate evaluations would be prespecified as much as possible, since the objectives of the study would be given and since the controls, interventions, and definition of constructs common to this type of study need to be arranged at the outset. Designs for responsive evaluations would be more open-ended and emergent, building to narrative description, rather than aggregating measurement over cases. Controls and program interventions would seldom be planned. The evaluator would intend, throughout the study, to discover and respond to those questions deemed important by various clients.

Coinciding with the difference in types of design is a marked difference in the *methodological approaches* used by the two types of evaluation. Preordinate evaluations, in general, would employ the "research model." Here the evaluator usually intervenes with two or more treatments, observes their relative impact on students or clients as measured by a few criterion variables, and tests hypotheses about their differential effects. According to Stake, preordinate evaluation reflects more a "stimulus-response model" and responsive evaluation reverses the sequence. Responsive evaluation is "response-stimulous" evaluation in the sense that the evaluator responds first, that is, observes a naturally occurring program while avoiding any kind of intervention and then stimulates or intervenes by reflecting what has been observed back to the client. In general, the methodologies of preordinate evaluation and responsive evaluation are experimental and naturalistic, respectively.

Accordingly, different *techniques* are preferred in the two approaches. In preordinate evaluation the techniques of choice are experimental designs, behavioral objectives, hypotheses, random sampling, standardized tests, inferential statistics, and research-type reports. Techniques preferred by responsive evaluators are case study, expressive objectives, purposive sampling, observation, adversarial hearings, and narrative reports.

Communications between evaluator and client in the two types of studies play different roles. In preordinate studies communication is employed to reach advance agreements about how and why the study will be conducted, to check periodically during the study to ensure that the participants are fulfilling their responsibilities, and to present the final report. In general, the preordinate evaluator tries to communicate formally and infrequently with the client. Conversely, the communications between the responsive evaluator and client are intended to be informal and frequent. As opposed to being prearranged, communication in responsive evaluation should occur naturally. A more relaxed and continuous exchange between evaluator and client is seen by Stake to be essential, since the intent is to carry on a continuous search for key questions and to provide the client with useful information as it becomes available.

The two types of evaluation also differ in their approach to *valuational interpretation.* In attaching value meaning to observed outcomes, the preordinate evaluator refers to prestated objectives or to the performance level of a norm group or students in a competitive program. The responsive evaluator would not necessarily exclude these sources, but would be sure to refer to the different value perspectives of those people actually involved in the specific program under study. Moreover, the responsive evaluator would not seek a single conclusion about the goodness or badness of the program, but instead would try to reflect all the interpretations obtained from the reference groups.

Stake consistently acknowledged in his writings that evaluations serve a wide range of purposes and legitimately may follow different approaches. While he explained why he usually preferred responsive evaluation, he also noted that there are always *trade-offs* with any approach. Specifically, he said that preordinate evaluations sacrifice direct service to those in the program in order to produce more rigorous, objective research reports. Responsive evaluations, on the other hand, sacrifice some precision in measurement in order to increase the usefulness of the reports for those involved in the particular program.

Our eleventh and final distinction between preordinate evaluation and responsive evaluation concerns *provisions for reducing bias.* Obviously, this topic is a dominant theme in preordinate evaluation. Objective procedures and independent perspectives are employed to ensure that the obtained information will stand certain tests of technical adequacy. Responsive evaluation also has tests of technical adequacy but less easily verified. Responsive evaluation emphasizes the importance of subjective information and deemphasizes the use of standardized, objective techniques, allowing some greater bias. Stake maintained that there are other ways of reducing bias.

Especially, he charged responsive evaluators to check for the existence of stable and consistent findings by employing redundancy in their data-gathering activities and replicating their case studies. He also advised them to promote understanding of their reports by presenting operational definitions of ambiguous terms. But, all in all, Stake has been more willing to leave bias for the reader to identify and interpret.

In table 7-1 we presented our perception of the main distinctions between preordinate and responsive evaluation. Table 7-2 contains a different kind of comparison. In this one, Stake estimated the percentages of time the preordinate and responsive evaluators would devote to different evaluative activities in a typical case. Stake's estimates reflect, so far as we know, only his opinion and may be considerably at odds with other views of reality.

According to the hypothetical comparisons, both preordinate and responsive evaluators might devote 10 percent of their time to identifying advance organizers. But this time for preordinate evaluators would be a search for goals, whereas for responsive evaluators it would be a search for concerns and issues. Preordinate evaluators might spend 30 percent of their time selecting and constructing instruments in order to ensure technical adequacy, but responsive evaluators might invest only 15 percent in this activity.

The greatest discrepancy of all is in observation of the program: 5 percent in preordinate evaluation versus 30 percent in responsive evaluation.

Table 7-2. Stake's Estimates of How Preordinate and Responsive Evaluators Allocate Their Time

Tasks	Preordinate Evaluation	Responsive Evaluation
Identifying issues, goals	10%	10%
Preparing instruments	30%	15%
Observing program	5%	30%
Administering tests, etc.	10%	—
Gathering judgments	—	15%
Learning client needs, etc.	—	5%
Processing formal data	25%	5%
Preparing informal reports	—	10%
Preparing formal reports	20%	10%
	100%	100%

Source: Robert E. Stake, 1975b, *Program Evaluation: Particularly Responsive Evaluation, Occasional Paper Series,* No. 5, Evaluation Center, Western Michigan University; Kalamazoo, Michigan.

According to Stake, responsive evaluators must invest heavily in observation activities in order to uncover and study issues and portray how the program is actually operating, whereas discovery of issues and portrayal of program operations are seldom priority concerns for preordinate evaluators.

Stake estimated that 10 percent of the typical preordinate evaluator's time might be spent administering tests, with little such activity on the part of the responsive evaluator, whose data collection might be mainly through naturalistic observation and examination of existing records. In addition, Stake estimated that 15 and 5 percent of the responsive evaluator's time might be devoted to gathering judgments and searching out client information requirements, respectively; the preordinate evaluator, who is interested more in objective assessments of outcomes related to the program developer's objectives, might engage in neither activity. The preordinate evaluator might not need to search out the client's needs, since preordinate evaluations are assumed consistently to be aimed at ascertaining whether the program objectives were achieved.

Because of the large investment in gathering objective data, Stake estimated that preordinate evaluators of a typical program might devote 25 percent of their time to the analysis of formal data, while estimating that responsive evaluators might devote 5 percent. Conversely, responsive evaluators might invest 10 percent of their time in preparing and submitting informal reports in order to fulfill the commitment to provide continuous feedback, whereas preordinate evaluators might have no comparable obligation and might invest negligible time in informal communications.

Finally, preordinate evaluators might invest heavily in preparing formal reports — about 20 percent of their time — since this is their main means of compiling and communicating findings. Responsive evaluators, having already invested considerable time and effort in providing continuous feedback to the client, might devote only about 10 percent of their time to formal reporting.

In discussing his comparison of preordinate evaluation and responsive evaluation, Stake emphasized that a main thematic difference is in the purposes, amounts, and kinds of communications with the client. The preordinate evaluator communicates with the client before the study to establish the conditions necessary to carry it through, little or not at all during the study because such communications then might bias the way the program operates, and formally at the conclusion of the study through a printed report conveying a detailed description of what was done and learned. In contrast to this characterization of stilted, basicallly one-way communications, Stake depicted the responsive evaluator as engaging continuously in two-way communications in order to learn of important issues that the client wants investigated and, as information becomes available, to provide useful feedback to the client.

Stake charged that reporting by preordinate evaluators is too focused and limited. He said its formal and technically sophisticated appearance causes its client to mistake too easily its message for truth. He said, because of its dependence on mathematical equations and formalistic prose, it is also unlikely to tell the client what the program was like.

To avoid the pitfalls of preordinate reporting, Stake advised responsive evaluators to develop their powers of communication. He said they should use whatever communication techniques are effective in helping their audiences to gain vicarious feelings of the nature of the program. He suggested using "story-telling" (see Denny, 1978) to portray complexity and said that more ambiguity rather than less might be needed in their reports. In general, he said, evaluation reports should reveal the "multiple reality" of an educational experience, that is, the different views and understandings that different participants and observers have regarding the experience.

In rounding out his comparison of the two approaches, Stake said that responsive evaluation will be criticized for sampling error, but that the size of the error may be small compared to the gains through improved communications with the audience. He acknowledged, however, that the preordinate approach sometimes is needed and does a more effective job.

Substantive Structure of Responsive Evaluation

Beyond contrasting preordinate evaluation and responsive evaluation, Stake expanded on his concept of responsive evaluation. He did so, especially, by describing its substantive and functional structures.

Stake identified *advanced organizers* as the first part of the substantive structure. In responsive evaluation, he saw these as *issues*. We infer that he meant areas of disagreement, uncertainty, and concern. He said an issue is a useful advance organizer because it reflects a sense of complexity, immediacy, and valuing. While it provides direction for investigation, it militates against the narrowly focused gathering of quantitative data. In order to identify and address issues, Stake advised the evaluator to become familiar with the program by talking to people, to reach a mutual understanding of the existence of certain issues, and then to use the issues as a structure for further discussions and for developing data-collection plans. He emphasized that the evaluator should identify and respond to issues throughout the evaluation.

Stake identified the second part of the substantive structure of responsive evaluation as consisting of the data-collection format in his countenance paper. In addition to issues, he saw this format as providing additional structure for data gathering. Through the use of the data-gathering format of the countenance model, the evaluator would seek to identify multiple, even contradictory perspectives and to check on congruences and contingencies. The relevant observations include the program's rationale; its intended and observed antecedents, transactions, and outcomes; various standards that different groups believe it should meet; and their different judgments of it.

Stake identified *human observers* as the third part of the substantive structure of responsive evaluation. He underscored their importance and claimed that they are the best instruments for investigation of many evaluation issues.

The fourth and final part of the substantive structure of responsive evaluation is *validation*. Stake charged the responsive evaluator to get information in sufficient amount from numerous independent and credible sources so that it effectively represents perceived status of the program, however complex.

Turning from the substantive structure of the responsive evaluation approach, Stake next considered its functional structure. In discussing how to evaluate "responsively," he said that the approach requires a large expenditure on observation. He said further that there are no linear phases: observation and feedback are important throughout the evaluation.

Evaluation Clock. Given these provisos, Stake presented the functional structure of responsive evaluation in the form of the evaluation clock, which appears in figure 7-4. He emphasized that this is not a standard clock; it moves clockwise, counterclockwise, and crossclockwise in whatever way is required to best meet the needs of the client. We presume that he intended the clock only as a heuristic, not a set of technical guidelines, since in the article he neither explained nor illustrated its use. At the risk of taking the clock too seriously and misperceiving what Stake had in mind, we offer the following interpretation.

12 o'clock: The evaluator *talks with client, program staff, and audiences.* These exchanges occur often during the evaluation and touch on a wide range of topics. These might include whether they want an evaluation and if so, why; what they see as the important questions; what they think of the evaluator's representations of value questions, activities, curriculum content, student products; and the like. Apparently, this step is one means to complete most if not all of the other tasks identified on the clock. A generalized suggestion, offered by Stake, is that the evaluator might keep a record of these exchanges and of the audiences' actions based on the

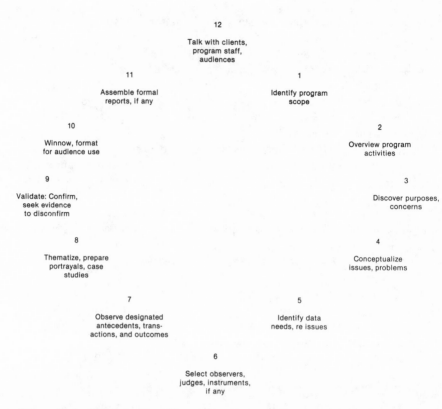

Figure 7-4. Stake's Functional Structure of Responsive Evaluation: The Evaluation Clock.
Source: Stake, Robert E., 1975b. *Program Evaluation: Particularly Responsive Evaluation. Occasional Paper Series,* No. 5, Evaluation Center, Western Michigan University; Kalamazoo, Michigan.

exchanges; such a record would be of use in such tasks as clarifying issues, focusing observations, and preparing reports.

1 o'clock: The evaluator, in collaboration with the client, examines the *scope* of the program to be evaluated. Often what is inside and outside a program is perceived variously and ambiguously. We presume the evaluator would try to bring some clarity and appreciation of the complexities by defining geographic boundaries, time periods and durations, population characteristics, content areas, and the like. In effect this involves placing some constraints on what will be looked at and focusing the investigation. We infer that in responsive evaluation such decisions would be flexible and revisited periodically during the course of the study.

2 o'clock: The evaluator *overviews* program activities. We take this to be a rather unstructured, exploratory, characterizing, activity, since the step at 7 o'clock calls for structured observations using some of the data-collection constructs provided by the countenance paper. The main point of observation at 2 o'clock, we think, is to see and come to know the program without imposing a substantive structure too quickly.

3 o'clock: The evaluator seeks to discover *purposes* for the evaluation and *concerns* that various people have about the program. (The purposes stated by certain groups might not be the purposes that they actually have in mind.) Different groups likely would see different purposes for the evaluation. One way of uncovering any different purposes for the evaluation is to list the concerns of various groups and then find out which concerns are most worrisome to which groups.

4 o'clock: The evaluator analyzes the *issues and concerns* and synthesizes them to provide a basis for determining data needs. To accomplish this conceptualization the evaluator might gather different viewpoints of what is and is not currently worthwhile in the program and what should be added. Also undoubtedly worthwhile would be obtaining reactions from audiences for each new conceptualization of issues. Stake cautioned evaluators not to pander to desires for only favorable or unfavorable information; he also warned them not to suppose that only the concerns of evaluators and external authorities are worthy of discussion.

5 o'clock: The evaluator identifies *data needs* with respect to investigating the *issues.* This would be a rather interactive derivation from the issues' conceptualization, working back and forth between data potentials and problem contexts. It would be aimed at ensuring that data pertaining to the issues deemed most important by the audiences would be gathered. Later checks on the comprehensiveness of these data are needed, of course, and so the evaluator returns to this point repeatedly.

6 o'clock: The evaluator plans the data-collection activities: makes a plan of observations, selects observers and instruments (if any), identifies records to be examined, selects samples (perhaps), and arranges for observations and other data-collection activities.

7 o'clock: The evaluator observes antecedents, transactions, and outcomes. We presume the evaluator would also examine the program rationale and collect standards and judgments pertinent to the program's antecedents, transactions, and outcomes.

8 o'clock: The evaluator *analyzes the obtained information* by developing *themes* seen in the information, using it to prepare *portrayals* of the program and perhaps doing *case studies.* With the help of observers, the evaluator might develop brief narratives, product displays, graphs, photographic displays, sketches, a sociodrama, taped presentations, and the like. In accordance with the procedures suggested in the countenance paper, the evaluator might also perform pertinent analyses of congruence between intentions and observations and of contingencies among antecedents, transactions, and outcomes.

9 o'clock: The evaluator *checks the validity* of findings and analyses. Various tests of record quality are conducted. Program personnel then react to the quality of portrayals. The evaluator might have different persons develop adversarial and advocacy reports regarding the merits of the program and possibly subject it to a "jury trial." He would go out of his way to seek evidence that would disconfirm his findings, as well as to seek triangulation and confirmation.

10 o'clock: The evaluator *winnows and formats information* in order to make it maximally useful to audiences. Audiences should be informed of the assembled data and queried regarding which would be of most value to them. Reactions should be collected from both authority figures and other members of the audience. The evaluator should then design communications so as to maximize available information in order to respond to the different needs of the different audiences.

11 o'clock: The evaluator prepares *formal reports* if they are required. Depending on prior agreements with the client and audience needs, a printed report may not be necessary. The evaluator might submit a video tape of a jury trial of the program or a script for a sociodrama intended to portray this finding. In general, media should be chosen that are accessible to the audiences and that would enhance communication and ensure fidelity of the message.

Description of the reporting step completes our discussion of the evaluation clock. We suspect that its main message is not to be found in its 12 steps but in the general strategy it implies. Stake elaborated on this strategy in terms of its *utility and legitimacy* compared to that of preordinate evaluation.

He observed that explicitness is not essential in order to indicate worth and that, in fact, the type of explicitness advocated in preordinate evaluation increases the danger of misstatement. In deciding how much and in what form to communicate, Stake saw the audiences' purposes as all important. He said that different styles of evaluation will serve different purposes and allowed that the evaluator may need to discover what legitimacies the audiences honor. But he claimed that responsive evaluation can be useful in both formative evaluation (when the staff needs help in monitoring its program) and summative evaluation (when audiences want understanding of program activities, strengths, and shortcomings, and when the evaluator feels a vicarious experience should be provided). He acknowledged that preordinate evaluation is the preferred approach when assessments of goal achievement, the keeping of promises, and tests of hypotheses are sought. He also agreed that the measures in preordinate evaluation are more objective and reliable. Nevertheless, Stake concluded all evaluation should be adaptive, and, obviously, he saw responsive evaluation as clearly superior in meeting this standard.

General Observations

In concluding this unit we have chosen to give our generalized observations concerning the contributions of Robert Stake. In some cases we have drawn from our reviews of his writings, in others we have reflected on our past encounters with him. We emphasize that these are our considered impressions and might not coincide with his own views of his philosophy, approach, and contributions.

Overall, we wish to emphasize that Stake has been a provocative, creative leader in evaluation. He has caught evaluators' attention with his thoughtful attacks on some of their "sacred cows" (e.g., standardized tests, experimental design, and performance contracting). He gave them new frameworks to guide their thinking about evaluation, and many evaluators have seriously considered and applied his ideas. He helped develop a new technique (adversary-advocacy reporting) and adapted existing ones not commonly used in evaluation (such as case study [1978] and sociodrama) to help people try out his approach. He has contributed substantially to the development of naturalistic evaluation and was early in raising the question as to what constitutes evidence. While he has contributed substantially to both the conceptualization and operationalization of evaluation, he sees the addressing of conceptual questions as probably more important (personal communication).

Stake also stimulated his students — Dennis Gooler, Steve Kemmis, Barry McGaw, Nick Smith, Peter Taylor, and Bob Wolf — to make substantial contributions to the field of evaluation. Examples are Wolf's adaptation of judicial proceedings to the task of collecting and analyzing judgments and his engagement in museum evaluation, as well as Nick Smith's exploration of various metaphors for evaluation. In addition, Stake charged his colleagues to think seriously about their ethical and social responsibilities and not to overestimate the importance of their services.

Stake's approach to evaluation, of course, has been influenced by his philosophy of education. He believes that education is organic, not produced. He sees all people striving to excel — but not necessarily at the education the state prescribes. He believes that formal education changes informal education very little, that context counts most, and that teachers are more a part of context than creators of education. He has said that goals of education cannot be other than the variation of aims embodied in the ideals and convictions of different communities, families, and students. He strongly favors local autonomy in the basic governance of schools. He regularly calls on the evaluator to search out the array of actual outcomes, noting standards tailored to the characteristics of the program being studied and of the community around it. He has said that few, if any, learning steps are truly essential for success in life's endeavors, that success and failure are largely overdetermined, and that, in any case, it is usually best not to think of the *instrumental* value of education as the basis for evaluating it. Consequently, he has charged the evaluator to look both to the instrinsic and extrinsic quality of educational practices. More specifically, he has advised the evaluator to note whether learning experiences had good content and were well arranged and to find out what appropriately selected people think are the costs and benefits of these experiences. He has said that teachers, parents, students, employers, and public leaders exercise the most relevant critical judgments, whether their criteria are in any way explicit, and charged the evaluator to collect and analyze their judgments. Finally, he has claimed that the alleviation of instructional problems is most likely to be accomplished by the people most directly experiencing the problems. He has charged the evaluator to consider the teachers and other educators involved in a program usually to be the primary client group, to focus at least in part on things that most concern them, and, to ensure that the evaluation orients largely to their purposes, whether or not it is ultimately critical of their work.

Stake's writings also reflect a relativist epistemology, which we think has undergirded his methodological suggestions. Tracing back perhaps to graduate study in Cantril's transactional psychology, he has said evaluators are "truth seekers," with many of them taking their role too seriously, for there are few (if any) objective truths in education. Instead, he has observed, there are "multiple realities"; that is, truth, like beauty, is in the eye of the beholder. Consequently, he has charged evaluators to collect and report the perspectives of various persons and groups. He cautioned them not to presume that only measurable outcomes testify to the worth of the program; he has said there are few critical data in a study and that student outcomes should be measured sometimes, but sometimes not. He has emphasized that evaluators can take different pathways to revealing program benefit and added that neither written tests nor other particular data should be seen as absolutely essential nor automatically excluded. He believes that internal evaluation is more useful than external and that self-evaluation is more useful than centralized evaluation. Overall, he has advised evaluators to use whatever techniques and information sources seem relevant to the task of portraying the complexities and multiple realities of a program, and to communicate the complexity even if the result instills doubt and makes decision making more difficult. Stake's methodology, as regards both data collection and reporting, in many ways, then, is divergent rather than convergent.

Regarding the role of the evaluator, Stake has said a fundamental task in any evaluation is to determine its purpose and the criteria to be assessed. He has said there are at least seven legitimate purposes for evaluation:

1. To document events.
2. To record student change.
3. To detect institutional vitality.
4. To place blame for trouble.
5. To aid administrative decision making.
6. To facilitate corrective action.
7. To increase our understanding of teaching and learning, or combinations of the above.

He has underscored the point that all the purposes cannot be served by a single collection of data and that only a few questions can be given prime attention in any one study. Thus, each evaluator has to decide on these matters, and so here too must be reductionist and convergent.

Stake advised evaluators not to work from preconceived notions of success. Instead, he recommended that they first give careful attention to "why the evaluation was commissioned," then look at what is happening in the program, and subsequently negotiate and choose the value questions and criteria. He further commented on the requisites of these choices:

1. Lead to discovery of the best and worst of program happenings.
2. Focus on things that most concern the people involved.
3. Not be preoccupied with a list of objectives or early choice of data-gathering instruments.

In a variety of ways Stake has conveyed a message concerning the evaluator's social and ethical responsibilities. He seems to have advised evaluators to promote equity and fairness in education, to help those with little power, to needle the powerful and deter them from misusing their power, to expose the huckster, to unnerve the assured, to reassure the insecure, and always to help people see things from alternative viewpoints. (This advice is reminiscent of the Beatitudes.) Stake advised both evaluators and clients to guard against bureaucratic, parasitic, and exploitive use of evaluations. Finally, he has advised that formal evaluation should be undertaken only when necessary, because he apparently perceives many formal evaluations to be nonproductive and to sap instead of give energy, and because he sees informal evaluation as being an integral part of personal and institutional behavior and regularly capable of informing and improving formal evaluation.

Perhaps this latter point provides some insight into Stake's skeptical reactions to the recently released *Standards for Evaluations of Educational Programs, Projects, and Materials* (Joint Committee 1981). He acknowledged that the advice contained in this document is generally consistent with his view that evaluation should provide useful service to clients, should employ multiple measures, should be above reproach, should be compatible with real-world conditions, and might legitimately employ different paradigms and methods. However, he expressed concerns that adoption of formal (procedural) standards by evaluators would (1) tend to legitimatize their professional service more than their record of achievements warrants, (2) imply a normative, convergent view of evaluation and possibly stifle creativity in development of the field, (3) focus attention on relatively trivial methodological points while diverting attention from major abuses, and (4) perhaps encourage bad practices not specifically attacked in the *Standards*.

Stake apparently has seen formalized evaluation in the American social system as inevitable, of limited value, and in need of improvement. While he cautioned educators to be highly frugal and selective in their purchase of evaluation services, he also offered evaluators a rich array of ideas designed to help them improve this service to clients.

Characterizing anyone's work and writings over a decade or more is a challenging and maybe impossible task. We obtained and responded to a very detailed reaction, from Dr. Stake, to a previous draft of this unit, and we believe this article is a faithful, although certainly not comprehensive, account of how he sees his own work. However, we think his overall assessment of the prior version provides a useful caveat for viewing this one and perhaps a better characterization of his main message than we have been able to provide. Hence, we close with Dr. Stake's summary assessment of the prior draft of this unit:

> You have done a fine job of a difficult task, trying to find consistency in what I say. I have made many comments and suggested changes — no doubt presuming things I said I don't like now were never said.
>
> As an overall criticism, I would say that your effort to be faithful to detail diminishes the overall sense of capitalizing on the experience and informal evaluation already going on, that is what responsive evaluation is supposed to be — honoring context, honoring pluralism — not only as an ideal — but as a constraint on

evaluator's quest for "enlightenment." You've got it here, but the quiz, for example, tells the reader that clocks and grids are more important than accommodating to situation and local history.

Knowledge Test for Unit 7

This knowledge test contains 19 multiple-choice questions. The purpose of these questions is to help you determine whether you have achieved the knowledge objectives of this unit. In each instance, select what you consider to be the best response and then compare your choice with the explanation for the correct and incorrect choices that follow.

When all knowledge questions have been completed, you will be instructed to score and interpret (and, if indicated, advised to remediate) your overall performance. Then you will be directed to attempt a number of application exercises.

Question 1.   Which of the following accurately identifies background factors that the authors believe influenced Robert Stake's thinking about evaluation?

a. His doctoral training was in cultural anthropology, he endorsed Scriven's view that evaluation involves judgment, and he saw first hand some of the difficulties involved in applying Tyler's model to the evaluation of federal projects.
b. Two of Tyler's students were among Stake's mentors. He got first-hand experience in evaluating federal projects through his work at the Center for Instructional Research and Curriculum Evaluation (CIRCE), and Hastings's research revealed misgivings concerning the usefulness of standardized tests.
c. He subscribed to Cronbach's preference for comparative evaluations, built on Tyler's suggestion that evaluators should compare intended and observed outcomes, and built on Scriven's view that evaluators must describe but not judge.
d. He was well grounded in statistics and measurements, studied law and social philosophy under Robert Wolf, and was influenced by Tom Hastings.

Correct response. You should have selected "b." Two of Stake's mentors were Tom Hastings and Lee Cronbach, who had studied under Tyler; Stake was involved at CIRCE in projects aimed at helping curriculum projects respond to federal evaluation requirements (which were largely Tylerian in nature), and Hastings's research influenced his views of measurement.

Incorrect Responses

a. Incorrect because Stake has had no formal training in cultural anthropology, though presently he is quite interested in ethnographic case studies; his doctoral program was in psychometrics.
c. Incorrect because Cronbach recommended against the use of comparative evaluations and because Scriven insisted that an evaluator must judge.
d. Incorrect because Stake was Bob Wolf's doctoral adviser not vice versa.

Question 2.   Why did Stake advise educators to "implore measurement specialists to develop a methodology which reflects the fullness, the complexity, and the importance of programs"?

a. He said, in effect, that measurement specialists had developed a technology based on standardized tests that offered a perspective on differences among students but ignored many of the variables that are important for describing educational programs.
b. He said measurement specialists had concentrated too little on predictive validity.
c. He said that standardized testing is totally unsuited to the information requirements of program evaluation and must be replaced by a naturalistic approach that employs such techniques as case study, observation, and judicial proceedings.
d. He emphasized that the field of psychometrics potentially offers the best theoretical base from which to develop a methodology of evaluation.

Correct Response. You should have selected "a." Stake charged that the testing approach, involving either norm-referenced tests or criterion-referenced tests, is much too narrow to serve as an adequate basis for describing and judging a program.

Incorrect Responses

b. Incorrect because, on the contrary, Stake said that the preoccupation of measurement specialists with the reliability of individual student scores and predictive validity was a questionable resource for program evaluation.

c. Incorrect because Stake advocated a broad methodology (to be used in describing and judging programs) that often would *include* standardized testing.

d. Incorrect because while he did not reject psychometrics as one of the areas from which to develop program evaluation methodology, Stake urged evaluators to look to other areas as well, such as history, art criticism, and ethnography, where language and concepts were more familiar to clients.

Question 3. The main purpose of the countenance approach is to assist evaluators who are trying to

a. decide what things to get data on.
b. state objectives behaviorally.
c. outline the procedures by which to identify, collect, and analyze relevant descriptions and judgments.
d. develop cost-benefit ratios.

Correct Response. You should have selected "a." Stake has emphasized that the purpose of the countenance paper was to portray the range of data that might be collected in an evaluation (while the purpose of his responsive paper was to provide guidance for obtaining those data).

Incorrect Responses

b. Incorrect because Stake said this practice — which had been advocated by Tyler — was too narrow.
c. Incorrect; this more nearly describes the purpose of the responsive paper.
d. Incorrect because the countenance paper is much broader in its view of relevant data and because it is not procedurally oriented.

Question 4. Which of the following is consistent with Stake's reaction to Tyler's conceptualization of evaluation, as reflected in the countenance paper?

a. He agreed with Tyler's inference that evaluators should not judge the developer's goals.
b. He shared Tyler's disinterest in student and parent aspirations.
c. He agreed with Tyler's view that evaluators should assess whether goals had been achieved but charged the evaluator to look broadly for additional kinds of outcome data.

d. He did not endorse Tyler's recommendation that objectives should be expressed in the language of the audience and might be presented, acceptably, either as expressive or behavioral objectives.

Correct Response. You should have selected "c." Stake's provision in his countenance paper for assessing the congruence between intended and observed outcomes is consistent with Tyler's view that evaluation involves determining whether objectives have been achieved; yet Stake called for a broader inquiry involving the observation of intended and unintended antecedents, transactions, and outcomes.

Incorrect Responses

a. Incorrect because Stake endorsed the judgment of goals advocated by Scriven and others.
b. Incorrect because both Stake and Tyler advocated evaluative interest in student and parent aspirations.
d. Incorrect because Tyler's recommendations were contrary to the use of expressive objectives, and also because Stake thought objectives in this form could provide useful and acceptable leads for gathering evaluative information.

Question 5. When plans indicate that 40 percent of class time should be spent in discussion and only 25 percent is spent that way, according to the countenance paper, you should

a. arrange for more discussion.
b. change the lesson plans.
c. gather judgment data on the discussion.
d. correlate discussion with outcomes.

Correct Response. You should have selected "c." Stake has emphasized that evaluation essentially involves a full portrayal of a situation that includes both descriptive and judgmental information.

Incorrect Responses.

a. Incorrect because Stake rejected the view that intentions should be accepted without question.
b. Incorrect because neither Stake nor any other writer on evaluation has offered the preposterous suggestion that plans must always conform to observed performance.

d. Not the best answer because while Stake suggested that "empirical contingencies" among observed transactions and observed outcomes should often be examined, the needed outcome data take more time to obtain than the immediately accessible judgment data, and because, in general, he feels that his suggestions for contingency analyses haven't worked out well.

Question 6. Which of the following questions best illustrates *analysis of congruence* between *intended and actual antecedents*?

a. What percentages of students successfully met at least 75 percent of the course objectives before entering the course and after completing it?
b. What percentage of teachers were judged to have carried out the project plan?
c. To what extent were the students' stated reasons for entering the program consistent with the needs and interests that program personnel had expected the students to have?
d. To what extent did the students devote the amount of time to the program that was required of them?

Correct Response. You should have selected "c." This item asks whether observed antecedents (the students' stated reasons for entering the program) are congruent to the intended antecedents (the teachers' expectations of the students' needs and interests upon entry to the program).

Incorrect Responses

a. Incorrect because this alternative calls for a pretest-posttest comparison (a comparison of observed antecedents and outcomes).
b. Incorrect because this option calls for a check on the congruence between intended and actual transactions (though antecedents could also be a part of the plan).
d. Incorrect because this option also calls for a check on the congruence between intended and actual transactions.

Question 7. What aspect of the countenance paper is involved when an evaluator assesses the extent to which the in-service program apparently caused the improved attitudes toward handicapped people that students were observed later to have?

a. Analysis of congruence.
b. Investigation of the program's rationale.

c.   Analysis of absolute standards.
d.   Analysis of empirical contingencies.

Correct Response. You should have selected "d." According to Stake, analysis of *empirical contingencies* involves identifying correlations between sets of observations (between observed transactions and outcomes or between observed antecedents and transactions) and assessing the extent to which the correlations can be defended as causal. In this question the evaluator has observed certain transactions (in-service program operations) and certain outcomes (measures of student attitudes) and is trying to determine whether the latter were caused by the former.

Incorrect Responses

a.   Incorrect because *analysis of congruence* involves comparing some intended condition with an observed condition and both sets of conditions in this example were observed.
b.   Incorrect because investigation of a program's *rationale* looks neither to congruences between intended and actual conditions nor to contingencies among antecedents, transactions, and outcomes, but to whatever philosophy, mission, and/or espoused principles undergird the program.
c.   Incorrect because reference to *absolute standards* (personal convictions about what is good and desirable in such a program) is unrelated to the search for correlations and causal relationships.

Question 8.   In a press release Dr. Howard Benjamin, executive secretary of the National Schoolmasters Association, said, "Teachers should not use instructional materials that are offensive to parents." In the countenance paper this comment is treated as

a.   hearsay.
b.   a standard.
c.   gospel.
d.   rationale.

Correct Response. You should have selected "b." This is an example of what Stake termed an *absolute standard* (a personal conviction about what is good and desirable in a program).

Incorrect Responses

a.   Incorrect because hearsay is supposition, second- or third-hand accounting, or simply gossip, not a conviction about what is good.

c. Incorrect because one person's belief about what is right, no matter how high his or her station, is not a God-given mandate for all.
d. Incorrect because this statement is presented as one person's belief (hence, it is an absolute standard), not as a statement of the philosophical background and general purpose of a program.

Question 9. Which of the following best reflects Stake's position concerning the role of judgment in evaluation?

a. A program has not been evaluated satisfactorily until it has been fully described and judged.
b. An evaluator's fundamental claim to professionalism is in the ability and willingness to render a final judgment of a program.
c. Evaluators are specially qualified to collect, analyze, and communicate descriptive information, but they have no special qualifications to provide judgmental information concerning the merit and worth of the wide array of programs to be found in education.
d. The members of the audience for an evaluation are not qualified to judge the program being investigated because, invariably, their judgments would be biased in favor of their vested interests.

Correct Response. You should have selected "a." Stake endorsed Scriven's position that an evaluation has not taken place until a judgment has been rendered. However, whereas Scriven said the evaluator should present his own judgment, Stake advised the evaluator to collect, analyze, and report the judgments of a broad reference group having interest in the program.

Incorrect Responses

a. Incorrect because Stake thought the evaluator, rather than featuring his own judgments, is well advised to collect, process, and emphasize other people's judgments.
c. Incorrect because Stake argued that evaluators do have special qualifications to collect and process judgmental as well as descriptive information.
d. Incorrect because Stake emphasized that the best source of wisdom about a program is often the group most involved in it, and he specifically advised the evaluator to gather and analyze their judgments.

Question 10. A teacher reports that all students have written excellent essays on "Air Pollution." According to the countenance paper, such teacher judgments

a. should be ignored.
b. should be replaced by standardized tests.
c. are valuable data.
d. are called transactions.

Correct Response. You should have selected "c." Stake has consistently encouraged evaluators to use judgments collected from a wide range of persons who in varying ways are knowledgeable of the object under study. Often such judgments reflect insights that could not be obtained from descriptive data alone.

Incorrect Responses

a. Incorrect because Stake advised evaluators to collect and analyze judgments from a wide range of interested parties.
b. Incorrect because Stake consistently advocated the use of both descriptive and judgmental data and because he sharply criticized educators' heavy reliance on standardized tests for evaluating programs.
d. Incorrect because transactions refer to the activities that go on in a program and because this item refers to much more: the judgment of an outcome of a writing activity.

Question 11. Which of the following is *most* consistent with the assumptions that Stake outlined for responsive evaluation?

a. Usually, responsive evaluations are aimed at teachers *in general,* since they are the ones who must carry out the programs their school systems adopt.
b. Usually, responsive evaluations are initiated when the program to be studied is already underway.
c. Responsive evaluations are intended to be self-evaluations, and there is usually no need for an "evaluator."
d. Responsive evaluation is a label that characterizes formal, externally-based evaluative activities only.

Correct Response. You should have selected "b." Stake said, in effect, that the responsive evaluator's point of entry is usually sometime after a program has started. Interestingly, this assumption is consistent with the notion in the countenance paper, that the evaluator would look at transactions, forward to outcomes, and backward to antecedents.

Incorrect Responses

a. Incorrect because on the contrary, Stake said that responsive evalua-
    tions serve specific clients, usually the people who are responsible for
    carrying out the program.
c. Incorrect because Stake directed his discussion of responsive evaluation
    to persons who have been commissioned, formally or informally, to
    evaluate a program.
d. Incorrect because while Stake's discussion of responsive evaluation
    assumed that a program evaluation had been commissioned, he mainly
    intended to characterize and provide some guidance for formalizing the
    normal occurrences in informal and self-evaluation. Also, he said in his
    countenance paper that the full countenance of evaluation encompasses
    both formal and informal evaluative activities.

Question 12.   Responsive evaluation

a. willingly trades off some measurement precision in order to try to in-
    crease the usefulness of the findings.
b. rejects the technology of standardized testing because of its narrow
    focus.
c. relies heavily on the use of published tests because of their estab-
    lished validity and the need to respond quickly to emergent informa-
    tion requirements.
d. uses measurement principles to develop needed data-gathering devices,
    but rules out the use of existing tests, interview guides, and observation
    protocols because existing instruments typically do not reflect the spe-
    cial information requirements of specific clients.

Correct Response. You should have selected "a." Stake identified this
trade-off as one of the main distinctions between preordinate evaluation
and responsive evaluation.

Incorrect Responses

b. Incorrect because while Stake described standardized testing as a nar-
    rowly focused activity, he included it along with a wide range of other
    techniques in the repertoire of the responsive evaluator.
c. Incorrect because Stake advised evaluators to use multiple data-
    gathering techniques and sources of information as a means of obtain-

ing valid information; in no way did he imply that responsive evaluation is heavily dependent on the use of published instruments.

d.   Incorrect because Stake charged the evaluator to use whatever is relevant.

Question 13. Which of the following is *not* a basis for distinguishing preordinate evaluation from responsive evaluation?

a.   The former views designs as static, whereas the latter views them as dynamic.
b.   The former is more subjective than the latter.
c.   The former calls for client feedback at discrete intervals, whereas the latter provides feedback more or less continuously.
d.   The former is typically concerned with single value perspectives, whereas the latter involves pluralistic value perspectives.

Correct Response. You should have selected "b." Stake characterized preordinate evaluation as highly constrained to the use of rigorous techniques because of its central concern for objectivity, whereas responsive evaluation features some of the subjective views of participants.

Incorrect Responses

a.   This is one of the essential differences mentioned by Stake.
c.   This is also true because preordinate evaluations usually provide feedback only at the end of the study, whereas responsive evaluators are supposed to interact continuously with their clients and audiences.
d.   This also is one of the essential distinctions mentioned by Stake.

Question 14. Which of the following does *not* coincide with Stake's estimates of how preordinate and responsive evaluators typically allocate their evaluation time?

a.   They spend about the same percentage of time identifying issues and goals.
b.   The preordinate evaluator devotes most of his time to observing the program, administering tests, learning client needs, and preparing informal reports.
c.   The responsive evaluator concentrates his efforts on observing the program, gathering subjective information, and issuing reports.
d.   A major difference is that the preordinate evaluator spends much more time preparing instruments than does the responsive evaluator.

Correct Response. You should have selected "b." Stake estimated that the preordinate evaluator typically might devote only 15 percent of his time to all of these tasks combined. Most of the preordinate evaluator's time typically might be allocated to activities associated with obtaining, analyzing, and reporting formal data.

Incorrect Responses

a. It does coincide with Stake's estimates because he estimated that both might spend 10 percent of their time in identifying issues and goals.
c. It coincides with Stake's view because he estimated that the responsive evaluator might devote 65 percent of his time to these activities.
d. It does agree with Stake's analysis since he estimated that the preordinate evaluator might devote 30 percent of his time to preparing instruments, whereas the responsive evaluator might devote 15 percent of his time to this activity.

Question 15. Which of the following is *not* consistent with Stake's advice to evaluators on how they should decide on the purposes to be served, questions to be addressed, and data to be obtained?

a. The evaluator should choose the value questions and criteria only after considering why the evaluation was commissioned and finding out what is happening in the program.
b. The evaluator should focus on questions and criteria that both lead to discovery of the best and worst of program happenings and focus on things that most concern the people involved.
c. The evaluator should not restrict the focus of study but instead should address the full range of purposes and questions that are of interest to the audience.
d. The evaluator should consider that there are a variety of purposes that might be served by an evaluation, but in any given study he should restrict his attention to one or a few of the purposes of interest to the audiences.

Correct Response. You should have selected "c." Stake observed that not all potentially relevant purposes for an evaluation could be served by a single collection of data, that only a few of the potentially interesting questions could be given prime attention in any one study, and that the evaluator, therefore, must be selective in specifying purposes and questions.

Incorrect Responses

a. Essentially this is the advice Stake gave to evaluators regarding how they should go about choosing the purposes, questions, and criteria to be addressed in a given study.
b. These are the criteria that Stake offered for assessing alternative questions and criteria that an evaluator might choose to guide a particular study.
d. Whereas Stake advised evaluators to search out and address issues continually during the course of a study, he also advised evaluators to place realistic constraints on the purposes to be served by any particular study.

Question 16. Which of the following is *not* consistent with the author's characterization of Stake's views regarding the evaluator's social and ethical responsibilities?

a. Evaluators should be keenly sensitive to issues of equity and fairness in education.
b. Evaluators should adopt and adhere to formal standards of sound evaluation practice.
c. The evaluator should honor and portray the multiple value perspectives of the persons and groups who are involved and interested in the program being studied.
d. Evaluators should help their clients consider avoiding a formal evaluation.

Correct Response. You should have selected "b." Stake argued against the adoption of formal standards of evaluation.

Incorrect Responses

a. Stake viewed this to be one of an evaluator's social responsibilities.
c. Stake's writings consistently reflect a philosophy of pluralism.
d. This statement is consistent with Stake's recommendation that formal evaluations should be undertaken only when they are clearly likely to justify their cost and bother.

Question 17. Which of the following is *most* consistent with the authors' characterization of Stake's philosophy of education?

a. The purpose of education generally is to pass on culture and help maintain a national identity.

b.   Local interests must be determined and constrained by the common interest.
c.   Education must always be viewed as a means to some practical end.
d.   Instructional problems are most likely to be solved by the people most directly experiencing the problems.

Correct Response. You should have selected "d." Stake said that such persons exercise the most critical judgments, are the ones most likely to alleviate instructional problems, and therefore should be considered by evaluators as their primary clients.

Incorrect Responses

a.   Incorrect because Stake said that the generally agreed-upon purpose of education is excellence. He sees the higher aims of education as service and provisioning of respect and internal integrity.
b.   Incorrect because Stake said this position embodies the questionable assumption that a program judged best is best for all people. In opposition to this position, Stake advocated a pluralistic approach to evaluation.
c.   Incorrect because Stake said it's not always best to evaluate a program based on its *instrumental* value; he implied that in some cases it might be more appropriate to look at its intrinsic value.

Question 18.   Which of the following is *most* consistent with the general advice that Stake offered for implementing the evaluation clock?

a.   The evaluator should strive to make his messages to his various audiences explicit.
b.   Evaluation can and should be a fairly straightforward, step-by-step process.
c.   The evaluator should employ subjective approaches to collecting, analyzing, and reporting information and should avoid the use of such narrow, artificial, and so-called objective techniques as standardized testing and rating scales.
d.   The audiences' purposes should be given primary importance in deciding how much and in what form to communicate.

Correct Response. You should have selected "d." Stake said that the audiences' purposes are "all important" in the evaluator's determinations.

Incorrect Responses

a. Incorrect because, on the contrary, Stake said that explicitness is not necessary to indicate worth and that the explicitness in much of the preordinate evaluation increases the danger of misstatement.
b. Incorrect because Stake said that evaluation is not a linear process and cautioned readers not to follow his evaluation clock in any consistent clockwise process.
c. Incorrect because Stake advocated the use of any techniques that would be relevant to the given situation; he also reminded the evaluator that he should find out and honor what his audience considers to be legitimate ways of gathering data.

Question 19. Which of the following is *most* consistent with the authors' characterization of Stake's epistemological orientation?

a. The evaluator should collect and report back multiple perceptions of what a program is and what it is achieving so that the audience can see how distorted their views are and be moved to see the objective reality of the program.
b. The worthiness of a program is determined by its outcomes (good and bad). If they exist, they can be measured. But the evaluator will surely fail to discover and measure the outcomes if a great deal of subjective information isn't obtained first.
c. Evaluation involves truth seeking, and evaluators should take this vital aspect of their role more seriously than they do.
d. In general, evaluators should aim at helping their audiences to see an expanded array of questions and possible answers about a program, as opposed to helping them develop a summary judgment of the program.

Correct Response. You should have selected "d." Stake said there are "multiple realities" and that the evaluator should help audiences to see the complexity of a program and view multiple interpretations of its worth.

Incorrect Responses

a. Incorrect because Stake said there are multiple realities, not one objective reality.
b. Incorrect because he charged evaluators not to presume that only measurable outcomes testify to the worth of a program. He advised them to gather whatever seems likely to illuminate the way people view the program, including their subjective judgments of it.

c. Incorrect because Stake said that many evaluators take their role as truth seeker too seriously. He advised them to search out "multiple truths" about a program, helping each reader to come to his/her own informed understandings of the program.

Interpreting the Knowledge Test. Having completed the knowledge test, total the numbers of correct and incorrect responses. Ideally, you got them all correct. For each question you missed, we suggest that you reread the question, then review the text to strengthen your understanding of the concepts involved.

Application Exercises

This section contains essay questions designed to help you assess whether you have understood the substantive structure of responsive evaluation and the steps in the evaluation clock.

Exercise 1. Identify and illustrate each of the main elements of the *substantive structure* of responsive evaluation.

Response to Exercise 1 should approximate the following:

Elements	Illustrations
1. Advanced organizers: issues are the most useful ones, since they reflect a sense of complexity, immediacy, and valuing.	Busing students versus other forms of integration. Treatment of evolution and creation in the school's science textbooks.
2. Countenance framework.	Using it as a guide to collecting comprehensive descriptive and judgmental data about a school district's program for integrating students.
3. Human observers.	Arranging to have a "resident researcher" conduct a case study of a school's science instruction over a six-month period.
4. Validation: ensuring that the obtained information is	Checking whether information has been obtained in relation to all of the

Elements	Illustrations
sufficient in quantity and reflects the use of multiple data sources.	important purposes, questions, and issues that were selected for study. Checking the extent to which the obtained information covers all aspects of the countenance framework. Checking to assess whether each question was addressed by multiple data sets.

Exercise 2.   Describe and illustrate each task in the evaluation clock.

Response to Exercise 2 should approximate the following:

Task	Elaboration	Illustration
1. Identify program scope.	Determine constraints by defining geographic boundaries, population to be studied, time frame, content area, main locations, and so forth.	The evaluator and client agree that the evaluation will consider the "Arts Impact Program" at the Cranbrook School from its inception in 1966 to the present time.
2. Overview program.	Explore the program to develop a general idea of its main features.	Examine the budget for the program; review newspaper clippings; talk to some of the teachers, students, special staff, parents, and administrators who are involved; observe program activities; and ask to see some of the students' work products.
3. Discover purposes, concerns.	Purposes: different reasons for wanting the evaluation; concerns: worries about the program.	Ask various persons whether they think anything would be lost by aborting the evaluation; and if so, to identify the potential benefits of doing the study; and, further, to give their judgment about whether these benefits would be worth the likely costs.

Task	*Elaboration*	*Illustration*
		Also ask these persons to identify any special concerns they might have about the program under consideration. Listen.
4. Conceptualize issues, concerns.	Identify the relevant perspectives; review the worries and hopes expressed by each group; list the pervasive and idiosyncratic uncertainties, hopes, fears, and disagreements; synthesize the information into a list of problems that might be studied; define each problem with as much clarity as possible; and get the client and representatives of other audiences to rate the importance of the defined problems and to interpret them further.	In an evaluation of a university's budgeting process, the evaluator identified many relevant perspectives: the central administration, the college deans, the professors' union, the student council, the board of trustees, the department chairpersons, personnel involved in instructional services, personnel involved in non-instructional services, the office of instructional research, the grants office, the accounting department, students at large, the state board of education, the governor's office, the state legislature, and federal auditors. He interviewed representatives of each group, kept notes on their assessment of the university's budgeting process, obtained and studied pertinent documents, developed a list of issues, and got persons with interest in each issue to help describe it. He then convened an advisory group, representative of the different perspectives, to go over the issues and help him decide on those that should receive most attention.

Task	*Elaboration*	*Illustration*
5. Identify data needs regarding issues.	Straightforward derivation of information requirements associated with investigating the issues identified previously.	Having assigned high priority to issues identified as (1) efficiency of the present departmental structure, (2) obstacles to reducing or eliminating investments in unproductive programs, (3) reliability and validity of formulas used to forecast income and expenses, (4) fairness of tuition increases, and (5) reasonableness of projected faculty salary increases — the evaluator listed questions, information sources, and data collection techniques that would be pertinent to the investigation of each issue. He then got an advisory group representative of the audiences to examine and help strengthen this initial data collection plan.
6. Select observers, judges, instruments, if any.	Based on the data needs identified, the evaluator would develop and/or select instruments, observers, and judges as required.	The evaluator might select specialists to help him conduct a case study, construct and administer a survey instrument, and hold hearings.
7. Observe designated antecedents, transactions, and outcomes.	Here the evaluator would use the countenance paper to systematize and probably expand his data-gathering activities.	The evaluator might analyze his data-gathering plan against the requirements of the countenance paper both for identifying gaps (e.g., there is no provision for studying the rationale of the existing program) and for planning analyses of contingencies and congruences.

Task	Elaboration	Illustration
8. Thematize, prepare portrayals, case studies.	Might develop brief overviews of the program, product displays, a video tape, etc.	Having studied the system used by the school district to "track students," the evaluation team prepared a video tape designed to convey the findings and stimulate discussion.
9. Validate: confirm attempt to disconfirm.	Run various tests on the quality of the obtained information, and get various people to examine and judge the procedures and data. Triangulate Have critical colleagues poke holes in the interpretation.	Having studied the "Summer Remedial Reading Program," the evaluator commissioned independent parties to use the findings to (1) attack the program and (2) support it. He commissioned a third party to "meta-evaluate" the entire study. Reports from all three of these activities were made available to the audience to help them interpret the results of the evaluation.
10. Winnow, format for audience use.	Prepare special communications that take maximal advantage of the available information in order to respond directly and differentially to the various audiences.	In a three-year study of a university's teacher education program, different members of the evaluation team were assigned to meet periodically with the cabinet of the university president, the council of the education dean, the college of education curriculum committee, and the department of teacher education. Each evaluation team member was assigned to attend regular meetings of these groups in order to learn continually of their emerging interests and in-

Task	Elaboration	Illustration
		formation needs and to present findings from the evaluation whenever they become available and might prove useful.
11. Prepare formal report if required.	These might be printed, taped, dramatized, or delivered orally.	Having completed an in-depth study of a district's "Learning Disabilities Program," the evaluator dramatized the results by presenting and assisting interested PTA groups to act out a sociodrama based on the results.
12. Talk with clients, program staff, audiences.	Throughout an evaluation, the evaluator should maintain communication with a wide range of interested parties in order to understand and stimulate their interests in the evaluation, and to get their advice on how best to conduct the evaluation.	At the start of an evaluation of a school district's bilingual education program, the evaluator organized an advisory group, representative of a wide range of interest groups, and held discussions with this group about once a month.

Questions Without Answers

Four questions are provided in this section, but answers are not given. The questions may be used as subjects for group discussions, as individual assignments, or as guides to exploring Stake's writings.

1. React to Glass's charge (1980) that Stake's advocacy of a responsive approach to evaluation is in conflict with his advocacy of a pluralistic stance in judging educational programs.
2. To what extent is responsive evaluation consistent with the recommendations embodied in *Standards for Evaluations of Educational Programs, Projects, and Materials* (1981)?

3. Discuss the appropriateness of labeling Stake's approach as "responsive," "reflective of the full countenance of evaluation," "client centered," "illuminative," and "naturalistic."
4. React to Stake's insistence that the concepts and advice contained in his countenance paper do not constitute a model of or for evaluation.

References

Clark, D.L., and Guba, E.G. 1965. An examination of potential change roles in education. Paper presented at the Seminar on Innovation in Planning School Curricula, Airliehouse, Virginia, October.

Cronbach, L.J. 1963. Course improvement through evaluation. *Teachers College Record, 64,* 672–683.

Cronbach, L.J. et. al. 1980. *Toward a reform of program evaluation.* San Francisco: Jossey-Bass.

Denny, T. 1978. Story telling and educational understanding. Kalamazoo: Evaluation Center, Western Michigan University. *Occasional Paper No. 12,* November.

Glass, G.V. 1980. Evaluation research. *Annual Review of Psychology, 31,* 211–228.

Hamilton, D., et al. 1977. *Beyond the numbers game.* Berkeley: McCutchan.

Joint Committee on Standards for Educational Evaluation. 1981. *Standards for evaluations of educational programs, projects, and materials.* New York: McGraw Hill.

MacDonald, B. 1975. Evaluation and the control of education. In D. Tawney (ed.), *Evaluation: The state of the art.* London: Schools Council.

Owens, T. 1973. Educational evaluation by adversary proceeding. In E. House (ed.), *School evaluation: The politics and process.* Berkeley: McCutchan.

Parlett, M., Hamilton, D. 1972. Evaluation as illumination: A new approach to the study of innovatory programs. Edinburgh: Centre for Research in the Educational Sciences, University of Edinburgh, *Occasional Paper No. 9.*

Provus, M. 1971. *Discrepancy evaluation.* Berkeley: McCutchan.

Rippey, R.M. (ed.). 1973. *Studies in transactional evaluation.* Berkeley: McCutchan.

Scriven, M. 1967. The methodology of evaluation. In R. Tyler, et al., *Perspectives of curriculum evaluation.* (AERA Monograph Series on Curriculum Evaluation). Chicago: Rand McNally.

_____. 1973. Goal-free evaluation. In E. House (ed.), *School evaluation: The politics and process.* Berkeley: McCutchan.

_____. 1976. Evaluation bias and its control. Kalamazoo: Evaluation Center, Western Michigan University, *Occasional Paper No. 4.*

Smith, L.M., and Pahland, P.A. 1974. Educational technology and the rural highlands. In L.M. Smith, Four examples: Economic, anthropological, narrative, and portrayal (AERA Monograph on Curriculum Evaluation). Chicago: Rand McNally.

Smith, E.R., and Tyler, R.W. 1942. *Appraising and recording student progress.* New York: Harper and Row.

Stake, R.E. 1967. The countenance of educational evaluation. *Teachers College Record, 68,* 523–540.

———. 1975a. *Evaluating the arts in education: A responsive approach.* Columbus, Ohio: Merril.

———. 1975b. Program evaluation: Particularly responsive evaluation. Kalamazoo: Evaluation Center, Western Michigan University, *Occasional Paper No. 5,* November.

———. 1976. A theoretical statement of responsive evaluation. *Studies in Educational Evaluation, 2,* 19–22.

———. 1978. The case study method in social inquiry. *Educational Researcher 7,* 5–8.

———. 1979. Should educational evaluation be more objective or more subjective? *Educational Evaluation and Policy Analysis.*

Stake, R.E., Easley, J.A., Jr. (eds.). 1978. *Case studies in science education.* Vol. 1, 2, Rep. NSF Proj. 5E-78-74. Urbana, Ill.: CIRCE, University of Ill. College of Education.

Stake, R.E., and Gjerde, C. 1971. An evaluation of TCITY: The Twin City Institute for Talented Youth. Kalamazoo: Evaluation Center, Western Michigan University, *Paper No. 1,* Evaluation Report Services.

Stufflebeam, D.L. 1966. A depth study of the evaluation requirement. *Theory into Practice, 5,* 121–133.

Stufflebeam, D.L., et al. 1971. *Educational evaluation and decision making.* Itaska, Ill: Peacock.

Tyler, R.W. 1942. General statement on evaluation. *Journal of Educational Research. 35,* 492–501.

Wolf, R.L. 1973. The application of select legal concepts to educational evaluation. Ph.D. thesis. University of Illinois, Champaign.

8 T. R. OWENS, R. L. WOLF: AN ADVERSARY APPROACH TO EVALUATION

Adversary evaluation moves a considerable distance toward the end of the continuum that begins with the Tylerian objectives-performance approach. Developed in the early 1970s, the adversary approach endeavors to illuminate all important aspects of a program being evaluated. Those aspects that are explored may extend beyond objectives originally set for the program. Quasilegal in its approach and structure, the adversary model follows a dialectic process. Two teams of evaluators explore the pros and cons of a program so that its major issues are clarified openly and honestly.

The end point of the adversary approach is to provide decision makers with sound evidence to act upon. Emphasis is placed on better decision making in education. For this reason, the adversary approach, according to one of its early developers, Thomas Owens, may work in conjunction with models proposed by Scriven, Stufflebeam, and Provus. It is claimed that the adversary model more capably meets the information needs of decision makers than earlier models.

There is far from universal acceptance of adversary evaluation. Stances both for and against the approach are being voiced in the literature.

The adversary model for educational evaluation was developed in the early 1970s. According to one of its early developers, Thomas Owens, the adversary approach has the methodology needed to provide information for decision makers to plan projects and to judge their intended and unintended effects once they have been implemented.

Basically, the approach involves the dialectic and legal processes. It attempts to examine openly issues surrounding a proposition by the presentation of cases for and against the proposition. The purpose is to clarify. With proceedings completed, and the many facets surrounding the object of the evaluation illuminated, decision makers have sufficient, sound evidence to make rational decisions.

The adversary model has taken various forms. One of the more conspicuous is the judicial model developed by Robert Wolf in 1973 and succeeding years. This brings to educational evaluation the techniques of a law court. There is no question, nevertheless, of rendering a guilty/not guilty kind of decision. The essence of the concept of judgment is the establishment of agreement in the context of disagreement. Again, the emphasis is on better decision making in education.

You can develop an understanding of the adversary approach to evaluation by working through the unit. As in earlier units, exercises have been set at the end to test your knowledge. The list of objectives for this unit is given next. Study these, read the unit, and then attempt the knowledge test, checking your answers against the keyed ones. Finally, complete the application exercises, comparing your responses with the salient points provided, and consider the section "Questions Without Answers."

Objectives

The objectives of the chapter are as follows:

1. To develop an understanding of the adversary model by
   a. showing the deficiencies of the psychological testing model for decision-making purposes.
   b. examining the adversary proceedings in their legal context.
   c. considering the applicability of adversary proceedings to educational evaluation.
   d. considering the practical implementation of the model as suggested by Owens.

   e. investigating the dimensions of the adversary proceedings as suggested by Owens.
2. To give an example of one form of the adversary approach, viz. Robert Wolf's "judicial model," by
   a. explaining briefly its rationale.
   b. outlining the four stages of its development.
3. To examine the status of adversary evaluation by
   a. discussing arguments favoring it.
   b. discussing arguments opposing it.

Intention of the Adversary Model

Writing in 1973, Owens pointed out that during the previous decade educational evaluation had undergone an expansion beyond that of judging final outcomes. Emphasis increasingly was placed on providing information for decision making. However, much of the methodology of evaluation had not kept pace with the expanded concept and broader administrative function.

Despite the fact that earlier writers were critical of the narrow function of evaluation based on the psychological testing model, the focus remained on the extent to which a project achieved its stated objectives Scriven in particular had emphasized (1967) the need to examine closely both the purported goals and assumptions on which a program is based. If assumptions entail the value of a program to individual students or to society, scarcely any methods existed to elicit this kind of information.

A further limitation of the psychological testing model noted by Owens was its suitability more for research than for practical decision making. While a comparative evaluation may show that one program is superior to another, this information does not necessarily mean that the superior program should be adopted. Its practical utility has not been proven. "Thus a gap exists between empirical findings and administrative decisions to implement certain practices." Moreover, the psychological testing model usually limits the number of variables that are examined. In particular, the easily quantifiable, tangible variables tend to be examined, while the more subtle, less tangible tend to be neglected. For example, the testing of students undertaking a new curriculum gives only part of the picture. Other variables influencing the program such as personal relationshps (e.g., student-teacher, teacher-administration), student attitudes, and community acceptance should be considered. The adversary model for educational evaluation was developed to overcome the kinds of problems raised.

Adversary Proceedings in Their Legal Context

In a legal context, the adversary proceedings were developed as an administrative hearing process for judging the merits of a case in which opposing parties were involved.

Owens (1973, pp. 296–297) has identified the following characteristics of the adversary proceedings as being appropriate for educational decision making.

1. The rules established for handling the adversary proceedings are quite flexible.
2. Complex rules of evidence are replaced by a free evaluation of evidence based solely upon whether the evidence is considered by the hearings officer to be relevant.
3. Both parties can be required before the trial to inform the hearings officer of all relevant facts, means of proof, and names of witnesses.
4. A copy of the charges is furnished to the hearings officer and defendant before the trial, and the defendant has the option of admitting in advance certain charges and challenging others.
5. Witnesses are allowed to testify freely and to be cross-examined.
6. Experts are often called upon to testify, even before the trial.
7. Pretrial conferences of the hearings officer with both parties tend to make the trial less a battle of wits and more of a search for relevant facts.
8. In addition to the two parties involved, other interested groups may be permitted to participate.

Applicability to Educational Evaluation

Writers generally agree that adversary proceedings in educational decision making do not necessarily replace existing designs for collecting and analyzing data. The proceedings provide an alternative method of presenting, interpreting, synthesizing, and reporting evidence. Presented data are considered to be more balanced than those obtained by psychological testing alone.

Translated into an educational milieu, many of the procedures outlined for the legal context of the adversary proceedings would allow structured consideration of important aspects of the program and of its evaluation. Underlying assumptions, goals, methods of data collection and their analysis, and the accuracy and adequacy of evaluation reports are all open to challenge. Both Owens and Wolf stress that the adversary approach keeps an evaluation "intellectually honest."

The legal adversary model is applicable to educational evaluation for other reasons. It enables a wide spectrum of people interested in the program to express their point of view either directly or indirectly (through advocates for one side or the other). Judgments do not rest on a program's original goals, but rather on a combination of these and relevant issues raised by those involved in the hearing. It also offers a method to assist in fair and open decision making. And most importantly, it presents an all-round, comprehensive view of the program, illuminating its strengths as well as its weaknesses. Decision alternatives and potential ramifications of these are aired publicly.

Practical Implementations

Owens has suggested seven major ways in which the adversary model could be implemented for educational evaluation purposes. These practical and useful suggestions will be briefly outlined.

Exploring the values of a new or existing curriculum. Comparative evaluations often fail to specify and investigate the theory, rationale, and assumptions behind a curriculum. An open debate about the "relevance of a particular curriculum to children's present and future needs, social needs, or disciplinary integrity may be a useful step before deciding whether or not it is wise to develop or implement the curriculum."

Selecting new textbooks. A school district's textbooks are too often chosen fortuitously or hastily. An adversary hearing by teachers from a selection committee could inform and enlighten teachers as an audience) about the worth of textbooks; based on arguments for and against each.

Estimating the congruence between an innovation and the existing system. Innovations may be introduced without reference to the wider school context. At an adversary hearing, evidence may be produced citing the likely detrimental effect of an innovation on the system as a whole, thus revealing potential barriers to the success of the program. Decisions could then be made to avert or overcome possible difficulties.

Revealing the different interpretations of the same data by various representatives. Owens has pointed out that a jury could comprise representatives of students, teachers, administrators, parents, and the community. Various members of the jury may interpret the same data differently; these differences, communicated to the decision makers, may very well improve their communication with the groups. Joint decision making could also be an outcome.

Informing teachers, supervisors, and administrators. As observers or participators, educators would gain new knowledge about the program which is the object of the hearing.

Resolving disputes about performance contracts. Disputes over the successful completion of performance contracts continue to arise. The adversary proceedings would help to resolve disputes based on expert testimony from a wide range of sources.

Arriving at the decision to be implemented. The educational decision maker may serve as the hearings officer, in which case his verdict is the decision. Or he may wish to implicate jurors, such as teachers and student representatives, in the decision making. Or the decision maker may wish to consider the jury's verdict as one piece of information to be used in conjunction with others, such as major arguments in the hearing and data collected by testing.

Owens considered that the adversary proceedings would be especially relevant to the implementation of the evaluation approaches developed by Daniel Stufflebeam, Robert Stake (his "countenance" model, 1967), and Malcolm Provus.

Dimensions of the Adversary Proceedings

Figure 8-1 displays applications and dimensions of the adversary proceedings as suggested by Owens. A perusal of the model clearly indicates the flexible manner in which it may be put into operation. The adversary approach is

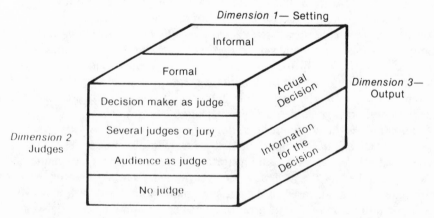

Figure 8-1. Applications and Dimensions of the Adversary Proceedings.

particularly useful when a policy decision involving large amounts of resources is at stake. In such an evaluation it is possible that the following aspects of the Owens cube would operate: formal setting, judge(s) and jury, and information to guide a decision. If the evaluation is to discover the most preferable of several textbooks for a particular grade-level course, the following aspects of the cube would most likely obtain: informal setting, any aspect of the judges dimension except "several judges or jury," and an actual decision as the output.

One Form of the Adversary Approach: Wolf's Judicial Model

The judicial model was developed by Robert Wolf in 1973 and subsequently was placed on trial to evaluate a teacher education program at Indiana University. With a variety of persons offering or witnessing testimony, pertinent information can be assembled quickly and a balanced account of the program obtained for decision-making purposes.

Rationale

Wolf (1975) stated that "educational evaluation has become an increasingly sophisticated element in the accountability movement." He went on to say that educators at all levels must justify their decisions, must grasp the complexities of instructional programs, and must realize the importance of effective communication with the public over such matters.

Wolf maintained that conventional evaluation approaches do not meet these "newly recognized needs." The solution to such a problem lies not in the compilation of impressive arrays of technical data, but in the illumination of all aspects of program alternatives. This would benefit both the educator and the consumer. Wolf's judicial evaluation model was developed to illuminate and inform.

The model adapts and modifies concepts from both jury trials and administrative hearings in law. The legal methodology offers a useful system of procedures aimed at producing alternative inferences from data before judgments are made. Evaluators can focus clearly on a set of issues, rely on testimony from individuals, explore different aspects of issues by using two evaluation teams, enable a balanced point of view to develop, and structure the deliberations of the program decision makers.

Moreover, the model (like any adversary approach) explores many of the assumptions and rationales of programs, as well as the methods by which evaluation data were collected and analyzed. In brief, the evaluation is kept "intellectually honest and fair."

The Four Stages of the Judicial Model

Before any adversary evaluation occurs, it is possible that evaluation activities have already taken place. For example, ongoing formative evaluation may have occurred to promote program development. Any records of evaluation data arising from such activity are likely to enhance the process of the adversary evaluation, which occurs at a time useful for important decision making.

Wolf has identified four stages for the implementation of the judicial model.

The issue-generating stage. Initially, a broad range of issues are identified relating to the evaluation of the program as perceived by as many involved personnel as possible. These issues need not be the same as the program's original objectives. Through interviews, and other means, issues considered important are identified.

The issue-selection stage. During this stage, the number of issues is narrowed to a manageable size for a hearing. Program and other involved personnel could help establish a priority ranking of the issues. A special review panel, consisting of representatives of groups important to the program, then checks the issues for relevance, makes necessary modifications, and puts them in written form.

The preparation of argument stage. Formal arguments are then prepared by both evaluation teams. Specific points of contention are developed around each issue. Developed arguments stem often from gathered evaluation data that addressed the strengths and weaknesses of the program. Statements supporting one side or other of an issue may be gathered from witnesses involved in, or affected by, the program. In addition, relevant evaluation records (for example, of earlier formative evaluations), documents, and reports are studied for possible use in final arguments.

The hearing stage. This stage involves two sections. During a prehearing session, both teams review their major arguments and in conjunction with the hearings officer, develop rules and procedures for the hearing. Areas such as number of witnesses to be called, scope of cross-examination, and criteria for determining the admissibility of evidence (e.g., relevance) are agreed upon. Finally, specific questions are drafted to guide panel deliberations.

The hearing itself, which may follow months of preparation of the first three stages, may be of more than one session, depending on the nature of the evaluation. Following the presentation of arguments and cross-examination, the panel deliberates. If the panel itself is not the decision-making body, it makes recommendations upon which decisions are made.

Wolf has stated that the judicial model "offers a forum for communication and dissemination as well as evaluation." The process certainly has the potential to illuminate decision alternatives and consequences, which very often cannot be anticipated prior to the hearing.

The Pros and Cons of Adversary Evaluation

It is probably true to say that no other evaluation model has attracted so much pro and con comment as the adversary approach. Typical comments by adherents of both points of view are given.

The Argument For

In her article "An Adversary Model for Educational Evaluation," Marilyn Kourilsky (1973) lists some advantges of the model.

Information Scope. "The decision maker tends to receive a *wider array of information* because both sides (by definition) are being represented." Confrontation between the two opposing advocates encourages a thorough substantiation of the adopted position.

Quality of Evidence. The adversary relationship encourages advocates to develop better quality evidence for the decision maker. Advocates are well aware that their statements will be challenged and therefore these must be strongly supported by evidence. Wide-sweeping statements such as "surveys have indicated" hold little currency in adversary proceedings.

Unwitting bias diminishes. The process diminishes the possibility of predisposed ideas of both program personnel and the evaluator concerning aspects of education obtruding and thus biasing conclusions. It is possible that the evaluator and decision maker may be unaware that biased approaches actually exist. Evaluation reports, however, can too easily contain the unconsciously biased views of the evaluator and those who have been implicated in the program being evaluated. Adversary evaluation provides the incentive to present the best possible case for both sides.

The "Yes Man" syndrome diminishes. It often occurs that the evaluator knows the decision maker's predilection toward the outcome of an evaluation study. Inadvertently, the evaluator "is unable to resist the temptation of appeasement," but the adversary proceedings guard against this kind of situation.

Hidden assumptions are exposed. The adversary approach helps expose, clarify, and eventually change underlying assumptions involved in a disagreement. When empirically verifiable evidence is produced, value premises underlying the collection of data are exposed and discussed. When underlying assumptions and value criteria (and judgments) are clearly shown, inconsistencies may be clarified. A sound basis for future decision making has therefore been established.

All of the points raised in this section emphasize that the benefits of the adversary approach arise from the enforced openness of both the dialectic and the legal processes. As a result, better and more rational decisions may be made.

The Argument Against

Some uneasiness about aspects of the adversary approach have been voiced in a number of quarters during the last few years. One such is that given by W. James Popham and Dale Carlson (1977) following their involvement in an adversary evaluation in Hawaii in the spring of 1976. Popham and Carlson list the weaknesses they believe are present in most adversary evaluations; they also offer, where warranted, suggestions for ameliorating these deficiencies.

Disparity in proponent prowess. It is easier to assume that both sides of an issue will be satisfactorily presented for the consideration of the decision maker(s) than to accomplish. It is also likely that disparity in the skill of the two competing individuals (or teams) will occur. Consequently, better defense may make the weak side of the case appear more attractive. When an incorrect decision is made on this basis, affecting large numbers of children, "it seems genuinely intolerable."

Popham and Carlson advocate that different procedures are necessary to remedy this deficiency of the model. They propose a process whereby both adversaries argue both sides of the issue. Thus, two sets of positive and two sets of negative arguments would be generated for the consideration of the decision maker. The poorer effect of disparity in proponent prowess would thus be overcome.

Fallible arbiters. Judges vary in their abilities. Unwise and ill-conceived decisions by judges can improperly sway the outcomes of the hearing one way or the other. This may too easily occur in new areas of evaluation, where no set of ground rules exists for the conduct of such evaluations.

Excessive confidence in the model's potency. Because unwarranted potency can be ascribed to fields not fully comprehended, there has been a tendency to assume that the adversary approach will always lead toward improved decisions. Inexperience with the law is most often the reason for giving unreserved praise to the efficacy of the model. While the adversary model may, on occasions, be a useful addition to the array of evaluation devices, it may also ride roughshod over political considerations, which will remain to disrupt decisions made as outcomes of the process.

The only remedy offered by Popham and Carlson "to bridle the enthusiasm of recent converts" is to ensure that the reality of the program being evaluated is not obscured by fastidious adherence to legal procedures (which too often are not fully understood).

Difficulties in framing the proposition in a manner amenable to adversary resolution. Educational issues cannot always be cast in such a way that the outcomes of an advocate-adversary dialectic will yield suitable guidance for decision makers. Decision makers often have to reach conclusions on the basis of complex and interrerlated information. A framework producing simple winner/loser outcomes may evade the complex and subtle nature needed to reach successful decisions about educational and social program issues.

As a remedy, Popham and Carlson advocate applying the adversary evaluation model only to those educational situations "in which the two decision options are in direct opposition to one another."

It may nevertheless be argued that the decision maker, having a wide scope of information available as a result of the adversary proceedings, will select the information that he considers most relevant to decision areas. This may arise from either of the opposing presentations.

Excessive costs. It is likely that adversary evaluation will cost more than a conventional evaluation of a similar program. The main reason is that the cost of two teams and a coordination/arbitration staff, required for adversary evaluation, is well in excess of that for other approaches to evaluation, for which considerably fewer specialized personnel are needed.

If an adversary evaluation is to be thoroughgoing, a great amount of time must be expended on clarification of working rules and operating procedures. Popham and Carlson advise entertaining thoughts of an adversary approach only when it can be afforded.

Although the benefits of the adversary approach to evaluation may be considerable, it is clear that careful consideration must be given to its potential usefulness for decision-making purposes before it is employed. In general terms, it appears that it should be closely considered as a possible evaluation approach when a policy decision involving larger amounts of resources is at stake.

Knowledge Test for Unit 8

This knowledge test contains two parts: five true-false questions and two multiple-choice questions. In the first part, having decided whether a statement is true or false, you will then be directed to answer a further question based on that decision. Correct responses are given after each question: compare your answer with the response that follows each question.

The multiple-choice section should also determine whether you have a sufficient grasp of the knowledge objectives of the adversary model. In each instance, select what you consider to be the best response. A comparison may then be made with the explanation for correct and incorrect choices that follows each question. When all seven knowledge questions have been completed, you will be instructed to score your performance.

Question 1. The adversary model for evaluation emphasizes better decision making by clarifying issues surrounding a proposition.

　　　　True＿＿　　　　　　　　False＿＿

If true, state the basic methodological approach on which the model is based. If false, what is the real purpose of adversary evaluation?

Correct Response. The statement is true. The adversary model has been developed to illuminate important facets of a program (or proposed program) so that decision makers have sufficient, sound evidence to make rational decisions. There is a movement away from the function of evaluation based on the psychological testing model and toward a dialectic approach that employs the legal model.

Question 2. Adversary proceedings for decision-making purposes replace existing designs for collecting and analyzing data.

　　　　True＿＿　　　　　　　　False＿＿

If true, give your opinions about the wisdom of the adversary proceedings replacing formerly used designs and approaches to evaluation. If false, state the place of earlier designs for evaluation in respect to adversary proceedings.

Correct Response. The statement is false. Although data arising from an adversary approach are considered to be more balanced than those obtained by psychological testing alone, the latter are nevertheless admissible evidence in a hearing. The extent to which testing outcomes are used in final evidence may be decided in prehearing sessions.

Question 3.   Owens insisted that the decision maker should not serve as the hearings officer, as his verdict would constitute the decision.

True____   False____

If true, state what you consider the true role of the decision maker to be during a hearing. If false, discuss the role of the decision maker in respect to judging evidence; include the possibility of involving others in making judgments.

Correct Response. The statement is false. The educational decision maker may serve as the hearings officer, in which case his verdict is the decision. Owens points out that jurors such as teachers and student representatives may also be involved. However, the jury's verdict may be only one form of judgment to be used in conjunction with other information when the decision maker reaches a conclusion about the fate of a program.

Question 4.   The Wolf approach to evaluation involves quasilegal procedures that present the pros and cons of a program.

True____   False____

If true, mention the "newly recognized needs" that Wolf claimed the model would meet. If false, state the real purpose of the Wolf judicial model.

Correct Response. The statement is true. Wolf believed that evaluation will play an increasingly important part in the accountability movement. Educators and other professionals will have to justify their decisions. To do so, they must grasp the complexities of instructional programs; evaluation is a significant help in this respect.

Question 5.   According to Wolf, during a prehearing session, both teams review their major arguments and, in conjunction with the hearings officer, develop rules and procedures for the hearing.

True____   False____

If true, mention some of the likely areas to be discussed at a prehearing session. If false, state which procedures, if any, precede the actual hearing.

Correct Response. The statement is true. During a prehearing session it is likely that areas such as the following are agreed to: number of witnesses to be called, scope of cross-examination, criteria for determining the admissibility of evidence, and the drafting of specific questions to guide panel deliberations.

Question 6.   To overcome disparity that may exist in proponent prowess, Popham and Carlson advocate

a.   insuring that selected evaluators have identical background and experience in evaluation.
b.   using a process whereby both adversaries argue both sides of the issue.
c.   making clear to the decision maker(s) that a hearings verdict is not binding and that this presents only one piece of evidence (albeit a very large one) about the object of the evaluation.
d.   arranging subsequent hearings when it becomes apparent that proponent prowess is badly unbalanced.

Correct Response. You should have selected "b." If this occurs, two sets of positive and two sets of negative arguments would be generated for the consideration of the decision maker.

Incorrect Responses

a.   Incorrect; such a proposition verges on the impossible.
c.   Not the best response; although the statement may be accurate, there is no guarantee that such action would necessarily overcome the disparity between proponent prowess.
d.   Incorrect; an action such as this is likely only to exacerbate an already unfortunate situation (unless action suggested in "b" occurs).

Question 7.   With which of the following statements would Wolf *not* agree?

a.   The judicial model modifies concepts from both jury trials and administrative hearings in law.
b.   The legal methodology offers a useful system of procedures aimed at producing alternative inferences from data before judgments are made.

c. Evaluators need not necessarily focus on a set of issues; in this way a flexible and balanced array of information can be gathered to help illuminate the truth about a program.
d. The judicial model explores many of the assumptions and rationales of programs.

Correct Response. You should have selected "c." Wolf's stance was that evaluators must clearly delineate a set of issues; two evaluation teams should enable a balanced point of view to develop and structure the deliberations of the program decision makers.

Incorrect Responses

a. Incorrect; this is an accurate statement of the quasilegal nature of the judicial model.
b. Incorrect; this description is an accurate depiction of the methodology of the judicial model.
d. Incorrect; one of the strengths of the judicial model is its ability to explore the assumptions and rationales of programs being evaluated.

Interpreting the Knowledge Test. Having completed the two sections of the knowledge test, we suggest that you review your performance and your understanding of the keyed responses and that you review pertinent sections of the unit.

Application Exercises

This section contains two essay exercises that should further determine your understanding of the adversary approach. Both exercises require a grasp of the implications of applying the model to real or hypothetical situations.

Following each exercise is a list of points that should have been included in your response. A review of these should help you assess your work. You may wish also to reread the relevant parts of this unit when you have completed an exercise to gain a more complete assessment of your answers.

Exercise 1. Select a program, real or hypothetical, to be evaluated. Imagine that you intend to organize the evaluation using the Wolf judicial model.

If you wish, incorporate any ideas of Owens — for example, you may wish to make use of his dimensional cube. Write an essay outlining the procedures that would occur. Your answer should include these main elements:

a. The issue-generating stage.
b. The issue-selection stage.
c. The preparation of arguments stage.
d. The hearing stage.

Response to Exercise 1 should include the following:

a. The issue-generating stage:
    1 . A broad range of issues are identified relating to evaluation of the program.
    2. Outcomes of any formative evaluation processes are used to help identify issues.
    3. Personnel involved in program development are invited to help identify issues for evaluation.
    4. Issues may vary from original program objectives.
    5. Interviews, and other means, are used to identify issues.
b. The issues selection stage:
    1. Issues are narrowed down to manageable size for the hearing (these should be specified).
    2. The part to be played by program and other personnel in establishing the priority ranking is outlined.
    3. A special review panel (which should be described) checks the issues for relevance and puts them in written form.
c. The preparation of arguments stage:
    1. Two teams of evaluators are selected; they prepare contrary formal arguments.
    2. Specific points of contention are developed around each selected issue.
    3. Statements and data relating to issues are collected from various sources.
    4. Reference is made to data from any earlier evaluation(s) of selected issues.
d. The hearing stage:
    1. In a prehearing session, both teams review major arguments.
    2. With the hearings officer, rules of debate are determined.
    3. Specific questions are drafted to guide panel deliberations.

4. Details of panel composition, decision-making body, and the number of sessions for the hearing are all determined.
5. The hearing occurs and the panel deliberates.
6. Recommendations ensue, upon which decisions are made.

Exercise 2. In an essay answer discuss the pros and cons of adversary evaluation. Complete your response with a brief paragraph containing balanced opinions about the worthwhileness of the adversary approach in the light of your discussion about its pros and cons.

Response to Exercise 2 should include the following:

a. The pros of adversary evaluation:
   1. Information scope; a wider array of information arises from both sides being represented, and confrontation encourages thorough substantiation of stances adopted.
   2. Quality of evidence; the ever-present possibility of challenge encourages precise documentation of evidence and a wariness of widesweeping statements.
   3. Predisposed ideas of both program personnel and evaluator are diminished; the adversary approach encourages evidence free of personal bias.
   4. The "yes-man" syndrome diminishes; the approach guards against appeasement by the evaluator of the decision maker's known leanings.
   5. Hidden assumptions are exposed; the approach helps reveal, clarify, and eventually change underlying assumptions involved in opposing points of view; value premises come to light, and inconsistencies are clarified.
   6. Enforced openness; as a result, better decisions may be made.
b. The cons of adversary evaluation:
   1. Disparity in proponent prowess; a better defense may make the weak side of a case appear more attractive.
   2. Fallible arbiters; judges vary in their ability, and poor decisions will sway the outcomes of the hearing.
   3. Excessive confidence in the model's potency; inexperience with the law may give rise to undeserved praise for the efficacy of the model.
   4. Political matters receive too little contemplation; the evaluators may ride roughshod over political considerations, but these will re-

main no matter what decision is reached and disruption of future plans may result.

5. Difficulties in framing the proposition in a manner amenable to adversary resolution; issues are not always approached in a manner helpful to uneventual decision making because decisions are often reached on the basis of complex and interrelated information.

6. Excessive costs; almost invariably, the adversary evaluation costs more than a conventional evaluation of a similar program.

c. A balanced argument:

1. Remedies may be proposed for many of the arguments against the model.

2. When finance is available, adversary evaluation may be considered, particularly when large programs need to be evaluated.

3. Careful consideration must precede any study using the adversary approach.

4. The model's enforcement of an open and honest approach, with bias held to a minimum, makes it unique among evaluation models.

Questions Without Answers

Three questions are given in this section but answers are not provided. The questions may be used as subjects for group discussions or as individual assignments. You may prefer to gain deeper insight into the adversary model by reading the articles and books recommended in the reference section. However, questions may be answered on the basis of material contained in this and earlier units.

1. In what ways does the adversary model differ from earlier approaches to evaluation?

2. To what extent does the adversary model work harmoniously with the approaches proposed by Stufflebeam, Scriven, and Stake?

3. Describe three or four situations in which the adversary approach could be usefully employed. On the basis of cost, decide whether another evaluation approach would be more suitable in each instance.

References

Auerbach, C.; Garrison, L.K.; Hurst, W.; and Mermin, S. 1961. The adversary system. In *The legal process*. San Francisco: Chandler.

Frank, H.N. 1949. *Courts on trial*. Princeton, N.J.: Princeton University Press.

Kourilsky, M. 1973. An adversary model for educational evaluation. *Evaluation Comment* 4, 2, June.

Levine, M. 1974. Scientific method and the adversary model. *American Psychologist* (September), 666–677

Owens, T.R. 1973. Educational evaluation by adversary proceedings. In House, E.R. (ed.), *School evaluation: The politics and process*. Berkeley: McCutchan.

Popham, W. James and Carlson, Dale. "Deep dark deficits of the Adversary Evaluation Model." *Educational Researcher* (June 1977), American Educational Research Association, Washington, D.C.

Scriven, M. 1967. The methodology of evaluation. In R.E. Stake (ed.), *Perspectives of curriculum evaluation*. Chicago: Rand McNally.

Stake, R.E. 1967. The countenance of educational evaluation. *Teachers College Record 68* (April), 523–540.

Stufflebeam, D.; Foley, W.; Gephart, W.; Guba, E.; Hammond, R.; Merriman, H.; and Provus, M. 1971. *Educational evaluation and decision making*. Itasca, Ill.: Peacock.

Wolf, R.L. 1974. The citizen as jurist: A new mode of educational evaluation. *Citizen Action in Education* (Winter), 4.

_____ . 1975. Trial by jury. A new evaluation method. *Phi Delta Kappan, 57,* (November), 185–187.

9 ILLUMINATIVE EVALUATION: THE HOLISTIC APPROACH

In order to answer the question whether there are alternatives to the Tylerian (objectives) model of evaluation, a group of 14 men met for a conference at Churchill College, Cambridge, in December 1972. The aim of the conference was to explore "nontraditional modes of curriculum evaluation" and to set out guidelines for future developments in this field. Participants, who included Robert Stake from the United States, and David Hamilton, Malcolm Parlett, and Barry MacDonald from the United Kingdom, were chosen because of their known reservations about established evaluation practices or because they had suggested or experimented with new approaches.

The result of the conference was to produce a manifesto of aims that advocated a total reappraisal of the rationale and techniques of existing program evaluation. These basic concepts were to lead to the development of what was to become known as "illuminative evaluation."

Characteristically, conventional approaches to evaluation had followed the experimental or psychometric traditions dominant in educational research. Illuminative evaluators believe that such an approach is restricted in scope and inadequate for elucidating the complex problem areas confronting evaluators.

285

Illuminative evaluation is introduced as belonging to a contrasting anthropological research paradigm. Attempted measurement of educational products gives way to intensive study of the program as a whole — its rationale, evolution, operations, achievements, and difficulties.

The crucial criticism of the objectives model is that it assesses without explaining, whereas illuminative evaluation methodology, viewing the program as a whole, values literacy rather than numeracy.

At the conclusion of the Cambridge conference, referred to above, members decided to make available the summary of their conclusions. The points of this summary, although they have an historical ring about them today, have endured and have directed the pathway pursued by evaluators who favor the illuminative approach. The salient features of the aims and procedures of educational practice agreed to by the conference are summarized:

1. Previous efforts to evaluate educational programs have, in general terms, not adequately served the needs of those who require evidence of the effects of such practices for the following reasons:
   a. Too little attention to educational practices, including those of the learning milieu.
   b. Too much attention to psychometrically measurable changes in student behavior.
   c. The existence of an educational research climate that rewards accuracy of measurement and generality of theory, but overlooks both mismatch between school problems and research issues and tolerates ineffective communication between researchers and those outside the research community.
2. Future efforts to evaluate these practices should be designed to meet the following criteria:
   a. Responsive to the needs and perspectives of differing audiences.
   b. Illuminative of the complex organizational, teaching, and learning processes.
   c. Relevant to public and professional decisions forthcoming.
   d. Reported in language that is accessible to their audiences.
3. That, increasingly,
   a. observational data, carefully validated, be used.
   b. the evaluations be designed sufficiently flexibly to allow for response to unanticipated events.
   c. the value position of the evaluator, whether highlighted or constrained by the design, be made evident to the sponsors and audiences of the evaluation.

4. Those who design evaluation studies should give careful attention to the following:
   a. The sometimes conflicting role of the same evaluator as guide and teacher of decision makers on the one hand, and as technical specialist and servant of decision makers on the other.
   b. The degree to which the evaluator, his sponsors, and his subjects should specify in advance the limits of an inquiry.
   c. The advantages and disadvantages of intervening in educational practices for the purpose of gathering data or of controlling the variability of certain features in order to increase the generalizability of the findings.
   d. The complexity of educational decisions, which inescapably have political, social, and economic implications.
   e. The degree to which the evaluator should interpret his observations rather than leave them for different audiences to interpret.

It is interesting to note that the conference took a stance very similar to that promulgated by Cronbach, namely, that different evaluation designs will serve different purposes and that even for a single educational program many different designs could be used.

You will be able to develop an understanding of the illuminative approach to evaluation by working through the unit. As was the case earlier, exercises have been set at the end to test your knowledge. The list of unit objectives is given next. Study these, read the unit, and then attempt the knowledge test, checking your answers against the keyed ones. Finally, complete the application exercises, comparing your responses with the salient points provided, and consider the section dealing with questions without answers.

Objectives

The objectives of the chapter are as follows:

1. To outline some doubts about aspects of traditional evaluation by considering emphasis on learning processes or measurement, the agricultural-botany paradigm, MacDonald and the holistic approach, and Stake's concept of evaluation as portrayal.
2. To gain an understanding of illuminative evaluation as a social-anthropological paradigm by considering the context of educational programs, the instructional system, and the learning milieu.

3. To study organization and methods of illuminative evaluation by considering salient features of illuminative evaluation, observation, interviews, questionnaire and test data, and documentary and background information.
4. To consider reporting and decision-making: who receives a report, communication of the spirit of the program, and, diversity among reports.
5. To point out some problems of illuminative evaluation by considering Stenhouse's reservations, experimenter bias, and illuminative evaluation and large-scale studies.

Traditional Evaluation: Seeds of Doubt

Emphasis on Learning Processes for Measurement

As early as 1969, Weiss and Rein, concerned about the association of "the numbers game" with evaluation, stated that they considered that a far more effective methodology would be more descriptive and inductive. By describing the unfolding form of the experimental intervention, the reaction of individuals and institutions subject to its impact, and the consequences (so far as they could be learned by interview and observation), much would be learned about the total program. Emphasis would thus be placed more upon learning processes than upon measuring per se. These statements, repeated by others at about that time, indicated that there was concern that conventional objective-type evaluations were not addressing themselves to understanding the educational process. They dealt in terms of success or failure, whereas a program is most likely to be a mixture of both, and a mixture which varies from setting to setting.

Cronbach (1963) was thinking along similar lines when he wrote:

Old habits of thought and long-established techniques are poor guides to evaluation required for course improvement. Traditionally, educational measurement has been chiefly concerned with producing fair and precise scores for comparing individuals. Educational experimentation has been concerned with comparing score averages of competing courses. But course evaluation calls for a description of outcomes. This description should be made on the broadest possible scale, even at the sacrifice of superficial fairness and precision.

The Agricultural-Botany Paradigm

Parlett and Hamilton have likened the Tylerian (objectives) approach to evaluation to an agricultural-botany paradigm. (T.S. Kuhn in 1970 described a paradigm as "an over arching concept which prescribes problem areas, research methods and acceptable standards of solution.") Students — something like plant crops — are given pretests (the seedlings are weighed or measured) and then submitted to different experiences (treatment conditions). Subsequently, after a period of time, their attainment (growth or yield) is measured to indicate the relative efficiency of the methods (fertilizers) used. Studies of this kind are designed to yield data of an objective numerical kind that permits statistical analyses. Isolated variables like I.Q., social class, test scores, personality profiles, and attitude ratings are codified and processed to indicate the efficiency of new curricula, media, or methods.

These writers point out, however, that this paradigm has notable shortcomings:

1. Educational situations are characterized by numerous relevant parameters that cannot be strictly controlled. If an attempt is made to stimulate laboratory conditions by manipulation, a situation arises that is not only dubious ethically, but also may lead to "gross administrative and personal inconvenience."

2. Before-and-after research designs assume that innovatory programs undergo little or no change during the period of study. A premise rarely upheld in practice. However, it remains fundamental to the design, constraining the researchers from adapting to the changed circumstances that so frequently arise.

3. Methods used in traditional evaluations impose artificial and arbitrary restrictions on the scope of the study. Parlett and Hamilton point out, for instance, that a concentration on seeking quantitative information by objective means may lead to neglect of other data, perhaps more salient to the innovation but that are disregarded as "subjective," "anecdotal," or "impressionistic." The evaluator, however, most likely will need to utilize information of this sort if he is to explain his findings satisfactorily and give proper weight to their importance in the full context.

4. Recent research of this type, by employing large samples and seeking statistical generalizations, tends to be insensitive to local "perturbations and unusual effects." Atypical results are seldom studied in detail as a consequence.

5. This type of evaluation often fails to respond to the varied concerns and questions of participants, sponsors, and other interested parties. Since classical evaluators believe in "objective truth" equally relevant to all parties, their studies rarely reflect the diversity of questions posed by different interest-groups.

As Parlett and Hamilton point out, the objectives-type evaluation falls short of its own tacit claims to be controlled, exact, and unambiguous. Particularly in the case of innovations, the programs are vulnerable to manifold extraneous influences, as the evaluator's definition of empirical reality is narrow. As a consequence, the evaluator may well divert attention away from questions of educational practice toward those of greater concern to sponsors and others with bureaucratic concerns.

MacDonald and the Holistic Approach

In posing a holistic approach to evaluation, MacDonald offered a response to the agricultural-botany paradigm. He has adopted the stance that evaluation should not start from the assumption that certain data (such as pupil outcomes) should be its area of concern, but that the evaluator should accept as potentially relevant all data concerning the program and its contexts. He has pointed out that human action in educational institutions differs widely because of the number of variables that influence it. This runs contrary to the assumption held by many that what was intended to happen is what actually happens, and that which happens varies little from setting to setting.

The holistic approach also implies that innovation of a program is not a set of discrete effects, but an organically related pattern of acts and consequences. Thus, a single act must be located functionally within a total context. MacDonald points out that it follows from this proposition that curriculum interventions have many more unanticipated effects than is normally assumed. Moreover, if a program is offered in different settings, historical and evolutionary differences alone make the innovation gap a variable that has significance for later decision making. Finally, the holistic approach implies that the goals and purposes of the program developers are not necessarily shared by its users.

MacDonald is also concerned about audiences who receive an evaluation report and particularly those who have to make decisions as a result of it. He considers that the traditional style of evaluation would not promote understanding of the considerations that should bear upon curricular action. His orientation is much more toward developing an empirical rather than a normative model of educational decision making and its consequences. This follows logically from MacDonald's emphasis upon what could be described as an anthropological approach to the illumination of an educational program.

Stake's Concept of Evaluation as Portrayal

Some distinct resemblances are found between MacDonald's position and that of Stake, particularly in respect to his concept of evaluation as portrayal and his "responsive evaluation." Similarly, in his "countenance of educational evaluation," Stake aspires to an evaluation "orientated to the complex and dynamic nature of education, one which gives proper attention to the diverse purposes and judgments of the practitioner." Having noted the deficiences of an evaluation based on traditional tests, which stress reliability of individual students scores and predictive validity, he suggests that "attention to individual differences amongst students should give way to attention to the contingencies among background conditions, classroom activities, and scholastic outcomes."

Stake's concept of evaluation as portrayal anticipates Parlett's and Hamilton's notion of illumination. It, too, is a reaction against the tradition of attempting to capture tight experimental control over the innovatory situation. He describes the traditional evaluation strategy as "preordinate" because it relies on prespecification and emphasizes statement of goals, use of objective tests, standards held by program personnel, and research-type reports.

In advocating responsive evaluation, Stake explains his position:

> Education evaluation is a "responsive evaluation" if it orientates more directly to program activities than to program intents, if it responds to audience requirements for information, and if different value-perspectives present are referred to in reporting the success of the program.

Stake's emphasis, then, is on the presentation of results. If evaluation is to be addressed to the decision makers rather than the research workers, the evaluator must attempt to portray the program in a way that communicates to an audience more naturally and more effectively than does the traditional research report.

The unit on Robert Stake's work does, of course, explain in far greater detail the "countenance" and "responsive" approaches to evaluation. The point emphasized here, in the context of illuminative evaluation, is Stake's claim that research-style information may not be the kind of information that is useful for decision makers.

Illuminative Evaluation: A Social-Anthropological Paradigm

This section, and the next, adheres strongly to Parlett and Hamilton (1977). In these two sections, the authors discuss an alternative model to the traditional forms of evaluation. They named their alternative model "illuminative evaluation," a term that grew out of research at the Massachusetts Institute of Technology in 1969.

The Context of Educational Programs

Illuminative evaluation takes account of the wider context in which educational programs function; thus its primary concern is with description and interpretation rather than with measurement and prediction. Parlett and Hamilton state, "It stands unambiguously within the alternative anthropological paradigm where historical, cultural, and social effects cannot be ignored."

The aims of illuminative evaluation are as follows:

1. To study the innovatory program — how it operates, how it is influenced by the various school situations in which it is applied, what those directly concerned regard as its advantages and disadvantages; and how students' intellectual tasks and academic experiences are most affected.
2. To discover and document what it is like to be participating in the scheme, whether as teacher or pupil.
3. To discern and discuss the innovation's most significant features, recurring concomitants, and critical processes.

Thus, it seeks to address and to illuminate a complex array of questions, helping the innovator and other interested parties to identify those procedures and those aspects of the program seen to have had desirable results.

As Parlett and Hamilton point out, the adoption of illuminative evaluation requires more than an exchange of methodologies (from the traditional ones); it also involves new suppositions, concepts, and terminology central to the understanding of illuminative evaluation of two concepts, the "instructional system" and the "learning milieu."

The Instructional System. Educational prospectuses and reports usually contain a variety of formalized plans and standards relating to particular teaching arrangements. Each of these may be said to constitute, or define, an instructional system and to include a set of pedagogic assumptions, a new syllabus (most likely), and details of techniques and equipment. A catalogue is an idealized specification of the scheme, a set of elements arranged to an optimistic, coherent plan.

Parlett and Hamilton point out that the traditional evaluator builds a study around innovations defined in this way. Having examined the blueprint or formalized plan and having extracted the program's goals, objectives, or desired outcomes, the evaluator next derives the tests and attitude inventories to be administered. The aim is to evaluate the instructional system by examining whether it has attained its objectives or met its performance criteria.

This technological approach, however, fails to recognize the prospectus or report for what it is:

> It ignores the fact that an instructional system, when adopted, undergoes modifications that are rarely trivial. The instructional system may remain as a shared idea, abstract model, slogan or shorthand, but it assumes a different form in every situation. Its constituent elements are emphasised or de-emphasised, expanded or truncated, as teachers, administrators, technicians, and students interpret and reinterpret the instructional system for their particular setting. In practice, objectives are commonly reordered, redefined, abandoned or forgotten. The original "ideal" formulation ceases to be accurate, or indeed, of much relevance. Few in practice take catalogue descriptions and lists of objectives very seriously, save — it seems — for the traditional evaluator.

The move from the discussion of the instructional system in its idealized form to a description of its implementation in practice may well represent moving into a new realm. This brings us to the second concept, the learning milieu.

The Learning Milieu.   The learning milieu is the "social-psychological and material environment in which students and teachers work together." It represents a network of cultural, social, institutional, and psychological variables that interact in complicated ways to produce, within groups or courses, a unique pattern of circumstances (e.g., pressures, opinions, conflicts) which suffuse the teaching and learning that occur there.

According to Parlett and Hamilton, the configuration of the learning milieu, in any particular classroom, depends on the interplay of numerous different factors. As an example, there are numerous constraints (legal, administrative, and financial) on the organization of teaching in schools; there are pervasive operating assumptions (about the arrangements of subjects, teaching methods, and student assessment) held by teaching staff; there are the individual teacher's characteristics (experience, attitude to teaching and learning styles, and private expectations); and there are student perspectives, needs, and motivations.

It is important that the diversity and complexity of learning milieux is seen as a basis for the serious study of educational programs. Any program, and particularly an innovation, should not be thought of as being a self-contained and independent system. The introduction of an innovation sets off a chain of repercussions throughout the learning context. Most likely, unintended consequences arise that affect the innovation itself, changing form and moderating its impact.

Parlett and Hamilton stress that an attempt to form a nexus between changes in the learning milieu with intellectual experiences of students is one of the chief concerns for illuminative evaluation. As they say, students do not confront knowledge "in naked form; it comes to them clothed in texts, lectures, tape-loops, etc." For its part, the management framework is embedded within wider departmental and institutional structures, each with its own set of procedures and professional and societal allegiances. These aspects of the learning institution, although apparently removed from the assimilation of knowledge at the classroom level, must not be ignored. Thus, the learning-milieu concept is necessary for analyzing the interdependence of learning and teaching as it relates the organization and practices of instruction with the immediate and long-term responses of students.

Moreover, there are phenomena of significant educational influence, such as student interest, concentration, and boredom, that debilitate the traditional psychological distinction between "cognitive" and "affective." These customarily arise in response to the total learning milieu, not to single components of it. Students respond to hidden as well as the visible curriculum; they assimilate the customs, conventions, culture, and models of the reality of the learning situation.

Organization and Methods of Illuminative Evaluation

Salient Features of Illuminative Evaluation

Illuminative evaluation is not a standard methodological approach but a general research strategy. It aims to be both adaptable to meet the size, aims, and techniques of the evaluation and eclectic to give the evaluator a choice of research tactics. Decisions about the strategy to be used in a particular instance arise from the problem to be investigated. No one method is used exclusively or in isolation; different techniques are combined to throw light on a common problem. Initially, as Parlett and Hamilton point out, the evaluator's concern is to become thoroughly familiar with the day-to-day reality of the setting being studied. This pursuit is similar to social anthropologists or to a natural historian. He makes no attempt to manipulate or control or elimiante situational variables, but takes as given the complex scene which he finds:

> His chief task is to unravel it; isolate its significant features; delineate cycles of cause and effect; and comprehend relationships between beliefs and practices and between organizational patterns and the responses of individuals.

Because illuminative evaluation emphasizes the examination of the program as an integral part of the learning milieu, there is a definite emphasis both on observation at the classroom level and on interviewing participating teachers and students. Parlett and Hamilton state that there are three characteristic stages of an illuminative evaluation:

1. The observation phase, in which the full range of variables affecting the outcome of the program or innovation are investigated.
2. The inquiry stage, in which the emphasis changes from being knowledgeable (the observation phase) to the focusing and directing of questions in a coherent relaxed fashion so that a systematic and selective list of important aspects of the program in its context is further understood.
3. The explanation stage, in which general principles underlying the organization of the program are brought to the light of day and in which patterns of cause and effect within its operations are delineated.

Within this three-stage framework, an information profile is compiled using data collected from four areas: observation, interviews, questionnaires and tests, and documentary and background sources.

Observation.   The observation phase occupies a central place in illuminative evaluation. Importantly, the investigator compiles a continuous record of events, transactions, and informal remarks. The data must be organized where they arise and interpretative comments on "both manifest and latent features of the situation" must be added. In addition to documenting these activities, the evaluator may also document a wide variety of other events, including staff, student and parent meetings, school community days, and the like.

This observation involves recording discussions with and between participants to provide additional information that otherwise might be obtained from more formal interviews. The language conventions and metaphors that characterize conversations within each learning milieu can reveal tacit assumptions, interpersonal relationships, and status differentials and hidden curriculum.

Parlett and Hamilton also say that there is a place for codified observation, making use of schedules for recording patterns of attendance, seating, utilization of time and facilities, interpersonal interactions, and the like. The illuminative evaluator must be cautious, however, in the use of such techniques, a they are not likely to uncover underlying features of the program.

Interviews.   Discovering the views of participants is crucial in the assessment of the impact of a program. In this process students and teachers are asked about their work, how it compares with their previous experience, and also about the use and value of the program (or innovation). A wide range of approaches to interviewing are available, but those chosen must be the most appropriate to elicit the type of needed information or comment. Brief, structured interviews are convenient for obtaining biographical or demographic information, while more open-ended and discursive forms are suitable for less straightforward topics. If shortage of time or finance preclude interviewing each participant (and this most likely will be the case), a random sample of interviewees must be made and care must be taken to ensure that informants or particular groups who have special insight or whose position makes their viewpoints noteworthy are included within the sample.

Questionnaire and Test Data.   Although the illuminative evaluator concentrates on observation and interview, paper-and-pencil techniques must not be disregarded where these may prove useful. Their advantage in larger-scale studies is especially evident, although they may be used profitably in smaller studies. Where survey-type questionnaires are used later in the study to sustain or qualify earlier tentative findings, open-ended questions may be included with fixed questions so that both quantitative summary data and unexpected commentary may be obtained.

Questionnaires should be used only after careful thought. Parlett and Hamilton point out that there are valid objections to some aspects of questionnaires. Their main concern, however, is that questionnaires are not used in isolation. Parlett and Hamilton state that besides completing questionnaires, participants may also be asked to prepare written comments about the program, to go through checklists, or to compile work diaries over a period of time.

Evaluators may also wish to use custom-built tests of attitude, personality, and achievement, although these will enjoy no privileged status within the study. The test scores must never be used in isolation. For reporting purposes, interest lies not so much in relating different test scores, but in accounting for them, using the study's findings within the total context.

Documentary and Background Information.   The historical antecedents of a program should be recorded, as these do not arise by chance. Primary sources can be tapped, such as confidential data held on file, together with autobiographical and eye-witness accounts of the program. Tape recordings of meetings and examples of students' work may also prove useful, as such information can provide a historical perspective of how the innovation was regarded by different people before the evaluation began. It may also indicate areas for later inquiry or point to topics for intensive discussion. It may also expose aspects of the innovation that would otherwise be missed.

Reporting and Decision Making

Who Receives a Report?

As early as 1971 MacDonald had developed his holistic approach to evaluation, which was based on decision making. All writers and practitioners of the illuminative style of evaluation agree that the principal purpose of evaluation studies is to contribute to decision making. The evaluator's report is addressed to three separate but related groups of decision makers: the program's participants, the program's sponsors or administrators, and interested outsiders, such as researchers and school committees.

Each group will look to the report for aid in making different decisions. For this reason, the evaluator cannot, even if so requested, provide a simple go/no-go about the program's (or innovation's) future. It may well be that a decision based on one group's evaluative criteria will be disputed by other groups whose priorities differ.

Communication of the Spirit of the Program

As has been pointed out earlier, Stake emphasizes that it is the task of the evaluator to communicate to an audience in a more natural fashion and, indeed, one more effective than the traditional research report. This suggests that a formal written report is not always necessary and, in fact, may defeat its own purpose by being too formal. Data overload is therefore to be avoided in reporting. Instead, as Stake puts it, "we need to portray complexity. We need to convey holistic impression, the mood, even the mystery of the experience."

The competition between the evaluator's natural desire to mirror what is seen and, by contrast, to explain it or account for it is sometimes acute. On the one hand, the evaluator may wish to capture the intimate flavor, the complexity, and the idiosyncrasy of the real-life program, but may also wish to lean toward interpretation in order to generalize or to seek patterns or even to capture the essence of what is being studied.

Diversity Among Reports

One of the principal strengths of illuminative evaluation is its versatility. A diversity among reports is an inevitable and desirable consequence of this approach. Traditional evaluations were built around requirements of methodology, whereas illuminative evaluations emphasize methods built around problem definitions and contracts made between evaluator and sponsor. Thes studies, therefore, tend to be directed to specified groups to discuss questions and problems and policy issues important to those groups. In the case of multiple audiences, the evaluator's task may well be to direct different groups to specific sections of the report. No matter what form the report takes, it should be readable, brief, and full of interest.

Illuminative evaluation thus stresses information-gathering rather than decision-making aspects of evaluation. The reporting task, for decision making, is to provide a comprehensive account of the complex realities of the program. From this account should arise sharpened discussions leading to disentangling of complexities and isolating the trivial from the significant.

Problems Associated with Illuminative Evaluation

Stenhouse's Reservations

Although he is entirely sympathetic to the criticism of the old-style, product-testing evaluation from which the illuminative style of evaluation has arisen, Laurence Stenhouse expressed reservations about this approach. His concern is the problem of criteria, as he feels that the general position assumed by some illuminative evaluators is likely to block progress in research-based innovation.

It appears to Stenhouse that illuminative evaluators seem to be concerned with "merit" or "worth" in a curriculum or educational practice, but their criteria are not clear and their concern with audiences and presentation of results appears to him to mask their problem:

> They aspire to "tell it as it is," and they often write as if that is possible if they allow for some distortion due to their own values. But there is no telling it as it is. There is only a creation of meaning through the use of criteria and conceptual frameworks. The task of briefing decision makers in language they readily understand can too easily lead to the casual importation of unexamined assumptions and criteria. Audience response can be seductive, especially if the audience is politically powerful. And it is too easy for the evaluation which aspires to the condition of the novel to degenerate into the novelette.

Stenhouse goes on to suggest that an important element in adequate evaluation of the curriculum is the philosophical critique. The object of such a critique should be to disclose the meaning of the curriculum rather than to assess its worth, though disclosure of meaning naturally invites assessment of worth. It follows that his concern about illuminative evaluation is that too much attention may be given to the political dimensions of a study and the presentation of results therefore channeled in vivid and acceptable but often oblique forms, and this may tend to make the discussion of such criteria "part of the privateness of the evaluators." He points out that such issues are too important to be regarded as "domestic issues in the evaluation household."

Experimental Bias

Parlett and Hamilton raise the question, Can personal interpretation be scientific? They are well aware (as is Stenhouse) that the collection, analysis, and reporting of data by an illuminative evaluator appear to be discretionary. The authors argue, however, as has Stake elsewhere, that no form of research is immune from prejudice, experimenter bias, and human error. Any research study, they maintain, requires skillful judgments and is thus vulnerable; even in evaluation studies that handle automatically processed numerical data, judgment is necessary at every stage.

Nevertheless, as Parlett and Hamilton admit, the extensive use of open-ended techniques, progressive focusing, and qualitative data in illuminative evaluation still raises the possibility of gross partiality on the part of the investigator. They suggest, therefore, that a number of precautionary tactics are possible. Consultants to the evaluation can be charged with challenging preliminary interpretations, and members of the research team can be commissioned to develop their own interpretations. Even with such precautions, the subjective element remains. Parlett and Hamilton argue that this is inevitable:

> When the investigator abandons the agricultural-botany paradigm, his role is necessarily redefined. The use of interpretative human insight and skills is, indeed, encouraged rather than discouraged.

In a similar fashion, it may be argued that the presence of the evaluator inevitably has an effect on the conduct and progress of the program. The evaluator must therefore attempt to be unobtrusive, supportive, and if possible, nondoctrinaire. This leaves the important point that an evaluator needs not only to call on intellectual capabilities, but also interpersonal skills. An illuminative evaluator seeks cooperation but does not demand it. Because the illuminative evaluator receives richer and more informative data than the traditional evaluator, the illuminative evaluator must be vigilant to ensure that professional standards are constantly maintained.

Large-scale Studies

The question may also be asked whether (bearing in mind the investigator's special position) the illuminative evaluation must necessarily be confined to small-scale innovations. Parlett and Hamilton firmly believe that illuminative evaluation may be applied on a wider scale. They base this assumption on a number of points, the most important being that learning milieux, despite their diversity, share many characteristics. Thus, instruction is often constrained by similar conventions and teachers encounter similar sets of problems; there may be a wide range of overlapping social and behavioral phenomena that accompany teaching, learning, and innovating programs. Illuminative evaluation may contribute to pinpointing and describing these phenomena adequately by providing abstracted summaries, shared terminology, and useful concepts.

Knowledge Test for Unit 9

To help determine whether you have achieved the knowledge objectives for the unit, this section contains six multiple-choice questions and explanations for correct and incorrect responses. You are requested to select the letter for what you consider to be the best response and then compare your answer with the responses that follow. After you have completed all of the questions, you will be assisted to interpret your performance.

Question 1. Which of the following statements best describes the illuminative approach to evaluation?

a. An investigation of the extent to which the outcomes of a program correlate with its expressed aims and objectives.
b. A study focusing on providing information for the major types of educational decisions.
c. The discovery of the extent of success of a program by collecting all possible admissible details related to it, and by debating the merits of these details.

d. An adaptable and eclectic investigation of the program, where the researcher, having become familiar with the setting, observes, inquires further, and then seeks to explain.

Correct Response. You should have answered "d." Although this is not a complete definition of illuminative evaluation, the statement contains the four main elements required for an evaluation using this approach, that is, becoming familiar with the context, observing, inquiring, and explanation.

Incorrect Responses

a. Incorrect; this statement comes close to the approach used by the Tylerian school of evaluators, that is, the "objectives approach." It is almost the antithesis of the aims of illuminative evaluation.
b. Incorrect; this is the definition of evaluation espoused by advocates of decision-oriented evaluations. It is similar to illuminative evaluation in that information is to be presented to decision makers, but it differs methodologically in many significant ways (as a further reading of the Stufflebeam unit will indicate).
c. Incorrect; this statement approximates the approach used in adversary evaluation, for which the methodology and intent of the investigation differ markedly from the illuminative approach.

Question 2. Because illuminative evaluation is not a standard methodological package but a general research strategy, it requires that the evaluator

a. be flexible in his approach to both the design and procedures used for the study.
b. attempt to control situational variables.
c. make early decisions about the nature of the inquiries to be pursued.
d. be wary of forming (or conjecturing) patterns of cause and effect within the operation of the program being studied

Correct Response. You should have selected "a." This statement is in keeping with the avowed intent that an illuminative evaluation must be both adaptable and eclectic. The choice of research strategies does not follow from research doctrine, but from decisions about the most appropriate technique to use in each particular case.

Incorrect Responses

b. Incorrect because the illuminative evaluator acts more like an anthropologist when becoming familiar with the setting being studied; no attempt is made to manipulate variables.

c. Incorrect; the illuminative evaluator surveys the field with an open mind at some length before selecting topics or aspects of a program for closer and more sustained study.

d. Incorrect; the illuminative evaluator must endeavor to spot patterns of cause and effect within the operation of a program and, by so doing, place individual findings within a broader, explanatory context.

Question 3.   Which of the following statements about the role and importance of observation in illuminative evaluation is most accurate?

a. The investigator may or may not develop a continuous record of on-going events, transactions, and informal remarks.

b. The value of observation is that it provides a basis for organizing data collected by other means.

c. On-site observation should not be biased by recording opinions of program participants.

d. The observation phase occupies a central place in illuminative evaluation.

Correct Response. You should have selected "d." The chief task of the evaluator is to observe the complexities of the scene and to isolate its significant features, including cycles of cause and effect.

Incorrect Responses

a. Not the best response because the statement does not stress the central function of observation.

b. Not the best response, and only partially accurate because in illuminative evaluations observational data are of primary interest.

c. Incorrect because the illuminative evaluation "dossier" of data is built on recording discussions with and between participants.

Question 4.   Concerning the gathering of data (for analysis by paper-and-pencil techniques), Parlett and Hamilton hold which of the following opinions?

a. Such techniques may be included with advantage.

b. Such techniques should be used only in larger-scale studies.

c. Such techniques should not include questionnaires because there are valid objections to this data-gathering method.

d. Such techniques as questionnaires and tests should not be employed, but instead participants should be asked to prepare written comments and compile work diaries.

Correct Response. You should have responded with "a." While concentrating on observation, the illuminative evaluator may use pencil-and-paper techniques with advantage, particularly as their analyzed outcomes may either sustain or qualify findings from observation and interviews.

Incorrect Responses

b. Incorrect; while paper-and-pencil techniques are most likely more useful in large-scale studies, they nevertheless may be used profitably in smaller studies.
c. Incorrect; while bearing in mind the shortcomings of this data-gathering method, the evaluator may use questionnaires but *not* in isolation.
d. Incorrect; written comments and the like, together with pencil-and-paper techniques, help to complete the illuminative evaluator's information bank.

Question 5. Which of the following is a major reservation expressed by Stenhouse about illuminative evaluation?

a. Reports are open to various (political) interpretations, as conclusions have not been based on "hard" data.
b. Outcomes may be questioned, as the study's design is not a standard one (as, for instance, is the case with one based on the Tylerian model).
c. The opinions, assumptions, and experience of the evaluator may bias the report and subsequent decisions too markedly.
d. These evaluators aspire to "tell it as it is" — but that is not possible.

Correct Response. You should have selected "d." Stenhouse asserts: "There is no telling it as it is. This can only occur by the creation of meaning through the use of accepted criteria and conceptual frameworks. Unexamined criteria and assumptions, casually imported by the evaluator, lead to doubts about the validity of the study and its outcomes."

Incorrect Responses

a. Incorrect because this point has not been raised as a criticism by Stenhouse.
b. Incorrect for much the same reason as given in response to question "a."

c. Not the best answer as this statement could also pertain to many evaluators using modes of evaluation different from the illuminative. Parlett and Hamilton, however, point out that illuminative evaluators, particularly, need to heed the necessity for "professional standards and behavior."

Question 6.   If it is true that one of the strengths of illuminative evaluation is its versatility, it follows that

a. the competition between the evaluator's desire to mirror what is seen, on the one hand, and the wish to explain it, on the other hand, is often very real.
b. all reports should make allowance for audience response, which may lead to a revision of the report.
c. the final report must be simple and easily understood by audiences.
d. a diversity among reports is an inevitable and desirable consequence.

Correct Response. You should have selected "d." This statement is an important example of versatility of illuminative evaluation. Studies, and their reported outcomes, are directed to specified groups. Thus, various reports relating to a particular study contain questions, problems, and policy issues important to various interest groups.

Incorrect Responses

a. Although an accurate statement about an illuminative evaluation, this is not the best response, because it does not explain the versatile approach, which is the hallmark of this mode of evaluation.
b. Not the best response; it is doubtful whether illuminative evaluators would be willing to change one of their completed reports even though few would expect universal acceptance of their findings.
c. Incorrect; although the report(s) must be written in a fashion that is both intelligible and appealing to audiences, oversimplification is to be avoided. As Stake comments: "Oversimplification obfuscates."

Interpreting the Knowledge Test.   Having completed the knowledge test, total the number of correct and incorrect responses. We suggest that you use this examination as a guide to reviewing and strengthening your grasp of the material presented in this unit.

Application Exercises

This section contains two essay exercises that should indicate whether you have understood the two major aspects of illuminative evaluation. Following each exercise is a list of points that should have been included in your response. Reviewing these points should help you assess the completeness of your essay.

Exercise 1. With specific references to writers such as Cronbach, Parlett and Hamilton, MacDonald, and Stake, write an essay outlining the reservations and doubts about traditional approaches to evaluation that led to their reevaluation and the consequent development of the illuminative approach. Your answer should include these main elements:

a. Cronbach's concern about "the numbers game."
b. Parlett and Hamilton and the agricultural-botany paradigm.
c. MacDonald and the holistic approach.
d. Stake's concept of evaluation as portrayal.

Response to Exercise 1 should include the following:

a. Cronbach's concern about "the numbers game"
    1. Description would capture the reaction of individuals and institutions subjected to an experimental intervention, and much would be learned about the total program.
    2. With emphasis upon the learning processes, evaluations would have to address themselves to an understanding of the educational process.
    3. Cronbach expressed concern about the traditional emphasis in evaluation on educational measurement and on the production of "fair and precise scores for comparing individuals."
    4. Cronbach stressed that description should be made on the broadest possible scale, even if superficial precision was thereby lost to some extent.
b. Parlett and Hamilton and the agricultural-botany paradigm.
    1. Parlett and Hamilton likened the objectives approach to evaluation to an agricultural-botany paradigm.
    2. For this reason, traditional evaluation studies yielded data of an objective and numerical kind to permit statistical analyses.

3. The writers point out, however, that educational situations are characterized by numerous relevant parameters that cannot be controlled
strictly.

4. A further criticism is that before-and-after research designs assume
that innovatory programs undergo little or no change during the
period of study, though this premise is rarely upheld in practice.

5. Moreover, traditional evaluations impose artificial and arbitrary
restrictions on the scope of the study, as subjective anecdotal or impressionistic data are disregarded.

6. Traditional evaluation has failed to respond to the varied concerns
and questions of participants and others interested in the educational program.

7. Parlett and Hamilton also have pointed out that traditional evaluation has fallen short of its own tacit claims to be controlled and
unambiguous, as programs are vulnerable to a great number of extraneous influences.

c. MacDonald and the holistic approach
1. The holistic approach offers a response to the agricultural-botany
paradigm.

2. The evaluators should accept as potentially relevant all data concerning the program and its context.

3. The holistic approach implies that a program is an organically related pattern of acts and consequences, and thus a single act must
be located functionally within a total context.

4. MacDonald states that programs may have more unanticipated effects than is normally assumed and that programs offered in different settings are likely to evolve differently.

5. MacDonald's orientation is more toward developing an empirical
rather than a normative model of educational decision making and
its consequences.

d. Stake's concept of evaluation as portrayal:
1. In his countenance of educational evaluation, Stake looks to a
study that portrays the complex and dynamic nature of education
and gives attention to the diverse purposes and judgments of the
practitioner.

2. Criticizing the undue emphasis placed upon measurement in education, Stake suggests that closer attention should be given to the contingencies among background conditions, classroom activities, and
scholastic outcomes.

3. Stake's concept of evaluation as portrayal anticipates Parlett's and
Hamilton's notion of illumination; it, too, stresses the restricting

influence of prespecification, and emphasis placed upon concentrating only on stated program goals.

4. Responsive evaluation orientates more directly to program activities than to program intents and brings to the surface value perspectives that influence the program.

5. The program must communicate to an audience as naturally and effectively as possible what actually occurs.

6. Stake's claim is that research-style information may not be the kind of information that is useful for decision makers.

Exercise 2. Write an essay about the salient features of illuminative evaluation and its procedures (except reporting). Your answer should include these main elements:

a. Illuminative evaluation as a general research strategy.
b. The observation phase.
c. The place of interviews.
d. Questionnaire and test data.
e. Documentary and background information.

Response to Exercise 2 should include the following

a. Illuminative evaluation as a general research strategy
   1. Illuminative evaluation aims to be both adaptable to meet the size, aims, and techniques of the evaluation and eclectic to give the evaluator a choice of research tactics.
   2. The choice of strategy to be used arises from the problem to be investigated.
   3. No one method is used exclusively or in isolation.
   4. The evaluator makes no attempt to manipulate or control or eliminate situational variables, but takes as given the complex scene that is found.
   5. The evaluator endeavors to delineate cycles of cause and effect and relationships between belief and practices.
b. The observation phase
   1. The observation phase occupies a central place in illuminative evaluation.
   2. The investigator compiles a continuous record of events, transactions, and informal remarks.
   3. The evaluator also documents a wide variety of other events such as meetings.

4. Discussions with and between participants are recorded and language conventions and metaphors discerned.

5. Parlett and Hamilton believe that there is also a place for codified observation, which makes use of schedules for recording patterns of attendance, seating, utilization of time and facilities, and the like; this information, however, must be used with caution, as it is not likely to uncover underlying features of the program.

c. The place of interviews

1. Discovering the views of participants is crucial in the assessment of the program's impact.

2. Course participants are asked about their work and also about the use and value of the program from their perspective.

3. The type of interview chosen must be the most appropriate to elicit the type of information or comment sought.

4. Brief, structured interviews are convenient for obtaining biographical or demographic information, while more open-ended and discursive forms are suitable for less straightforward topics.

d. Questionnaire and test data

1. Though concentrating on observation and interview, the illuminative evaluator must not disregard paper-and-pencil techniques where these may prove useful.

2. Their advantage in large-scale studies is especially evident (although they may be used in small studies).

3. The results of questionnaires may be used later in a study to sustain or qualify earlier tentative findings.

4. Questionnaires should be used only after careful thought — and never in isolation.

5. Besides completing questionnaires, participants may also be asked to prepare written comments about the program or to compile work diaries of their activities over a period of time.

6. Custom-built tests of attitude, personality, and achievement may be used (but without privileged status within the study) — and again, never in isolation.

e. Documentary and background information

1. The historical antecedents of a program should be recorded, as these do not arise by chance.

2. Primary sources may be tapped, such as confidential data held on file, together with autobiographical and eye-witness accounts of the program.

3. Tape recordings of meetings and examples of students' work may also prove useful in providing an historical perspective.

Questions Without Answers

Three questions are offered in this section, but answers are not provided. The questions may be used as subjects for group discussions or as individual assignments. Before attempting these questions, you may wish to gain deeper insight into illuminative evaluation by reading sections of the third book in the reference section, *Beyond the Numbers Game*, edited by David Hamilton et al. Nevertheless, questions may be answered on the basis of material contained in this and other units.

1. "Evaluators of the Tylerian persuasion, such as Hammond and Michael and Metfessel, are likely to report outcomes of evaluative studies differently than evaluators of the illuminative mode." Discuss this statement, giving special emphasis to comparative methods of communication.
2. What are some of the problems associated with illuminative evaluation? Are there satisfactory methods to overcome these problems, or is illuminative evaluation doomed to failure because of them?
3. Suggest a hypothetical, innovatory program to be evaluated. Compare the methodology used by a traditional evaluator to that likely to be employed by an illuminative evaluator. Give reasons why one approach may be more convincing to a decision maker than the other.

References

Cronbach, L. J. 1963. Course improvement through evaluation. *Teachers College Record, 64* (8), 672–683.

Hamilton, D. F., and Delamont, S. 1974. Classroom research: A cautionary tale. *Research in Education, 11* (May), 1–16.

Hamilton, D. et al. (eds.). 1977. *Beyond the numbers game.* London: MacMillan Education.

Hastings, J. T. 1966. Curriculum evaluation: The why of the outcomes. *Journal of Educational Measurement, 3* (1), 27–32.

House, E. R. 1972. The conscience of educational evaluation. *Teachers College Record, 72* (3), 405–414.

MacDonald, B. 1971. The evaluation of the Humanities Curriculum Project: A holistic approach. *Theory into Practice, 10* (3), 163–167.

———. 1973. Humanities curriculum project. In *Evaluation in curriculum development: Twelve case studies* (Schools Council Research Studies). Macmillan Education.

Parlett, M. R. 1972. Evaluating innovations in teaching. In H. J. Butcher and E. Rudd (eds.), *Contemporary problems in research in higher education.* New York: McGraw-Hill.

Parlett, M. R., and Hamilton, D. 1977. Evaluation in illumination: A new approach to the study of innovative programmes." In D. Hamilton et al. (eds.), *Beyond the numbers game.* London: MacMillan Education.

Scriven, M. 1967. The methodology of evaluation. In R. W. Tyler, R. M. Gagne, and M. Scriven, *Perspectives of curriculum evaluation* (American Educational Research Association Monograph on Curriculum Evaluation no. 1). Chicago: Rand McNally.

Stake, R. E. 1974. Responsive evaluation. *New Trends in Evaluation, 35* (January), 41–73 (Institute of Education, University of Goteborg).

Stufflebeam, D. L., and Guba, E. 1968. Evaluation: The process of stimulating, aiding and abetting insightful action. Address to the Second National Symposium for Professors of Educational Research, 21 November, at Boulder, Colorado. Evaluation Center, College of Education, Ohio State University.

Stufflebeam, D. L., et al. (Phi Delta Kappa National Study Committee on Evaluation). 1971. *Educational evaluation and decision making.* Itasca, Ill.: Peacock.

Suchman, E. A. 1967. *Evaluative research.* New York: Russell Sage Foundation.

Tawney, David (ed). 1976. *Curriculum evaluation today.* London: MacMillan Education.

10 SCRIVEN'S CONSUMER-ORIENTED APPROACH TO EVALUATION

The proper role of the evaluator, according to Michael Scriven, is that of "enlightened surrogate consumer." Armed with skills in obtaining pertinent and accurate information and with a deeply reasoned view of ethics and the common good, the evaluator should help professionals to produce products and services that are of high quality and of great use to consumers. More importantly, the evaluator should help the consumers to identify and assess alternative goods and services. Scriven has been sharply critical of evaluation ideologies that focus on achieving the developer's objectives as opposed to meeting the needs of consumers; he has proposed a number of concepts and methods that are designed to move evaluation from its objectives orientation to one based on needs.

Summative evaluation may serve to enable administrators to decide whether the entire finished curriculum, refined by the use of the evaluation process in its first (formative) role, represents a sufficiently significant advance on the available alternatives to justify the expense of adoption by a school system.

Michael Scriven is a philosopher of science who has contributed extensively to the growth of the evaluation profession. He has sharply criticized both

311

classical and more recent conceptualizations of evaluation. He has grounded his consumerist view of evaluation in a basic philosophical position and has evolved concepts and methods to help articulate and apply his approach. He has also been one of the foremost leaders in the effort to professionalize evaluation work.

He was born and raised in Victoria, Australia. He took his master of arts degree in applied mathematics and symbolic logic at the University of Melbourne and completed his Ph. D. in philosophy of science at Oxford University. He served in professional roles at the University of Minnesota from 1952 to 1956, at Swarthmore College from 1956 to 1960, Indiana University from 1960 to 1965, University of California at Berkeley from 1965 to 1975, and University of San Francisco from 1975 to 1982. At this writing, he was Distinguished University Professor at the University of Western Australia in Perth.

We chose to label Dr. Scriven's approach as "consumer-oriented evaluation" in order to characterize his basic philosophical approach. He has defined evaluation as the systematic assessment of the worth or merit of things and has emphasized that evaluators must be able to arrive at defensible value judgments rather than simply to measure things or determine whether goals have been achieved. Instead of accepting a developer's goals as given, an evaluator, according to Scriven, must judge whether achievement of the goals would contribute to the welfare of the consumers. Irrespective of the goals, the evaluator must identify actual outcomes and assess their value from the perspective of consumers' needs. For Scriven, the professional role of the evaluator is that of "enlightened surrogate consumer," serving as informed social conscience is what he sees as the "foundation stone of professional ethics in evaluation work." His practical approach to evaluation, in general, calls for identifying and ranking the optional programs and products that are available to consumers, based on their relative costs and effects and in consideration of the assessed needs of the consumers. He has often identified the magazine *Consumer Reports* as exemplary of what professional evaluation should contribute.

In this unit we trace and discuss Dr. Scriven's theoretical, methodological, and professional contributions. His critical appraisal of alternative approaches are identified and discussed. We discuss his formative-summative conceptualization and identify his main working concepts. His 1983 attack on prevailing evaluation ideologies and a few of his methodological suggestions are discussed. We conclude the chapter by noting his achievements in establishing the Evaluation Network and *Evaluation News*.

The unit's instructional objectives are listed below. Please review these, read the subsequent text, then complete the knowledge test and application questions that appear at the end of the unit. Assess your answers against the keyed ones, and if any of your answers are incorrect, review pertinent sections of the unit. You may want to conduct further independent investigation by attempting the "Questions Without Answers" (or discussing them with your fellow students or colleagues) and consulting the sources of information about Dr. Scriven's work that are listed at the back of the unit.

Objectives

This unit is designed to help you achieve the following objectives:

1. To identify and explain Scriven's definition of evaluation.
2. To identify and assess his critiques of other views of evaluation by Tyler and Cronbach.
3. To explain his position regarding the role of judgment in evaluation.
4. To explain the role of needs assessment in his approach.
5. To explain his distinctions between evaluation and estimation of goal achievement, the goal and roles of evaluation, formative and summative evaluation, intrinsic and payoff evaluation, amateur and professional evaluation, goal-based and goal-free evaluation, and evaluation and metaevaluation.
6. To discuss the Key Evaluation Checklist by identifying the guiding rationale, listing and defining the steps, and explaining how the formative-summative conception relates to the Key Evaluation Checklist.
7. To explain his assessments of the evaluation ideologies labeled separatism, positivism, management, and relativism.
8. To identify his role and main contributions in professionalizing evaluation.

These objectives may be achieved merely by reading the material in this unit. To enrich your understanding of Scriven's ideas, however, study his original writings, especially those listed at the end of this unit. Some of the material here is not readily available in the published literature and reflects one author's close working relationship with Dr. Scriven over a period of more than 10 years.

Evaluation Defined

Over the years, Dr. Scriven has evolved his suggested definition of evaluation, but its basic message has remained the same. In a classic article (1967) he defined evaluation as a methodological activity that "consists simply in the gathering and combining of performance data with a weighted set of goal scales to yield either comparative or numerical ratings, and in the justification of (1) the data-gathering instruments, (2) the weightings, and (3) the selection of goals." In discussing the thrust of his intended meaning of evaluation, we have often heard him say that evaluation essentially is the systematic and objective determination of the worth or merit of some object, and that evaluations are best executed by engaging an independent evaluator to render a judgment of some object based on the accumulated evidence about how it compares with competing objects in meeting the needs of the consumers. According to this view, evaluation is preferably comparative; by implication it looks at comparative costs as well as benefits; it is concerned with how to best meet the needs of consumers; optimally, it is a professional activity involving systematic procedures; it should be conducted as objectively as possible; and it must culminate in judgments and recommendations.

Critique of Other Persuasions

In consideration of the preceding definition, Scriven has sharply criticized other views of evaluation and has used his critical analysis to extend his own position. He has charged that the Tylerian tradition — which sees evaluation as determining whether objectives have been achieved — is fundamentally flawed, since it is essentially value-free. He sees evaluations based on this approach as potentially invalid, since the developer's goals may be immoral, unrealistic, not representative of the assessed needs of consumers, or too narrow to foreshadow possibly crucial side effects. Instead of using goals to guide and judge effects, Scriven has argued that evaluators should judge the goals and not be constrained to them in the search for outcomes. Whether the program was guided by meritorious goals, he believes, evaluators should search out all of the results of a program, assess the needs of consumers, and use both sets of assessments to arrive at conclusions about the merit and worth of programs.

Scriven also took issue with the advice offered by Cronbach (1963). Cronbach had criticized the prevalent practice of evaluating programs by using norm-referenced tests to compare the performance of experimental and control groups and had counseled the use of a more developmentally oriented approach. Cronbach advised against exclusive use of comparative experimental designs and suggested that a variety of measures should be used to study a particular program in depth while it is being developed and that the results should be used to help guide the development. Scriven said that this advice by Cronbach clouded the important distinction between the goal and roles of evaluation and in fact equated evaluation to only one of its roles, or what Scriven labeled "formative evaluation." Building on this critique, Scriven extended his view of evaluation in his classic article, "The Methodology of Evaluation" (1967).

Formative and Summative Evaluation

In this article, Scriven argued that the evaluator's main responsibility is to make informed judgments. He emphasized that the goal of evaluation is always the same — to judge value. But, he continued, the roles of evaluation are enormously varied. They may "form part of a teacher-training activity, of the process of curriculum development, of a field experiment connected with the improvement of learning theory, of an investigation preliminary to a decision about the purchase or rejection of materials . . . ," and so forth. He reasoned that the failure to distinguish between evaluation's goal (to judge the value of something) and its roles (constructive uses of evaluative data) has led to the dilution of what is called evaluation so that it no longer achieves its goal of assessing value. In other words, he said that evaluators too often, in trying to help educators improve their programs, become co-opted and fail to judge the programs. For Scriven, an objective assessment of value is the sine qua non of evaluation.

With the paramount importance of the goal of evaluation firmly established, Scriven proceeded to analyze the roles of evaluation. He concluded that there are two main roles: formative, to assist in developing programs and other objects; and summative, to assess the value of the object once it has been developed and placed on the market.

Formative evaluation is an integral part of the development process. It provides continual feedback to assist in planning and then producing some object. In curriculum development it addresses questions about content validity, vocabulary level, usability, appropriateness of media, durability of materials, efficiency, staffing, and other matters. In general, formative evaluation is done to help staff to improve whatever they are operating or developing.

In the summative role, evaluation "may serve to enable administrators to decide whether the entire finished curriculum, refined by use of the evaluation process in its first (formative) role, represents a sufficiently significant advance on the available alternatives to justify the expense of adoption by a school system." Summative evaluation usually should be performed by an external evaluator in order to enhance objectivity, and the findings should be made public. This type of evaluation searches for all effects of the object and examines them against the assessed needs of the relevant consumers. It compares the costs and effects of the object to those of what Scriven has called critical competitors, especially cheaper alternatives. In case the audience might be predisposed to judge only outcomes against the developer's goals, the summative evaluation provides judgments about the extent to which the goals validly reflect assessed needs. Overall, summative evaluation serves consumers by providing them with independent assessments that compare the costs, merits, and worths of competing programs or products.

Amateur versus Professional Evaluation

In the early stages of curriculum development, Scriven prefers "amateur evaluation" (self-evaluation) to "professional evaluation." Developers, when they serve as their own evaluators, may be somewhat unsystematic and subjective, but they are also supportive, nonthreatening, dedicated to producing a success, and tolerant of vague objectives and exploratory development procedures. Hence, they are unlikely to stifle creativity in the early stages of development. Professional evaluators, if invovled too early, may "dampen the creative fires of a productive group," slow down the development process by urging that objectives be clarified, or lose their objective perspective by becoming too closely aligned with the production effort, among other considerations. Professional evaluators are needed, however, to perform both formative and summative evaluation during the later stages of development. Both types of evaluation require high-level technical skills and objectivity seldom possessed by persons on the development staff who haven't been specially trained in the theory and methodology of evaluation. Scriven recommends that a professional evaluator be included on the development staff to perform formative evaluation, and he has often advised that external professional evaluators be commissioned to conduct and report summative evaluations.

Intrinsic and Payoff Evaluation

Scriven also distinguishes between intrinsic and payoff evaluation. Intrinsic evaluation appraises the qualities of an instrumentality, regardless of its effects on clients, by assessing such features as goals, structure, methodology, qualifications and attitudes of staff, facilities, public credibility, and past record. Payoff evaluation is concerned not with the nature of the program, textbook, theory, or other object, but rather with its effects on clients. Such effects might include test scores, job performance, or health status. Scriven acknowledges the importance of intrinsic evaluation, but emphasizes that one must also determine and judge outcomes, since causal links between process and outcome variables are rarely if ever known for certain. He explains that both types can contribute either to formative or summative roles. He has been particularly critical of accrediting boards because of their preoccupation with intrinsic criteria, such as number of books in an institution's library, and their failure to assess the performance of graduates.

Goal-free Evaluation

In yet another move against the widespread preoccupation with goals-based evaluation, Scriven introduced a counter proposal under the label of "goal-free evaluation." According to this approach the evaluator purposely remains ignorant of a program's printed goals and searches for all effects of a program irrespective of its developer's objectives. There are no side effects to examine, since data about all effects, whatever the intent of the program, are equally admissible. If a program is doing what it was supposed to do, then the evaluation should confirm this, but the evaluator will also be more likely to uncover unanticipated effects that the goal-based evaluators would miss because of their preoccupation with stated goals. In any case, Scriven says that goal-free evaluation is reversible and complementary: one can start out goal free in order to search for all effects, then shift to the goal-based approach to ensure the evaluation will determine whether goals were achieved; or both types of evaluation can be conducted simultaneously by different evaluators. Advantages of goal-free evaluation, according to Scriven, are that it is less intrusive than goal-based evaluation; more adaptable to midstream goal shifts; better at finding side effects; less prone to social, perceptual, and cognitive bias; more professionally challenging; and more equitable in taking a wide range of values into account. In general, we see goal-free evaluation as an innovative technique — not a model — that is helpful in implementing the consumer-oriented approach to evaluation.

Needs Assessment

One of the difficulties in using goal-free evaluation concerns how to assign value meaning to findings. If outcomes are identified without regard for what one is trying to accomplish, then how can one sort out the desirable from the undesirable consequences? Scriven's answer is that one must compare the observed outcomes to the assessed needs of the consumers. But if a need is a discrepancy between something real and something ideal and if an ideal is a goal, then aren't needs assessments goal based, and therefore aren't goal-free evaluations also goal based? Scriven says no. First of all, a developer's goals aren't necessarily consistent with some set of ideals such as those embodied in democracy. In any case, he maintains that the classic conception of need as a discrepancy between something real and something ideal is wrong, since ideals are often unrealistic. Because the needs of consumers are a fundamental concept in his approach, he and his students extensively conceptualized and researched this concept.

For Scriven a need is "anything essential for a satisfactory mode of existence, anything without which that mode of existence or level of performance would fall below a satisfactory level." The examples he typically uses are vitamin C and functional literacy. In the absence of these things, a person would be physically ill or socially and intellectually debilitated; hence the person needs them. For Scriven, needs assessment is a process for discovering facts about what things if not provided or if withdrawn would result in very bad consequences, by any reasonable standards of good and bad. Given the results of such a needs assessment, one can then judge outcomes observed for a given program as good, bad, or indifferent depending on whether they do or would contribute to meeting the identified needs. In our experience, this argument is presently more compelling on philosophical than on practical grounds. Much development at the technical level will be needed before needs assessment will offer both a feasible and appropriate means of judging outcomes.

The Key Evaluation Checklist

The Key Evaluation Checklist synthesizes Scriven's earlier ideas. It reflects his view that evaluation involves multiple dimensions, should employ multiple perspectives, involves multiple levels of measurement, and must use multiple methods. Hence, he has sometimes referred to the Key Evaluation Checklist as the multimodel of evaluation. Its eighteen checkpoints are as follows:

1. *Description.* What is to be evaluated? The *evaluand*, described as objectively as possible. Does it have components? What are their relationships?

2. *Client.* Who is commissioning the evaluation? The *client* for the evaluation, who may or may not be the *initiator* of the request for the evaluation and may or may not be the *instigator* of the evaluand — e.g., its manufacturer or funding agency or legislative godparent — and may or may not be its *inventor* — e.g., designer of a product or program.

3. *Background and Context* of (a) the evaluand and (b) the evaluation. Includes identification of stakeholders (such as the nonclients listed in number 2, the sponsor, community representatives, etc.); believed nature of the evaluand; expectations from the evaluation; desired type of evaluation (formative vs. summative; organization charts; prior efforts, etc.).

4. *Resources* ("support system" or "strengths assessment") (a) available to or for use of the evaluand, (b) available to or for use of the evaluators. These are not what *is* used up, for example, in purchase or maintenance, but what *could* be. They include money, expertise, past experience, technology, and flexibility considerations. These define the range of feasibility.

5. *Function.* What does the evaluand do? Distinguish what it is *supposed* to do — *intended or alleged* function or role — from what it *in fact* does — *actual* function(s) both for the client and the consumer; both *could* be covered under *Description*, but it's usually best to treat them separately. Are there obvious dimensions or aspects or components of these functions?

6. *Delivery System.* How does the evaluand reach the market? How is it maintained (serviced)? How improved (updated)? How are users trained? How is implementation achieved/monitored/improved? Who does all this?

7. *Consumer.* Who is using or receiving the (effects of the) evaluand? Distinguish *targeted* populations of consumers — *intended market* — from actually and potentially *directly* impacted populations of consumers — the *true market* or customers or recipients (or clients for the evaluand, often called the clientele); these should be distinguished from the total directly *or indirectly* impacted *recipient* population, which makes up the *true consumers*. Note that the instigator, etc. (see numbers 2 and 3) are also impacted, for example, by having a job, but this does not make them consumers, in the usual sense. We should, however, consider them when looking at total effects and can describe them as part of the affected, impacted, or involved group.

8. *Needs and Values* of the impacted and potentially impacted population. This will include wants as well as needs, and also values such as *judged* or believed standards of merit and ideals (see number 9); the defined goals of the program where a goal-based evaluation is undertaken; and the needs, and so on, of the instigator, monitor, inventor, and the like, since they are indirectly impacted. The relative importance of these often conflicting considerations will depend upon ethical and functional considerations.

9. *Standards.* Are there any preexisting objectively validated standards of merit or worth that apply? Can any be inferred from *client* plus *consumer, function* and *needs/values*? (This will include *appropriate* ideals; see the felt ideals in number 8.) *If* goals are being considered, and *if* they can be validated as appropriate (e.g., from a needs assessment) *and* legal/ethical, and so on, they would graduate from being recorded in number 8 to being accepted, as *one* relevant standard, here in number 9.

10. *Process.* What constraints/costs/benefits apply to the normal *operation* of the evaluand (*not* to its effects or *outcomes* of number 11)? In particular, legal/ethical–moral/political/managerial/aesthetic/hedonic/scientific? One *managerial* process constraint of special significance concerns the "degree of implementation," that is, the extent to which the actual operation matches the program stipulations or sponsor's beliefs about its operation. One *scientific* process consideration would be the use of scientifically validated process indicators of eventual outcomes; another would be the use of scientifically (historically, etc.) sound material in a textbook or course. One *ethical* issue would involve the relative weighting of the importance of meeting the needs of needy target population people and the career or status needs of other impacted-population people, for example, the program staff.

11. *Outcomes.* What effects are produced by the evaluand (intended or unintended)? A matrix of effects is useful; population affected × type of effect (cognitive/affective/psychomotor/health/social/environmental) × size of each z time of onset (immediate/end of "treatment"/later) × duration × each component or dimension (if analytical evaluation is required). For some purposes, the intended (e.g., program monitoring, legal accountability), for others, the distinction should not be made (consumer-oriented summative-product evaluation).

12. *Generalizability* to other people/places/times/versions. ("People" means staff as well as recipients.) These can be labeled deliverability and salability/exportability/durability/modifiability.

13. *Costs.* Dollar vs. psychological vs. personnel; initial vs. repeated (including preparation-maintenance-improvement); direct/indirect vs. immediate/delayed/discounted; by components if appropriate.

14. *Comparisons* with alternative options — include options recognized *and* unrecognized, those now available and those constructable. The leading contenders in this field are the "critical competitors" and are identified on cost-plus-effectiveness grounds. They normally include those that produce similar or better effects for less cost, and better effects for a manageable (*resources*) extra cost.

15. *Significance.* A synthesis of all the above. The validation of the synthesizing procedure is often one of the most difficult tasks in evaluation. It cannot normally be left to the client, who is usually ill-equipped by experi-

ence or objectivity to do it; and the formula approaches — for example, cost-benefit calculations — are only rarely adequate. "Flexible weighted-sum with overrides" is often useful.

16. *Recommendations.* These may or may not be requested, and may or may not follow from the evaluation; even if requested it may not be feasible to provide any because the only types that would be appropriate are not such that any scientific evidence for specific ones is available in the relevant field of research. (*Resources* available for the evaluation are crucial here.)

17. *Report.* Vocabulary, length, format, medium, time, location, and personnel for its (or their) presentation need careful scrutiny, as does protection/privacy/publicity and prior screening or circulation of final and preliminary drafts.

18. *Metaevaluation.* The evaluation must be evaluated, preferably prior to (a) implementation, (b) final dissemination of report. External evaluation is desirable, but first the primary evaluator should apply the Key Evaluation Checklist to the evaluation itself. Results of the metaevaluation should be used formatively but may also be incorporated in the report or otherwise conveyed (summatively) to the client and other appropriate audiences. ("Audiences" emerge at metacheckpoint 7, since they are the "market" and "consumers" of the evaluation.)

These steps are not intended to be performed in any particular sequence, but all must be addressed before the Key Evaluation Checklist has been properly implemented. Also, an evaluator may cycle through the checklist several times during the evaluation of a program. Early cycles are formative evaluation; the last cycle is what Scriven terms "summative evaluation."

The rationale of the Key Evaluation Checklist is that evaluation is essentially a data-reduction process whereby large amounts of data are obtained and assessed and then synthesized into an overall judgment of value. In describing this data reduction process, Scriven suggests that the early steps help characterize a program or product and the later ones help to assess its validity.

Metaevaluation

The final item in the Key Evaluation Checklist calls for the evaluation of evaluation. Scriven introduced this concept in 1968, when he published an article responding to questions about how to evaluate evaluation instruments. He cited this as one of many concerns in metaevaluation and emphasized that evaluators have a professional obligation to ensure that their proposed or completed evaluations are subjected to competent evaluation. His rationale is that "evaluation is a particularly self-referent subject since . . . evaluation applies to the process and products of all serious human endeavor and hence to evaluation." He notes that metaevaluation can be either formative, in assisting the evaluator to design and conduct a sound evaluation, or summative, in giving the client independent evidence about the technical competence of the primary evaluator and the soundess of his or her reports. Scriven's methodological suggestions for conducting meta-evaluations include the use of his Key Evaluation Checklist to assess an evaluation as a product, the use of some other checklists, or the use of professional evaluation standards.

Evaluation Ideologies

As seen in the foregoing material, Scriven has been one of the most thoughtful and vocal critics of prevailing views of evaluation. Consistent with this critical stance, he has emphasized that evaluation is a particularly self-referent subject, which agrees with his advocacy of metaevaluation. In a recent paper he classified the prevailing views of evaluation into four groups and critiqued each one extensively in the hope of convincing evaluators to recognize and shed certain biases, which he said have debilitated evaluation work. Then he used his analysis of strengths and weaknesses of each approach to strengthen his rationale for the Key Evaluation Checklist. He has described this checklist model as one that encompasses the best features of all other serious proposals about how to do evaluation and one that avoids the flaws that he identified in the other proposals. We think it will help you to gain further insight into Scriven's philosophy of evaluation, in general, and the Key Evaluation Checklist, in particular, if you carefully consider his analysis of alternative ideologies. Therefore, we have attempted below to capture his most salient points regarding each of the four ideologies. These ideologies are the separatist ideology, the positivist ideology, the managerial ideology, and the relativist ideology.

The Separatist Ideology

Scriven sees the separatist ideology as rooted in the denial or rejection of the proposition that evaluation is a self-referent activity. This ideology is best reflected in evaluation proposals that require the appointment of evaluators who are totally independent of what is to be evaluated. Establishing and maintaining this independence of evaluator from the evaluand is often seen to be essential for ensuring that evaluation reports are unbiased. In addition, evaluators who practice this ideology, according to Scriven, often fail to recognize or address the need to have their own work evaluated. Quite possibly, many of them, in any case, see such metaevaluation as a concern of somebody else, since evaluators, according to their separatist view, couldn't be objective in evaluating their own work. Hence, Scriven pointed to the paradox of an evaluator who earns a living by evaluating the work of others but fails to seek, or may even resist, evaluations of his own services.

Underlying this kind of professional parasitism, Scriven sees a basic human flaw: "valuephobia, a pervasive fear of being evaluated." It is manifested when evaluators, who are in close contact with the persons whose work they evaluate, become co-opted, lose their critical perspective, and praise what they might have criticized had they maintained greater distance from the evaluand. Valuephobia may also be present when evaluators resist, or at least avoid, having their evaluations evaluated. And it is present when evaluators, in assessing programs, are careful not to evaluate the program's personnel.

In opposition to the separatist position, Scriven argued that professionals, including professional evaluators, need to acknowledge and deal straightforwardly with the self-referent nature of evaluation. The hallmark of a professional is subjecting one's work to evaluation. The fact that all evaluations are prone to bias should not deter one from evaluating one's own work or commissioning someone else to do the job. Instead, one should respond by conducting the evaluation in as unbiased a manner as possible and subjecting the evaluation to scrutiny against recognized standards of sound evaluation. In so-called program evaluations one should look realistically at the staff as well as the other aspects of the program, since, invariably, success and failure are inseparable from the work of the staff and since there will be little prospect for improvement through evaluation if guidance for improving the performance of staff is not provided.

The Positivist Ideology

Scriven saw a second ideology, that of logical positivism, as another overreaction to valuephobia. In their attempts to remove bias from scientific works, Scriven thought the positivists overreacted to the point of trying to render twentieth-century science, in general, and evaluation, in particular, as value-free. While the separatists reject the self-referent nature of science or evaluation, the positivists reject the evaluative nature of science. Scriven pointed to a number of contradictory cases, for example, educational psychologists who assert that no evaluative judgments can be made with objectivity, yet easily produce evaluative judgments about the performance of their students. Of course, Scriven's response to the flaws of positivism is to give central importance to the practice of assigning value meanings to the findings obtained in evaluation studies.

The Managerial Ideology

For Michael Scriven, the "well-managed evaluation" often means much more than one that is guided by a competent administrator. It can instead involve "a very self-serving indulgence in valuephobia" by both program managers and evaluators. Program managers may impose rigid controls over the evaluation they commission so that there will be no surprises. They may want only their program evaluated, not the personnel who operate it and especially not its administrator. And they might insist that the evaluation be limited to determining whether their stated goals for the program have been achieved and that it be restricted from judging their work based on somebody else's wishes for the program.

From the manager's perspective this managerial ideology clearly includes a bias toward producing favorable reports. According to Scriven, many evaluators are willing to fulfill the manager's wishes for favorable, predictable reports because of a parallel set of self-serving reasons. They want future contracts or to retain their evaluation position in the institution, and giving a favorable report, or at least one that doesn't make their client and sponsor nervous, is in the best interest of obtaining future work. They are often willing to partial out any concern for personnel evaluation because this helps to make the evaluation more independent of the different and often conflicting value positions that different persons involved in the program might hold. And the manager's request for limiting the assessment to what had been intended is especially congenial since then the evaluators not only will avoid having to assess the implementation of the program and especially the performance of staff members in it, but will also avoid having to deal with values, since they are presumed to be given in the program manager's goals.

In the managerial ideology we can, then, see the possibility of a confluence of the separatist, positivist, and managerial ideologies — all with bad effect. By avoiding evaluation of the manager and staff (consistent with the separatist ideology), by keeping the evaluation as a technical service devoid of value determinations (the positivist approach), and by helping the managers to get the good report they need on the accomplishment of their goals (the managerial ideology), the evaluator has effectively rendered evaluation as a disservice and not a contribution to society.

With the bent outlined above, the study, according to Scriven, would exclude many vital aspects of a sound evaluation. It would deter rather than assist clients to examine their goals and services critically. By concentrating on the developer's goals it would fail to ensure that the service had value for addressing the consumers' needs. It also would likely be myopic and not consider whether the service or program or product is a "best buy," when it could serve the client better by exposing and comparing alternatives. And it would likely skirt issues concerned with ethics and prudent use of scarce resources. For Scriven, the widely seen adherence to the managerial ideology and its connections to other bad evaluation practices is a travesty for society and for the evaluation profession. He has used his critical analysis of this stance as a platform from which to advocate a series of reforms, which are seen in his Key Evaluation Checklist. These include the following:

1. Performing needs assessments as a basis for judging whether a program has produced beneficial outcomes.
2. Evaluating "goal-free" so as not to become preoccupied with the developer's goals and thereby to miss finding important but unanticipated outcomes, good and bad.
3. Comparing what is being evaluated to viable alternatives.
4. Examining services for their cost/effectiveness.
5. Combining personnel and program evaluation.

The Relativist Ideology

Another ideology that Scriven has seen as flawed and debilitating in its influence on evaluation work is the relativist ideology. Scriven sees it as an overreaction to problems associated with the positivist ideology. Whereas the positivists often have put forth the view that there is an objective reality that can be known by anyone who can and will use unbiased assessment procedures, the relativists have charged that this construction is overly simplistic and can only lead to narrow assessments that give exclusive and undue prominence to the perspective of some group in power, under the mistaken view that their perspective and assessments are objective. In response to the hazards of positivism, the relativists assert that all is relative, that there is no objective truth. Therefore, they call for multiple perspectives, multiple criteria, multiple measures, and multiple answers.

Scriven has seen much of this movement in the evaluation field as an overreaction that sometimes denies the possibility of objective determinations of worth or even objectively correct descriptions of programs. While he also rejects the existence of a single correct description, he counsels us not to abandon the idea that there is an objective reality. While it may be a complex reality beyond our present capabilities to comprehend and describe thoroughly, we only delude ourselves if we therefore pretend it does not exist. He counsels, instead, that we may need to relativize our descriptions to different audiences. But he cautions us not to accept all conflicting descriptions as correct, as, we think, some of the more woolly-headed relativists seem prone to do. Instead we are advised, as evaluators, to seek out the "best," the "better," the "ideal."

Professionalization of Evaluation

Consistent with his concern for evaluating the ideas and works of fellow evaluators, Scriven has been a main force for professionalizing evaluation. He has been a leading advocate of the development and use of the *Standards for Evaluations of Educational Evaluation* (Joint Committee, 1981). He helped to establish and develop the Evaluation Network, a professional organization for evaluators from education, health, government, and social programs. And he developed the newsletter of this organization into the highly respected journal, *Evaluation News*.

This has been a brief summary of some of Michael Scriven's main contributions to evaluation. These contributions have spanned two decades, and they have influenced evaluation practice substantially. Serious students of evaluation should study his original writings and keep abreast of his future contributions.

Knowledge Test for Unit 10

Below are 16 multiple-choice questions and 5 matching statements. Each is followed by an explanation of the correctness or incorrectness of the alternative answers. These questions and explanations are intended to assist you to determine whether you have achieved the knowledge objectives of this unit. For each question, choose the response you consider to be the best one. After you have selected a response, evaluate your choice against the scoring key and the interpretive material that follows each question.

After you have completed all of the knowledge questions, you will be instructed to score and interpret (and, if indicated, advised to remediate) your performance. Then you will be presented with a number of application exercises. The concluding section of the unit lists "Questions Without Answers" and recommended supplementary readings.

Question 1. According to Scriven, evaluation is

a. the process of determining the extent to which valued goals have been achieved.
b. the process of delineating, obtaining, and providing useful information for a client's use in judging decision options.
c. the process of determining discrepancies between performance and given standards.
d. the assessment of value.

Correct Response. You should have selected "d." According to Scriven, evaluation is the assessment of value. It is consistent with the formal definition of evaluation that he presented in "The Methodology of Evaluation." ("Evaluation is . . . a methodological activity which . . . consists simply in the gathering of and combining of performance data with a weighted set of goal scales to yield either comparative or numerical ratings, and in the justification of (a) the data-gathering instruments; (b) the weightings; and (c) the selection of goals.")

Incorrect Responses

a. Incorrect because Scriven believes that evaluation guided by a given set of goals may miss important effects, and he believes that goals also must be evaluated.
b. Incorrect because it emphasizes that the evaluator should provide information for decision making but not actually make the decision, whereas Scriven believes that the evaluator must judge program options and thus make decisions about the program being evaluated.
c. Incorrect because it is a variant of "a." Scriven would not accept as sufficient a definition of evaluation that determined only discrepancies between given standards and performance. He would insist that the standards should be assessed and not be the sole basis for assessing performance.

Question 2. Over the years, Michael Scriven and Lee Cronbach have clashed in their published advice to evaluators. Which of the following best represents their essential disagreement?

a. Cronbach has advised evaluators to use multiple measures in each study, whereas Scriven has warned that such practice is wasteful and has instead advised evaluators to use a single summative measure.
b. Cronbach has emphasized that the primary obligation of evaluators is to settle fundamental decision questions concerning whether a program or product is a "best buy" for consumers, whereas Scriven has stressed that the evaluator's most important role is to serve as the "handmaiden to the developer."
c. Scriven charged that Cronbach's preference for formative evaluation as opposed to summative evaluation was fundamentally wrong.
d. Cronbach stressed the need for comparative evaluations, whereas Scriven argued that such practice would lead to superficial results and not provide the necessary level of in-depth information that is obtainable from an in-depth case study of a single program.

Correct Response. You should have selected option "c." Cronbach did advocate formative evaluation over summative evaluation, and Scriven said that this advice obscured the fact that essentially and ultimately each evaluation must produce a summative assessment of the worth or merit of an object.

Incorrect Responses

a. Incorrect because both writers advised evaluators to use multiple measures.
b. Incorrect because the opposite is more nearly true.
d. Incorrect because the opposite is more nearly true.

Question 3. With which of the following statements would Scriven most likely agree?

a. Evaluators should decide to judge or not to judge educational practices in accord with the role an evaluation study is to serve.
b. Evaluators should obviate the need for subjective judgment by employing designs with high degrees of internal and external validity and with preset decision rules.
c. Evaluators should judge the value of the educational practices they evaluate.
d. Evaluators should describe educational practices fully, but they should avoid passing judgments on the practices.

Correct Response. You should have selected "c." Scriven has asserted that evaluators must formulate and report their judgments of whatever they evaluate.

Incorrect Responses

a. Incorrect because Scriven has stated that evaluators must make judgments in formative as well as summative evaluation.
b. Incorrect because Scriven has noted that the evaluator usually must operate in ambiguous, uncontrolled situations. He notes that evaluators should expect that and not shy away from such assignments. Hence, evaluators cannot depend on preset decision rules or complete information. Therefore, they must generally perform the most professional of all evaluative functions: formulating and publicizing judgments in the face of inadequate and insufficient information. Scriven has offered the consolation that even though the judgments of evaluators will often be wrong, they will be right more often than those of any other group.
d. Incorrect because Scriven has noted that evaluators who fail to make judgments are failing to meet their full responsibilities as evaluators.

Question 4. Which of the following is not consistent with Scriven's position concerning the role of needs assessment in evaluation?

a. Goals provide the best basis for judging outcomes only if the goals have been developed as responses to assessed needs.
b. It is not necessary to consider the needs of consumers as a basis for assessing products and services, since, fundamentally, the evaluator's professional judgment is the determinant of worth or merit of an object.
c. Properly conceived, needs assessments determine gaps between ideals and realities in society and consequently are indistinguishable from any true evaluation study.
d. Needs assessments should determine what things if not provided or if withdrawn would prove harmful and should thereby provide a criterion for determining whether an identified contribution is valuable.

Correct Response. You should have selected option "d." Scriven, who advocated a comprehensive search for outcomes in an evaluation, argued that the identified outcomes should be judged good or bad, depending on the extent they contributed, *not* to achieving stated goals or closing gaps between realities and ideals (which he saw as often "pie in the sky"), but to remov-

ing or preventing forces that otherwise would place the client in an unsatisfactory state.

Incorrect Responses

a.   Incorrect because Scriven said that goals may be too narrow and reflect
     only the developer's selection of certain needs and may also be out-of-
     date, since by the end of a project the needs that formed the basis for
     choosing the project's goals in the first place may have changed sub-
     stantially.
b.   Incorrect because while Scriven sees the evaluator as responsible for
     rendering judgments and issuing recommendations, he also emphasizes
     that such judgments and recommendations should be derived by com-
     paring outcomes to assessed needs.
c.   Incorrect because Scriven explicitly argued against a conception of
     needs referenced to ideals, since they often are so unrealistic that they
     cannot assist in developing practical recommendations.

Question 5.   Which of the following best illustrates Scriven's differentiation
between role and goal relating to evaluation?

a.   The goal of evaluation may vary enormously, since any study may ad-
     dress a wide range of questions; the role of evaluation is always,
     however, the same: to facilitate decision making.
b.   By stressing the constructive part that evaluation can play in nonthreat-
     ening activities (roles), we neglect the fact that its goal always includes
     estimation of value.
c.   The goals of any evaluation study should be tempered according to the
     relative sensitivity of roles to be served by the study.
d.   The goal of any evaluative study is summative, while its role is usually
     formative.

Correct Response. You should have selected response "b." While evaluation may serve many roles (both constructive and destructive), its goal is
always the same: to judge value. This has been Scriven's main argument,
and it has led him to insist that evaluators render judgments.

Incorrect Responses

a.   Wrong because Scriven sees only one goal for evaluation (judgment of
     value), but many roles (public relations, record keeping, guidance for
     development, advice for purchasing a service, and so forth).

c. The opposite of Scriven's position. He believes that evaluators shirk their responsibility when they do not formulate and report judgments about the programs they evaluate.
d. Wrong because formative and summative evaluation are both roles to be served by evaluation.

Question 6. Which of the following best illustrates the use of formative evaluation?

a. Formulating judgments about the overall value of a new textbook.
b. Assigning credit or blame for the results of a completed project.
c. Assessing the implementation of a work plan.
d. Determining the payoff of a prior investment.

Correct Response. You should have selected option "c." Formative evaluation assists program personnel to carry through developmental efforts.

Incorrect Responses

a. Incorrect because the textbook has already been published and formative evaluation of it would have to occur during its development.
b. Incorrect for a similar reason.
d. Incorrect because the investment process has already been completed.

Question 7. Summative evaluation is best described as

a. assessing the early forms of a new product.
b. appraising a product already on the market.
c. improving a product while it is still fluid.
d. bridging the gap between intrinsic and payoff evaluation.

Correct Response. The best response is "b." Summative evaluation involves judging a developmental effort after the development work has been completed.

Incorrect Responses

a. Incorrect because it denotes an instance of formative evaluation.
c. Incorrect for the same reason.
d. Incorrect because it refers to a methodological as opposed to a role problem in evaluation. The problem in bridging intrinsic and payoff evaluation is how to make the causal link between independent and

dependent variables, not whether the evaluation aids development or judges its finished products.

Question 8. Intrinsic evaluation can briefly be defined as an appraisal of

a. change in students' attitudes.
b. the design of an instructional program.
c. the degree and intensity of student motivation.
d. effects of the teaching instrument on students' knowledge.

Correct Response. You should have selected "b." This is correct because intrinsic evaluation is the evaluation of qualities inherent in a treatment as opposed to results achieved by administering the treatment.

Incorrect Responses

a. Incorrect because "change in student attitude" is an effect produced by a program, as opposed to a quality, such as "the inquiry orientation," of the program that produced the change.
c. Incorrect for a similar reason. The "degree and intensity of student motivation" is an effect, not a characteristic, of an instructional program.
d. Incorrect because of its emphasis on effects on students.

Question 9. According to Scriven, the pure payoff approach to evaluation is characterized by concern for

a. results of the curriculum but not its goals.
b. the goals of the curriculum but not its results.
c. both the goals and the results of the curriculum.
d. neither the goals nor the results of the curriculum.

Correct Response. You should have selected "a." While it determines whether goals have been achieved, its main limitation is said by Scriven to be that it does not judge whether the goals are worth achieving.

Incorrect Responses

b. Wrong on both counts. Payoff evaluation does not assess goals, but it does assess results.
c. Wrong because payoff evaluation does not assess goals.
d. Wrong because payoff evaluation does assess results.

Question 10. Which of the following statements most correctly distinguishes between goal-free and goal-based evaluation?

a. Goal-free evaluation is intrinsic evaluation, whereas goal-based evaluation is the same as payoff evaluation.
b. Goal-free evaluation is subjective, whereas goal-based evaluation is data-based evaluation.
c. Goal-free evaluations assess all effects irrespective of stated goals, whereas goal-based evaluations search for effects that pertain to stated goals.
d. Goal-free evaluations assess outcomes, side effects, costs, feasibility, and other nongoal attributes of a teaching instrument, whereas goal-based evaluations assess the morality, clarity, and importance of goals.

Correct Response. You should have selected "c." According to Scriven, the rhetoric of goals should not dictate and constrain the search for results.

Incorrect Responses

a. Incorrect because intrinsic and payoff evaluations differentiate between variables that relate to the qualities of a treatment and its effects; knowledge of intrinsic and payoff evaluation concepts does not assist in distinguishing between goal-free and goal-based evaluation.
b. Incorrect because both goal-free and goal-based evaluation are data based and involve the development of subjective conclusions.
c. Incorrect because both goal-free and goal-based evaluations assess outcomes.

Question 11. Which of the following is *not* a part of Scriven's rationale for using goal-free evaluation?

a. Goal-based evaluations have consistently failed to produce sound and useful evaluative findings and must be replaced by a more effective evaluation strategy.
b. Goal-free evaluators likely will discover significant outcomes that usually are missed by goal-based evaluators.
c. So long as evaluations determine the positive and negative outcomes of a project, it is not necessary to assess particularly whether stated goals have been achieved.
d. In developing a mindset to check on the achievement of stated objectives, evaluators are likely to be insensitive to significant effects, that do not relate to the stated objectives.

Correct Response. You should have selected "a." The rationale for goal-free evaluations is not that they should replace goal-based evaluations. On the contrary, Scriven sees a continued role for goal-based evaluations. But he believes that findings from goal-free evaluations will add useful and unique information to that produced by goal-based evaluations.

b. A part of Scriven's rationale for goal-free evaluation is that goal-free evaluation supplements the data provided by goal-based evaluation.
c. Another part of the rationale for goal-free evaluation is that not knowing program goals is not a handicap as long as the evaluator systematically searches for all important effects of a program.
d. Also a part of the rationale for goal-free evaluation because Scriven has argued that knowing a program's goals can be a handicap insofar as this knowledge causes an evaluator to concentrate on results related to objectives to the exclusion of other results.

Question 12.   Which of the following best explains the meaning of side effects in the context of goal-free evaluation?

a. In goal-free evaluation side effects are the primary concern because goal-based evaluation will provide a thorough analysis of the main effect.
b. Goal-free evaluations are not concerned with side effects because these are intrinsic qualities of the teaching instrument and not the proper concern of evaluations designed to identify and assess outcomes.
c. In goal-free evaluation side effects are the effects that evaluative feedback has on the behavior of the audiences for the evaluation findings.
d. In goal-free evaluation there are no side effects because all effects, not just those related to stated goals, are of primary concern.

Correct Response. You should have selected "d." There is no concern for assessing side effects because from the outset of the evaluation all outcome variables, not just those related to the stated goals, are equally important.

a. Incorrect because in goal-free evaluation there is no distinction between side effects and main effects.
b. Incorrect because it contains an incorrect definition of side effects.
c. Incorrect because it also is based on an improper definition of side effects.

Question 13. Which of the following statements is most consistent with Scriven's rationale for metaevaluation?

a. Primary evaluation work should be granted a kind of evaluative immunity because the threat or fact of evaluating a service inevitably influences how the service is conceptualized and delivered and because such influence in evaluation inevitably would lead to biased evaluation results.

b. Since evaluation applies to the process and products of all human endeavor, it must be applied to itself.

c. Formal evaluation work must be carefully planned, and metaevaluation is the term Scriven introduced to reference the work that is involved in planning evaluations.

d. Metaevaluation is an important means of increasing evaluation assignments and the funds that are allocated to support evaluation work, and thus expands the opportunities for on-the-job training in evaluation.

Correct Response. You should have chosen "b." Since evaluation is an activity intended to help improve the human condition and since all such activities, by definition, must be evaluated, then evaluation itself must be evaluated.

Incorrect Responses

a. Incorrect because, on the contrary, metaevaluations, when properly conceptualized and conducted, should, according to Scriven, lead to better primary evaluations.

c. Incorrect because metaevaluations are intended to assess all aspects of the primary evaluation, not just evaluation plans.

d. Incorrect because, on the contrary, metaevaluations are intended among other things to eliminate wasteful evaluation practices.

Question 14. Which of the following is the *best* rationale for the Key Evaluation Checklist?

a. Evaluation is the process of formulating and executing a sequence of critical comparative experiments that lead to knowledge of certain phenomena such that outcomes of specified actions are predictable.

b. Evaluation is a data-reduction process that involves characterizing a project and synthesizing a judgment concerning the project's overall value.

c. Evaluation guides a project through five developmental stages by assessing and reporting discrepancies between performance and standards at each of the stages.
d. Evaluation involves the progressive comparison of a program's intended and actual antecedents, transactions, and outcomes.

Correct Response. You should have selected "b." Scriven sees evaluation as a systematic process involving the characterizing and assessing of a project. Essentially, evaluators gather and analyze large sets of data across a wide range of checkpoints and then synthesize the data so an overall judgment of value can be rendered.

Incorrect Responses

a. Incorrect because it refers to the rationale for programmatic experimentation and not to the rationale for the Key Evaluation Checklist.
c. Incorrect because it is more the rationale for Provus's discrepancy evaluation model than for the Key Evaluation Checklist.
d. Incorrect because it references Stake's countenance evaluation approach and does not provide a valid rationale for the Key Evaluation Checklist.

Question 15. Which of the following *best* explains the relationship between Scriven's formative-summative conception of evaluation and his Key Evaluation Checklist?

a. The checkpoints in the Key Evaluation Checklist are both formative and summative.
b. The first seven checkpoints — the characterizing steps — are formative; the last eleven validating steps are summative evaluation.
c. The Key Evaluation Checklist is a summative evaluation model.
d. The Key Evaluation Checklist is basically a formative evaluation model.

Correct Response. You should have selected "a." The last cycle through the 18 steps is summative evaluation, while prior cycles constitute formative evaluation.

Incorrect Responses

b. Incorrect because Scriven has not equated the characterizing and validating stages with formative and summative evaluations.
c,d. Incorrect because the Key Evaluation Checklist is both formative and summative.

Question 16.   Which of the following best explains the relationship between Scriven's goal-free evaluation conception and his Key Evaluation Checklist?

a. Goal-free evaluation and the Key Evaluation Checklist are two different but complementary evaluation strategies.
b. The Key Evaluation Checklist explicates the steps one follows in conducting a goal-free evaluation.
c. The Key Evaluation Checklist is a model of the development process, whereas goal-free evaluation is a model of the evaluation process.
d. Goal-free evaluation is an appropriate methodological strategy to be employed in the comprehensive check of program consequences.

Correct Response. You should have selected "d." This explanation of the relationship between goal-free evaluation and the Key Evaluation Checklist is correct because goal-free evaluation is a methodological strategy that checks for all program consequences and because checkpoint 11 of the Key Evaluation Checklist calls for a comprehensive check of consequences.

Incorrect Responses

a. Incorrect because the Key Evaluation Checklist is an overall approach to evaluation that subsumes strategies such as goal-free evaluation.
b. Incorrect because the Key Evaluation Checklist is not an explication of goal-free evaluation.
c. Incorrect because the Key Evaluation Checklist models evaluation and not development, and because goal-free evaluation is not an evaluation model but a particular methodological strategy.

Questions 17 to 21.   For each statement in numbers 17–21, select the appropriate ideology from the list below. Base your choices on your understanding of Scriven's analysis. Record your choices by writing the letter of the selected ideology in the space provided to the left of each numbered statement.

A. separatist ideology
B. positivist ideology
C. managerial ideology
D. relativist ideology

_____ 17. Opposes the proposition that a teacher could profitably and justifiably evaluate his or her own work.
_____ 18. Erroneously refers to the difficulty of fully and accurately

describing something as the basis for denying its existence in some objectively identifiable form.

____ 19. Constrains the evaluation to address only those questions that are sanctioned by the persons who have authority over the program that is to be assessed.

____ 20. Rejects the evaluative nature of science.

____ 21. Biased in favor of giving reports that demonstrate that goals were achieved.

Correct Responses. You should have responded as follows, for the reasons given:

__A__ 17. The separatist ideology rejects the self-referent nature of evaluation and would require that teachers' performance be evaluated by an external agent.

__D__ 18. According to Scriven, the relativists not only advocate multiple description of an object from different perspectives (which Scriven also advocates), but err by claiming a causal linkage between their claim that there is no objective reality and the difficulty of eliminating variability in description of a single thing.

__C__ 19. This clearly is the managerial ideology, which puts the manager of a program in charge of deciding how the program will be assessed: usually only against the manager's goals and not against the needs of the consumer nor in terms of the manager's style and job performance.

__B__ 20. According to Scriven, logical positivists are guided by a value-free conception of social sciences, in general, and evaluation in particular.

__C__ 21. This, again, is the managerial ideology, although concentration on identifying and assessing only those outcomes that pertain to the manager's goals is congruent with the positivist position that evaluators should avoid interjecting values of their choice into their evaluation efforts.

Scoring of the Knowledge Test. Now that you have completed the knowledge test over the Scriven assignment, total the number of correct responses. If your score was 16 or above, you have demonstrated a basic knowledge of Scriven's evaluation philosophy and concepts. Thus, you are ready to proceed to the application exercises in the next section. If your score was 11 to 15, you have shown some grasp of Scriven's ideas, but probably could benefit by a review of the prior material. If your score was lower than 11 and if you still do not understand why, before proceeding to the next section you should again work through the instructional material in the unit.

Application Exercise

This section contains two essay exercises designed to demonstrate whether you understand the basic premises and concepts in Scriven's formative-summative evaluation approach. Answer the questions on separate sheets of paper. Following each exercise is a list of points that should have been included in your response; reviewing them will help you assess your response. Complete the first exercise before proceeding to the second. Refer as often as needed to the assigned reading and the keys contained in the preceding knowledge test.

Exercise 1. Explain what Scriven means in the following quotation: "Formative evaluation is a necessary part of any rational approach to producing good results on the summative evaluation, but the question of whether and how professional evaluators should be employed depends very much upon whether they do more harm than good."

Responses to Exercise 1 should present and develop the following points:

a. Success in developmental efforts depends on feedback from ongoing formative evaluation.
b. Summative evaluations, in judging the success of completed developmental efforts, reflect whether formative evaluation existed and guided the effort to a successful conclusion.
c. Generally, professional evaluators are needed to conduct effective formative evaluations.
d. However, professional evaluators, when introduced very early in developmental efforts, can stifle creativity and lose their objectivity.
e. Hence, professional evaluators are needed to conduct formative evaluations, but since they may do more harm than good in the early stages of projects, it is best to do one's own formative evaluation early in a project and to employ a professional evaluator to take over this role after the project has developed a modicum of stability.

Exercise 2. Suppose you plan to evaluate a team-teaching program using the Key Evaluation Checklist. Summarize the steps you would follow.

Responses to Exercise 2 should include approximately the following:

a. Characterize as objectively as possible the nature of the team-teaching program to be evaluated.

b. Clarify the audiences for the evaluation findings, including the commissioner of the evaluation and all other stakeholder groups, especially students, administrators, and teachers.

c. Examine the background of the need for the evaluation and clarify the questions to be answered.

d. Inventory the financial and other types of resources that are available to support the development, maintenance, and evaluation of the program.

e. Perform a functional analysis of the team teaching as it actually operates, especially in terms of what the teachers and students actually do while participating in the program.

f. Analyze what the school district does to ensure that the team-teaching program is appropriately implemented, for example, orient and train students, parents, and teachers; update program plans; and monitor and improve implementation.

g. Carefully examine which students are actually using and benefiting from unique aspects of the program.

h. Assess the needs of students and teachers that might be addressed by a team-teaching approach.

i. Search out standards that might have been evolved by the education profession to assess team-teaching programs; also derive other standards of assessment by means of analyzing the program's functions and goals; and, in general, determine and assess the criteria of merit and the philosophical arguments pertaining to the team-teaching program.

j. Examine the implementation process to find what constraints attend the normal operation of the program and to help discern the parts of the program plan that are not feasible in the given setting or possibly workable only there.

k. Check all effects of the program comprehensively.

l. Examine the possibility and desirability of exporting the approach to other school situations.

m. Assess the various financial, psychological, and other costs of the team-teaching program.

n. Identify and assess critical competitors to team teaching.

o. Validate and synthesize all information obtained.

p. Form conclusions and recommendations regarding the future use of the program in its setting and elsewhere.

r.   Secure evaluation of the evaluation work and use it both to strengthen the primary evaluation and to inform audiences about its strengths and weaknesses.

Questions Without Answers

In the knowledge test, you were pretty much "spoon fed." In the essay test you had to do considerably more work and were given less help in assessing your responses. In this section you will be mainly on your own. This section presents several questions, but answers are not provided. The questions are important. Often they are perplexing. Even in appealing to authorities you will find that some of the questions are controversial. Hence, in the mold of a true Scriven-type evaluator, you must formulate your own judgments, that is, develop and be prepared to defend your own answers to the questions.

In this spirit we invite you to consider and respond to the following questions. Write your responses out so that you will have them available for discussion with others.

1.   Is all evaluation comparative? Why or why not?
2.   Are formative evaluation and summative evaluation conceptually and operationally distinct concepts? Why or why not? Support your answer with illustrations.
3.   If an evaluator judges a program at one point in time, does he lose his independence and objectivity regarding his future evaluations of the program? Why or why not? If yes, must an evaluator terminate his relationship to a program once he has submitted his judgment of it? If not, how can the evaluator not become co-opted by a program staff that acquiesces to his initial judgments and recommendations?
4.   Describe a summer in-service training program for second-grade teachers who work in schools with high concentrations of disadvantaged children. According to Scriven's conceptualization of evaluation, explain how you would evaluate the program.
5.   Now, evaluate some program, project, or product that you are familiar with, according to Scriven's approach to evaluation. Describe what you are evaluating. Summarize your design for evaluating it. Then present your evaluation results.
6.   As your final task, evaluate this unit according to Scriven's approach to evaluation.

References

Cronbach, L. J. "Course improvement through evaluation." *Teacher's College Record.* *64*, 672–683.

Joint Committee on Standards for Educational Evaluation. 1981. *Standards for evaluations of educational programs, projects, and materials.* New York: McGraw-Hill.

Scriven, Michael. 1967. The methodology of evaluation. *In Perspectives on Curriculum Evaluation, (AERA Monograph Series on Curriculum Evaluation,* No. 1). Chicago: Rand McNally.

_____ . 1974. Pros and cons about goal-free evaluation. *Evaluation Comment, 3,* 1–4.

_____ . 1975. *Evaluation bias and its control. Occasional Paper Series,* No. 4, Western Michigan University, Evaluation Center.

_____ . 1983. Evaluation ideologies. In Madaus, Scriven, and Stufflebeam, *Evaluation models.* Boston: Kluwer-Nijhoff.

Author Index

Subject Index